Out of My Mind

ANDY ROONEY

Out of My Mind

PublicAffairs
New York

Published in the United States by PublicAffairs™, a member of the Perseus Books Group.

Printed in the United States of America.

Library of Congress Cataloging-in-Publication Data
Rooney, Andrew A.
    Out of my mind / Andy Rooney.
       p. cm.
    Includes bibliographical references.
    ISBN-13: 978-1-58648-416-3 (hardcover : alk. paper)
    ISBN-10: 1-58648-416-8 (hardcover : alk. paper) 1. American wit and humor. I. Title.
    PN6165.R665 2006
    814'.54—dc22

                                                                2006023497

10 9 8 7 6 5 4 3 2 1

CONTENTS

PART 2.
FEELING PHILOSOPHICAL

PART 8.
ON MONEY

PART 9.
THE ENGLISH LANGUAGE

PREFACE

I thought to myself, lying in bed one night, in an uncharacteristic moment of modesty, "How much do I have to say that anyone cares about reading?"

If you write for a living, you have to put modesty out of your mind. It is a great privilege to have something you have written preserved in type and printed as a book.

One thing I know is, you can make an essay out of anything. There are times when I've written on subjects about which I know very little. A writer can do that. He has the advantage of being able to look things up, to ask questions of other people more knowledgeable than he. He can sit back and think before putting anything down on paper. This puts the writer one up on readers and often makes him sound smarter than he is. I try to do that. It doesn't seem dishonest. I comb my hair and try to wear decent clothes so I'll look better than I would naked, so why shouldn't I try to write in a style that makes me sound smarter and more interesting than I am?

This book is made up of all essays. The essay is a grand and classic writing format. Igor Stravinsky, the musician, tried to write at one point in his career. He said, "I experience a sort of terror if I sit down to work and find an infinity of possibilities open to me. No effort is conceivable."

Stravinsky said he conquered that terror by turning his creative urge to the seven notes of the scale and writing music. "For then I have something solid and concrete," he said. "I am saved from the anguish of unconditional liberty."

I turn not to the piano, but to the essay form. The essay offers a writer a great deal of freedom but falls short of offering the "unconditional liberty" that stopped Stravinsky. The essay provides a writer boundaries within which he can go to work. Confinement is conducive to creativity.

I am not a great writer, but I don't write badly very often. This passes for good writing. As a matter of fact, there's just so much good writing anyone can take. To some extent, it's like acting. If you notice the acting, it probably isn't good. Good writing shouldn't call a lot of attention to itself, either.

Something happens to a lot of people when they write. Their voice changes—even on paper. They tighten up and are not themselves. One thing of which I am certain is that no one writes as he speaks and no one speaks as he writes. When a writer is faced with the choice of styles, it is always better if he writes more like he speaks. If you know the writer, you should be able to hear his voice as you read the words.

You can't take the idea too far because when we talk we are hesitant, discursive and repetitive. If you make a verbatim transcript of a conversation, it invariably needs to be heavily edited before being printed.

The writer gets a good break in newspapers. His or her name is right there up front, available for credit or blame on whatever has been written. In the arts, it has always bothered me that the writer takes last place. The credits on a movie or a play almost always list the writer in small type where it's hard to find. I never knew why this was because actors are a dime a dozen and good writers are hard to find. The production of a play or a movie or the publication of a book stands still until the writer gets the words down on paper. No one can do anything until the manuscript appears. There are a dozen editors, publishers, directors, producers and investors waiting for one writer to get something down on paper. Then they change it.

Writing an essay is, for me, always a pleasure because people tend to leave it alone. An essay isn't important enough to change.

The essays in this book were written over the past four years. Some of them show their age. I have rewritten small parts of some of them for that reason. Margie, my wife of sixty years, died in 2004 and her name does not appear as often as it originally did because it hurts too much to write it.

—ANDY ROONEY

PART ONE

Daily Life

We all look for that perfect day when we have enough to do but not too much.

WE'RE WASTING AWAY

Last Saturday, I filled the trunk of my car and the passenger seats behind me with junk and headed for the dump. There were newspapers, empty cardboard boxes, bags of junk mail, advertising flyers, empty bottles, cans and garbage. I enjoy the trip. Next to buying something new, throwing away something old is the most satisfying experience I know.

The garbage men come twice a week but they're very fussy. If the garbage is not packaged the way they like it, they won't take it. That's why I make a trip to the dump every Saturday. It's two miles from our house and I often think big thoughts about throwing things away while I'm driving there.

How much, I got wondering last week, does the whole Earth weigh? New York City alone throws away 24 million pounds of garbage a day. A day! How long will it take us to turn the whole Planet Earth into garbage, throw it away and leave us standing on nothing?

Oil, coal and metal ore are the most obvious extractions, but any place there's a valuable mineral, we dig beneath the surface, take it out and make it into something else. We never put anything back. We disfigure one part of our land by digging something out and another after we use it and throw it away. I say "away," but there's really no such place as "away."

After my visit to the dump, I headed for the supermarket, where I bought $34 worth of groceries. Everything was in something—a can, a box, a bottle, a carton or a bag. When I got to the checkout counter, the cashier separated my cans, boxes, cartons, bottles and bags and put three or four at a time into other bags, boxes or cartons. Whatever came to her hand on the conveyor belt in a bag, she put in another bag. Sometimes she put my paper bags into plastic bags. One bag never seemed to do. If something was in plastic, she put that into paper.

On the way home, I stopped at the dry cleaners. Five of my shirts, which had been laundered, were in a cardboard box. There was a piece of cardboard in the front of each shirt and another cardboard cutout to fit the collar to keep it from getting wrinkled. Clipped to the front of each shirt was a cloth tag that identified the shirt as mine. The suit I had cleaned was on a throwaway hanger, in a plastic bag with a form-fitting piece of paper inside over the shoulders of my suit.

When I got home, I put the groceries where they belonged in various hiding places in the kitchen. With the wastebasket at hand, I threw out all the outer bags and wrappers. By the time I'd unwrapped and stored everything, I'd filled the kitchen wastebasket a second time, already getting ready for next Saturday.

It would be interesting to conduct a serious test to determine what percentage of everything we discard. It must be more than 25 percent. I drank the contents of a bottle of Coke and threw the bottle away. The Coca-Cola Company must pay more for the bottle than for what they put in it. Dozens of things we eat come in containers that weigh more and cost the manufacturer more than what they put in them.

We've gone overboard on packaging in the United States and part of the reason is that a bag, a can or a carton provides a place for the producer to display advertising. The average cereal box looks like a roadside billboard.

The Earth we inhabit could end up as one huge, uninhabitable dump.

You'd see me there Saturday mornings . . . throwing stuff away.

JUST ANOTHER DAY

"Days" don't move me much. Memorial Day is not a day I remember friends who died during World War II any more than I remember them other days. Fragmentary memories of them often come to mind, evoked by something I see, hear or experience.

I enjoy thinking of them for a moment, wince at the thought they're gone forever, then put them out of mind and go about my day. Tears come to my eyes unbidden ten times a year when I think of my boyhood friend Obie Slingerland, who died on the deck of the Saratoga when he landed his plane with a bomb hung up in its bay.

I don't need a Memorial Day to remember friends like Obie or Bob O'Connor, Bob Post, Bob Taft, Charley Wood or Bede Irvin. They died in World War II having lived less than half the life I've enjoyed.

We have so many "Days." Memorial Day used to be called Decoration Day when I was a kid. At some point, the name was changed to Memorial Day and set aside to honor all war dead. That seemed like a step in the right direction. Armistice Day, a federal holiday, was changed to Veterans Day in 1954.

It seems to me all these "Days" don't really do much for those they're intended to honor. When my mother was alive, I didn't love her more on "Mother's Day." I got caught up with the "Mother's Day" pitch by the card, flower and candy promoters but I always resented it. She would laugh if I bought her flowers or candy, dismissing it as silly and something I didn't have to do. However, I always suspected she might have missed it just a little if I hadn't done it. Margie doesn't sit by the phone waiting for it to ring on Mother's Day but when it did ring at 6 P.M. on May 12, she said, "There's the last one." She'd kept track.

If none of our four children ever called me again on Father's Day or my birthday, it wouldn't make me think they didn't like me. I know them too well.

Columbus Day, St. Patrick's Day and Martin Luther King Jr.'s birthday are good rallying days for the Italians, the Irish and black Americans. It's good for them to get together to indicate their pride in their heritage, but I don't think Columbus Day or Martin Luther King Jr.'s birthday should be federal holidays. The Irish, at least, have had the good sense to celebrate with their St. Patrick's Day Parade on Sunday when drivers are not trying to get to work.

Washington's Birthday is observed as a federal holiday on the third Monday of February. Twelve states have tried to make sense of honoring Lincoln and Washington by establishing "President's Day" to honor both of them but it isn't a federal holiday. The silly but good holidays are Halloween, Valentine's Day and Thanksgiving. I don't know how we let Thanksgiving in so close to Christmas. It's good if you don't mind having turkey on two occasions so close together.

The fastest-growing religion in the United States is Islam and you can bet the Muslims are going to demand holidays of their own before many moons.

I don't like to see days off proliferate. There are five great American holidays: Thanksgiving, Christmas, New Year's Day, the Fourth of July and Labor Day. We need Labor Day because it's the real New Year's Day and a signal that summer vacation is over.

STATES BY THE NUMBERS

Minnesota is the best state to live in, according to a book of statistics called *State Rankings*, put together by Kathleen and Scott Morgan, who live in Kansas, the thirteenth best state to live in.

After Minnesota come Iowa, New Hampshire, Virginia and Massachusetts.

The worst states to live in, according to the book, are Alabama, Louisiana and Mississippi. Florida is ranked way down as thirty-ninth best, which is strange, considering how many people choose to go there from some other state to live.

According to the U.S. Census Bureau, there are now about 300 million people in the United States. I'm glad we didn't decide to have a celebration when we hit 300 million because it's nothing to celebrate. Empty lots have been disappearing under houses, apartment buildings and office structures all my life. The more people we have, the more buildings we put up.

It hasn't been long since New York had the largest population of any state but it's been dwarfed in the last twenty years by California. California, with 34 million people, is almost twice as big as New York, with

18 million. Even Texas is bigger than New York now with 20 million people. Lucky Wyoming has fewer than half a million. There are seven other states with fewer than a million people.

The worst statistic is the number of people in state prisons. There were 1,236,476 people locked away in the year 2000, and that figure hasn't changed much. Most prisoners are men. There are only 93,000 women in the pokey. No one seems to know whether women are more honest or just smarter and don't get caught as often.

It costs approximately $60,000 a year to keep each prisoner. You'd think there might be some way prisoners could be put to work and pay their keep. The trouble with that is, of course, if you give a prisoner a job, someone will complain that this deprives an honest person of a job. It just seems like there's so much work to be done in the world that we ought to be able to find something useful for more than a million and a quarter people to do rather than sit in prison cells all day.

A lot of those prisoners probably were put away for stealing cars. In the whole United States, an amazing 1,165,559 cars were stolen in 2000. You wonder why we go to all the trouble of locking them. What good are locks if we have that many cars stolen every year?

People make the most money in Connecticut, where the average salary is $40,870. I live in Connecticut and make more than that and am surrounded by people who make more than I do. Massachusetts, New Jersey and New York are next. The lowest average incomes are in Mississippi, New Mexico and West Virginia. The average salary in those states is about half what it is in Connecticut.

In Massachusetts, 35 percent of the people have college degrees.

Maine is one of my favorite states but it has some unusual statistics. In almost every category, it's near the top or the bottom of the list. For example, more people vote in Maine than almost any other state. It has the most number of veterans per capita, the highest local taxes but a low crime rate.

More people own their own homes, 77 percent, in Michigan and Iowa, and fewest own them in New York, 53 percent. That's because in New York City, there are relatively few private homes. Most people live in rented apartments.

WEATHERING THE STORM

The financial experts who predict trends in the stock market's rise and fall have something in common with meteorologists who tell us what the weather is going to be: They are both wrong about half the time. This makes their guess as good as ours.

Last week, the weather reports we heard in New York were saying we could expect a dusting of snow over the weekend. By Saturday, the reports were upgraded, and on Monday morning, by which time we'd had 14 inches of snow, they were saying we could have as much as 14 inches of snow. All this was unusual because meteorologists are more apt to err on the side of excess to make their reports sound more interesting. Their guess is seldom less than the snow or rain that actually comes down.

On television, the weather reporters pad their parts by saying things like, "There will be an accumulation of 8 inches of snow on the roads tomorrow morning during the rush hour, so allow yourself extra time and drive carefully." Has any driver in history ever driven more carefully because of being admonished to do so by a radio or television announcer?

The traffic reporters and weather experts both give a lot of advice. The traffic reporter will say, "There's a four-car pileup with an overturned tractor trailer on I–90, so stay to your right."

The other advice they like to give, as though they were being helpful, is to travelers: "Kennedy Airport is closed to all traffic, so call your airline in advance for flight information." Have they ever tried to call an airline? Airlines don't have people answering telephones. You have as much chance of getting information about a flight from an airline as you have of finding out whether we're going to war with Iran by calling the White House and asking to talk to President Bush.

Because I had work to do and knew I wouldn't be able to get into New York from our home in Connecticut Monday morning, I drove to New York on Sunday. New York is good with snow, but there's always one building in a block where the tenants don't shovel and it makes it difficult to get around. Snowplows clear the streets but block the crosswalks in the process.

Taxi cabs are scarce after a snowstorm. Cabs have two-wheel drive and bald tires and can't move in snow. Buses come in clusters of three, then none for an hour.

A friend of mine was in town from Des Moines and couldn't leave because the airports were closed. He called me at the office to ask if I'd have dinner with him. His situation made me question how hotels handled incoming reservations when people already in the rooms couldn't get out. Most of the people employed in hotels probably couldn't get to work. How did they get the beds made, the sheets washed?

Monday night, most restaurants in the city were closed because their waiters, cooks and managers couldn't get to work. Suppliers had not supplied them. We found a good restaurant, but I felt guilty after dinner. At home the morning newspaper had been covered with snow and couldn't be found in the driveway. The oil company had come but couldn't get the tanker into our snowbound driveway. There was no way the mailman could get to the box on our front door.

Margie said she was going to try to get the car out in the morning and go to the store.

I wanted to be as nice to her as I knew how, so I told her to drive carefully.

FORGET THE BIRTHDAY GREETINGS

We are awash in remembrance. We need some special occasions in our lives. It's nice to make one out of some anniversary, but eventually, as we accumulate friends over the years and relatives proliferate, there become more special occasions in our lives than we can handle—or even remember.

There are people who never forget a birthday or wedding anniversary and others who never remember one. Some tidy people keep track of these dates in other people's lives in little black books. They spend more time remembering than is called for by the unimportance of many of these occasions. While it may be fitting to make an event out of a fifth, tenth, twenty-fifth or fiftieth wedding anniversary, those like the sixth, eleventh or forty-third would be better forgotten. I resent the remembers.

The idea of making a joyous event out of getting a year older doesn't make sense. We all hate our age. Not only that, we find it ridiculous and humiliating not to be able to blow out the burgeoning number of candles on a cake. And we shouldn't be eating cake anyway.

There are a few people who never mention their birthday because they don't want to call attention to it. This seems more sensible than setting off bells and whistles to proclaim to the world that you're a year closer to the end of your life. I'm more apt to be depressed than elated on the occasion of mine.

We've always tried to soften the blow for people getting old in every way except by ignoring the fact. Old age is called "the golden years," but anyone old enough to fall in that category knows there's nothing golden about them.

Then there's the commonly accepted notion that wisdom comes with age, as if this made aging an occasion for joy. We all know, however, in our heads if not in our hearts, that this is not true. We are as dumb at sixty, seventy, eighty or ninety as we were at twenty-one. We may know more but our brain doesn't work any better, and probably less well, than it ever did. Like the look of our face or the shape of our feet, we're stuck with the brain we came with and it functions with less and less agility as the years pass.

Annual celebrations probably ought to end the day a child blows out the candles on his or her twelfth birthday cake. We leave little monuments of special occasions throughout our lives but there isn't time to stop and celebrate all of them and we should stop trying.

We ignore some of the most important dates in our lives because they're not sentimental occasions. Depending on the state we live in, the fifteenth, sixteenth, seventeenth and twenty-first birthdays are vital because it is on those days we become old enough to marry, drive, vote or drink. They don't bring funny cards from friends.

What I most want is a couple of weeks during which there are no days to celebrate. That would be worth celebrating.

THE JUNK BUILDING BOOM

There are times when I yearn for a czar or dictator. It would have to be me because I'd disagree with the dictates of any other.

Today I'm thinking how badly we need someone with absolute power in charge of controlling the buildings people erect. I'd not only want to control new construction, I'd also want the power to tear down some of the buildings already up. I'd like to have the power to drive through our small town in Connecticut and mark certain homes and commercial buildings for demolition.

There are monstrosities in every city and town in America. The construction of many of these buildings could have been prevented if we didn't have this perverse notion that people can build anything they want as long as they own the land they put it on. Clearly there should be a law against some buildings. Fair-minded people who object might ask who would decide what could be built and what could not. I'll decide, that's who.

The accepted idea is that what someone does with an empty lot is strictly his or her own business but that isn't true. It's the business of everyone who lives anywhere nearby. An unattractive building intrudes on their lives every day they pass by and are forced to look at it. You could say no one is forced to look at an ugly building but this ignores the magnetic attraction anything unlovely holds for our eyes.

The construction of a home or business in a town should not be taken lightly. Buildings last. An ugly house is practically immortal. Badly built office towers often stand for a hundred years and the rent is still rising. A house may get painted, added to or subtracted from but once one is built, it's there for good as far as our lives are concerned.

There's not a community in America that doesn't have buildings so unattractive that they should be leveled and carted off to the dump in small pieces to raise the value of others in town. (It is incumbent upon me to say here that our house might be considered by some to be a candidate for destruction on grounds of its aesthetic shortcomings.)

"Developer" is a dirty word. Developers are moving in on open fields, wooded hills, vacant lots and even back yards everywhere. In many wealthy communities, they're tearing down perfectly good $500,000 homes to put up $5 million display houses. We need de-developers to undevelop places that were developed badly. As building dictator, I would prohibit the intrusion of one brick or 2-by-4 on a back yard for the purpose of enlarging an existing home. A back yard is more important than any additional bedroom or two-car garage.

The disappearance of back yards in city and suburb followed the demise of the front porch fifty years ago. There was a time when half the population of small-town America sat on its front porch watching the passing scene from a comfortable position in a hammock, swing or rocking chair. No longer. The inaction has moved inside to a position in front of the television set in the living room. People don't live in the living room, they watch there. It has become the watching room.

A city back yard is an oasis cordoned off from the parade of machinery passing by in the street out front. There can be quiet, grass, flowers, peace and tranquillity just a short distance from the frenetic world of moving machinery. In a back yard, flowers do not rush to grow, grass does not have a horn to blow, or radio to blare out. As the population multiplies and the demand for space increases, back yards, like front porches, will become a thing of the ancient past. They'll be replaced by brick and steel with no personality but a life expectancy of 500 years unless, of course, I am appointed the first czar of deconstruction.

LIFE BECOMES LESS NEIGHBORLY

Growing up, I knew everyone on our block and most of the people around the corner and up the street. The Duffeys were on one side, the McAnenys on the other. The Gordons lived next to the Duffeys and the Buckleys were next to them. Dick Stephens lived across the street. He had a chow named Chummy. The Hessbergs were next to the Stephens. Their German Shepherd was called a "police dog."

We have lived for more than fifty years in our present house. Don't ask me to name more than four of ten neighbors who live within 100 yards of us—or any of their dogs. People move more often than they used to. Neighbors have gone out of style in America. No one borrows a cup of sugar.

We are no longer active in many of the hometown organizations whose meetings we once attended regularly. Attendance at the meetings of all local organizations is dramatically lower. A notice in our current town bulletin says, "The Town Meeting scheduled for June 27 was canceled for lack of a quorum."

They're having a terrible time getting anyone to come to Parent-Teacher Association meetings. Even organizations like the American Legion, the Rotary, the Kiwanis and the Knights of Columbus have lost 25 percent of their membership in many communities. Most of the people listed as members no longer go to church. We don't chat over the back fence. We get in the car and go someplace, or stay inside and watch television. Not as many kids are playing Little League baseball.

If we needed a quart of milk, I used to walk down to the grocery store a block from our house. If Tom was in his yard, cutting the grass, I stopped and we talked. Now if we need milk, I get in the car and go to the supermarket.

Margie used to belong to a bridge club, a book club and an investment club. She never missed a meeting. Several years ago, Robert D. Putnam wrote a good book called *Bowling Alone*. He spoke about the virtues of "civic engagement and social connectedness," saying they produce better schools, economic progress, lower crime and more effective government.

Young people don't get married half the time until they're middle-aged, so many of them live in apartments with strangers next door, not neighbors. Gay Americans often keep to themselves, and half of all Americans who marry get divorced. They separate from both spouse and neighbor.

You can't beat a good, hometown newspaper as a cohesive force in a community, but hometown newspapers are having a tough time. The readership of *USA Today* and newspapers like the *New York Times*, the *Washington Post* and the *Los Angeles Times* is a problem for small papers that live in the shadow of their circulation.

Local newspapers have tried to become less local by not excluding neighboring towns with the paper's name. My hometown newspaper is no longer the *Norwalk Hour*. Now it's simply *The Hour*. A newspaper I used to deliver, the *Albany Times Union*, is now the *Times Union*. In the same area, the *Troy Record* has become *The Record* and the *Schenectady Gazette* is *The Gazette*. I wouldn't be surprised to see the *New York Times* drop "New York."

THE RETRACTABLE WEDDING

There isn't time to read everything in the newspaper, and we all pick and choose. I glance at page one to see if we're at war and to check on how many Israelis were killed by Palestinians or how many Palestinians were killed by Israelis.

The business section seems like someone else's business, not mine, and I don't read real estate because I have my house so I quickly turn to the editorials, letters, columnists and the sports section.

I skim the wedding announcements and try to guess, on very little evidence, whether the marriage will work or not. If there's a picture of the couple, they look happy together and the announcement is upbeat, but buried in the story there is often a sign of trouble lurking. When the parents of one of the couple are from two different places, you know that marriage didn't work out and I suspect statistics would bear out my suspicion that children of divorced parents are more apt to divorce.

In the Sunday newspaper I have in my hand, I see these sentences:

"Ms. Kirwan, 29, is keeping her own name."

"Ms. O'Hara, known as Nell, is keeping her name."

"Miss Woo, 29, is keeping her name."

"Miss Heins, 40, is keeping her name."

"Ms. Scop, 26, will keep her own name."

"Anna Mills Smith . . . was married to Robert Brett Hickman. . . . The bride and bridegroom will be known as Mr. and Mrs. Hickman-Smith."

If I was a young woman who had had some success starting a career before I met a guy I wanted to marry, I'd choose to keep my name. I don't know how the custom of the woman taking the man's name ever got started. However, while there are no statistics to back me up, I'd be willing to bet that there are more divorces in marriages where the woman keeps her name than in ones where she takes the man's name.

It seems apparent that the growing trend is for a woman to keep her own name. I approve but I don't know where it leads us. Having a name assigned to every person is a convenience for society and certainly friendlier if not so practical, as if we each had nothing but a number to identify us. Taking both names and inserting a hyphen, as the Hickman-Smiths have, may seem like the answer, but what happens when they have children who want to marry? Say they have a girl named Samantha Hickman-Smith. Samantha meets a boy whose parents merged their names just as hers did. Their name is Billingham-Watson. Their son's name is Rutherford. If Samantha and Rutherford marry, do they become Mr. and Mrs. Hickman-Smith-Billingham-Watson? And if they do, what will ever become of their children's names when they marry?

One newspaper, the *New York Times*, is now publishing news of gay unions. "Thomas John Michael Mirabile and William Edward Doyle, Jr. celebrated their partnership last evening at the Brooklyn Botanic Garden in a commitment ceremony."

Neither of the men in a gay union ever seems to take the other's name.

Wedding announcements are chock full of miscellaneous facts you don't get any place else.

"The couple was married at the Salsa del Salto Bed and Breakfast in Taos." I wonder if they slept there that night?

Or, "Her father is vice president for finance at Retractable Awnings.com in Miami."

Too many weddings, like awnings, are retractable.

BETTER BY FAR

Sometimes, when I worry about little things like the future of mankind, I deliberately turn my thoughts to how great life could be for us in the future.

I did a morning radio interview last week, and the interviewer asked if I thought things were better for people than they used to be.

I said "better," but I wasn't articulate explaining why I thought so.

Life is better than it was for our parents, grandparents, great-grandparents and ancestors because invention has enabled us to fill our lives with more good things and more interesting times, and with less onerous physical labor. We live much longer because our doctors know more and have better medicine. We're filling those extra years with five times as much living as people living in 1900 got into one year.

One hundred years ago, a woman never left the house most days. She got lunch and dinner ready for her working husband and children. She cleaned. There was no vacuum cleaner, no dishwasher, no clothes washer and drier. She scrubbed the clothes on a washboard after heating water on a wood-burning stove.

After dinner, 100 years ago, people either went to bed or sat in the dark. Some read with difficulty by the flickering light of a candle or oil lamp. The women knitted, men whittled. For music, they whistled. No word from the outside world entered the house. No radio, no television.

Sure, we have it better. Thomas Edison's light bulb turns night to day with a flip of the switch. We read the newspaper and watch what went on in the world on a picture box across from our chair. We are entertained, enlightened. If we don't like what we see, we can change what we're watching without moving any more than a finger.

We have done an amazing job delivering clean water and electrical power into our homes through unseen pipes and wires. Our waste is spirited away.

Houses that were once warmed in freezing winter weather by the spotty heat thrown off by wood-burning fireplaces are evenly heated by oil, electricity or coal.

I often look at old buildings in New York City that are five and six stories high. Someone had to live on the top floor a hundred years ago. The only way to get to the upper floors before elevators were invented in 1852 was to walk up carrying what you needed. In summer heat, a top floor apartment without air conditioning (invented recently in 1911) often reached 120.

We recently celebrated the 100th anniversary of flight. Travel that once took days or months by foot, horse-drawn carriage or sailing ship, now takes a small part of one day. Great as the Wright Brothers invention has been in providing us with mobility, airplanes do not compare with automobiles in the convenience they provide us moving around our own personal little world every day.

Traveling farther and more often doesn't necessarily add to our lives, but travel helps us get to know more about how others live.

Inventions have created a world our grandparents and great-grandparents could not have imagined. The good old days were not that good. That's what I should have told the man who interviewed me on radio.

WEDDING DUMBBELLS

President Bush wants to strengthen the institution of matrimony in America. As one way of doing this, he proposed an amendment to the Constitution that would ban gay marriages.

If Congress is going to consider this seriously, it ought to broaden the search for ways to strengthen marriage and look into all aspects of this custom that has developed in every part of the civilized world. The custom is that two people pair off to live together, love together, have children and help each other through life. Most problems develop when the issue arises about what role the man and the woman play in their relationship. Some men are carried away with their masculinity and some women are not satisfied with their femininity.

The great number of divorces make pretentious wedding vows, organ music and expensive bridal gowns seem silly. It's no longer just death that do them part. They part for dozens of other reasons long before they die.

The divorce rate varies by state. In Oklahoma, 70 percent of all marriages ended in divorce in 2000 . . . must be something in the water out there. Millions of Americans everywhere have been married twice and, while there are no statistics, millions more have been married three times. Someone who gets divorced twice is more apt to get divorced a third and fourth time than someone who's been divorced once. This is my own, homemade statistic.

There are no statistics yet on whether gay marriages will be any more successful than heterosexual marriages. The President feels strongly about the sanctity of marriage and maybe one way he could promote longevity in a union between a man and a woman would be to make divorce illegal. Along with banning gay marriage, the Constitution could be rewritten to ban divorce. If people knew they weren't going to be able to get out of it, they'd be more careful about getting into it.

There are too many happily divorced people for the President to make such an amendment retroactive, but once passed, henceforth and from that day forward, couples would be forbidden to divorce. There would be no such thing.

At the very least, it would be illegal for a couple with children to get divorced. Any man who left his wife with children to take care of would have to undergo an unpleasant operation to assure society that it didn't happen again. Any woman who had more than one child without being married would be subjected to a comparable procedure. We don't need a lot of children by people who don't know how to take care of them because the children grow up and have children of their own that they don't know how to take care of.

There's something else the President might do besides making it illegal for same-sex couples to marry and making divorce illegal. He could make it more difficult for anyone to get married in the first place. Obviously, when you look at our high divorce rate, you have to conclude that too many men and women are going into marriage without thinking it through first.

Two people who wish to get married should have to take a test to see whether or not they're going to be able to maintain the relationship. No one should be able to get married on a whim. You can't get a driver's license without taking a test to prove you're capable of driving a car. Why can you get a marriage license without first providing some evidence that you're capable of living with someone?

Still another possibility President Bush might consider is to make marriage licenses good for a limited time, perhaps five years. When a marriage license expired, it would have to be renewed. A couple would no longer be married for life.

A marriage board would study the application and approve or disapprove it.

President Bush should think through this whole custom of marriage before we start amending the Constitution.

A JOB EASILY DONE

It's a welcome relief to find yourself performing some job you know how to do. When I come on an easy one, it keeps me from despair over my ineptness at all the others I don't know how to do.

Shaving every morning might seem to a woman like a nasty little job for men. The fact is, shaving is easy, quick and men get a sense of accomplishment from it. He is so familiar with the job that he can preview the day's work while he's doing it without cutting himself. I know how to shave and I look better after I've done it. That's the most you can ask of a job.

Cutting the grass has not been hard work since the advent of power mowers. The operator directs a machine with whirring blades from a comfortable perch in a saddle behind the engine. The swath a mower cuts as it traverses a lawn becomes satisfyingly wider with each pass, and if there's anything at all difficult about mowing the lawn now, it's filling the tank of the mower with gas.

We had four or five inches of snow in Connecticut this week. Shoveling snow is overrated as hard work. All the alarm bells about snow shoveling and heart attacks have added prestige to the shoveler, but I have never once died moving snow with a shovel. I suspect more people die in their sleep on a snowy night than shoveling snow the next morning.

Many of the easy jobs are ones I save for the weekend when I seek the illusion I'm accomplishing something without actually doing any work. Shopping, of course, is the number one time-spending amusement in the country.

To say, "I've got to go to the store" or "I should do the shopping" makes it sound like work, which it isn't. Shopping is almost always an excuse for getting out of the house and away from the work you ought to be doing.

The best jobs to do are ones that look hard but aren't because you get more credit for doing those. I don't want to alienate women who do a lot of it, but vacuuming is imitation hard work. There is nothing in any way difficult about rolling a roaring wind machine around a room on its little wheels. The noise it makes seems unnecessary but adds to the suggestion that it's work.

The only hard part of vacuuming the living room rug is putting the damned vacuum back in the closet when you've finished. Vacuum cleaners are unwieldy. If he invented them, Hoover stopped too soon.

Washing the car in the driveway on a spring or summer day is another job that has the reputation of being hard but isn't. The only hard part of washing the average car is getting to the middle of the windshield with a sponge or cloth without getting your shirt and pants wet where you lean up against the car.

This morning, something happened to the computer on which I write. Finally, after a frustrating hour, I called for assistance and the technician came to fix it.

In an effort to help, I brought in a small lamp and put it on the desk near the computer. As I plugged it in, there was that familiar flash indicating the bulb had blown. I went to the closet, came back with a new bulb and screwed it in until it was snug. The bulb glowed. At last, a job I knew how to do: changing a light bulb.

SOME THOUGHTS ON VACATIONS

Taking a vacation isn't easy. There are all sorts of ways to do it wrong and I suspect that a lot of you make a mess of your vacation.

First, we all ought to face the fact that planning a vacation is more fun, more satisfying and more restful than actually taking one. It's certainly less expensive. Looking forward to a good vacation is one of the great pleasures of life, yet very few of us can say that about actually being on vacation.

In the first place, planning a vacation doesn't cost anything. Nothing goes wrong when you're planning. There are no endless hours of driving, no lines at the airport, no unexpected expenses, no rainy days to endure when you're in the planning stages.

I am something of an expert on ruining a vacation because I've done it often.

I know what's wrong, but I can't correct my mistake. I have made one of the basic vacation errors. I try to do too many things in too many different places.

Cramming it full is not the way to take a vacation. The things I planned all seemed good to me when I was thinking about them, but now that I'm halfway into my month off, I realize I'm not having a lot of fun or getting much rest because I keep going someplace. Wherever I am, I decide to pick up and go somewhere else.

The places I go all look good from a distance but once I get there, they're pretty much like where I came from but with different people and a different, unfamiliar bed to sleep in. I know now that I should have gone to a nice house we have in the country and stayed there. I shouldn't have done a lot of moving around. It might have been a good idea to have had the telephone disconnected but I'm too insecure for that. I'm afraid no one would have called me and I'd never have known they hadn't.

I'm already planning next year's vacation while I'm still on this one. I know what I'm going to do. I'm not going anywhere. I'm going to stay home, go to bed early, get up when I feel like getting up, watch some late-night television, eat what I feel like eating with no regard for the diet advice everyone is shoving down our throats in books and magazine articles. Next year, in order to have a real, restful vacation, I'd like to be bored for a few days because I had nothing to do. Being busy is never restful.

I hardly ever read a whole book anymore and even the morning newspaper is a challenge if you're on a busy vacation. If you're traveling, you have to read someone else's hometown newspaper and it's never the same as what you're used to. Next year, I'm going to spend two hours over breakfast, drink three cups of coffee and read the whole newspaper, including the Help Wanted pages. I may take a nap after breakfast instead of doing an errand. I'll do a lot of errands on my vacation, though, because buying something can be very relaxing.

I grew up with boats on a lake we went to summers, but boating is one of the most tense ways to relax. Unlike cars, boats very often don't work. There's often something wrong with a boat and boats are certainly one of the most expensive pleasures known to man. A boat is more expensive than a hotel and then you have to pay to put it away in winter.

I often pass a big boatyard or docking area with hundreds of boats just sitting there in the water, doing nothing. There's no single toy Americans own so many of that they use so infrequently, as their boats. The places you can go in a boat are much more limited than the places you can go in a car. There are no four-wheel drive boats.

I keep hearing about other people's vacations. Not many will admit they were terrible, but if you listen carefully, you can detect telltale signs that give it away. We had friends who went to Europe on the Queen Mary. We did that ourselves many years ago on the old Queen Mary. Call it luxurious, call it unusual, call it interesting, but don't call it a vacation. On board, they make you feel as though having a good time is compulsory. There's nothing restful about being on a boat.

A friend gave me a great hammock for Christmas several years ago. Hammocks are a genuine vacation item. They are hard to get into and hard to get out of, so once you're there, you tend to stay. That's vacation kind of time.

THE SMELL OF A NEW CAR

There are times other than birthdays, weddings, anniversaries and holidays that mark the personal history of each of us. In the past fifty years, I have bought fourteen new cars and each time was a special occasion in my life. I don't buy a new car lightly.

The price of a new car ought to be firmer than it is. I always have the feeling I could get the same thing for less if I shopped around more. It is obvious that car manufacturers have deliberately done things to obscure the price so that potential buyers can't figure out how much they are paying for what.

My old car, a 1999 model, had 86,000 miles on it and a few dings that needed paint. I usually drive a car for 100,000 miles before I trade it in, but I needed new tires and didn't want to put out $750 for four new tires on a car with that many miles on it. Tires last about 40,000 miles and I knew I'd never drive it another 40,000 miles.

My new car is from another manufacturer. It's a lot like the old one but three inches shorter. Many of the features on the car I bought—which I'm not going to name—were what they called "optional." My dictionary says: "Optional: left to choice. Not compulsory." In the car dealer's lexicon, "optional" means "take it or leave it" because you can't buy the car without most "optional" equipment.

I did not want the "Panorama Moonroof." My old car had one (called a "sunroof" by that manufacturer) and I never—not once—used it. I had to take the "Moonroof."

"If you want that," the salesman said of another feature, "it's $350 extra."

"What if I don't want it?" I asked.

"Well, you don't have to take it, but we don't have a car on the floor right now without it."

In every case, when they say something is "optional," they mean it costs extra if you want it. And if you want the car, you have to take it.

"Do I get four wheels?" I asked, "or are wheels optional?"

Car salesmen are deaf to attempts at humor.

The only "optional" equipment I seem to have avoided was the "genuine leather-wrapped steering wheel."

There are so many variations on basic models that I question whether manufacturers ever make two cars alike. Anyone looking to buy a car can't compare prices of two different kinds of cars or two different cars in the same showroom because no two are the same.

Years ago, when I was buying my first car, it was simple. I had the choice of buying a Ford, a Chevrolet, a Buick or an Oldsmobile. Maybe

I'd look at a Pontiac or a Chrysler, but I wasn't faced with 19 different models of each make. It was either a Ford or it wasn't.

Now every manufacturer puts out a dozen models, each with a different number. My car comes in an X3, an X5 or an X7. I asked why they skipped model X4 and model X6 and the salesman didn't know. He thought it was strange that I asked.

At the bottom of many of the pages in the glossy brochure for my car, there are explanations for the asterisks like:

"Optional: included in X3 3.3Oi Premium Package."

"Halogen free-form fog lights (std on 3.3 Oi, opt on 2.5i)."

"Included in Optional Premium Package."

What "optional" means in every case is, it isn't included on the basic car or if it is included you can't buy the car without the optional features because they don't make a car without it. I am perfectly willing to have car salesmen make a decent living. Most of them have good personalities and are pleasant to deal with, but what we all want and can't get from them is a firm price that we can compare with the price of a car we're looking at somewhere else.

EXPENSIVE BED, BAD BREAKFAST

I don't know what it is about them, but I remember hotels I've stayed in and I was saddened to read that the Rossiya Hotel in Moscow is being closed and torn down.

I stayed at the Rossiya twice years ago and I've never forgotten because it was the worst hotel I was ever in. The Rossiya was built by the Communist regime in 1967. At the time, it was the biggest hotel in the world—3,000 rooms. That's a lot of little cakes of soap in an American hotel but the Rossiya didn't have soap.

When you left your room at the Rossiya, you turned in your key to a woman sitting at a desk by the elevator on every floor. When you came back, you stopped and got your key from her. The Communists always wanted to know when foreigners were coming and going.

They were proud to tell you there was a telephone in every room in the Rossiya, but they didn't tell you there was no switchboard in the hotel. If anyone wanted to call you, they had to know the number. No one knew the number, of course.

If the Rossiya was the worst hotel I ever stayed in, the best was a suite I once had on the top floor of the Fairmont in San Francisco. I had a four-way view of the city, including the Golden Gate Bridge. Even breakfast was good.

The year after I was discharged from the Army after World War II, I wrote a book with a friend, which we sold to MGM. We went to Hollywood and our agent put us up at the Beverly Hills Hotel. It was such a grand experience that I've never stayed anywhere else when I go there. It's cost me dearly over the years. The hotel is owned by the royal family of Brunei, who probably took the money for it from the people of Brunei. I have breakfast in the Polo Lounge and always hope Clark Gable or Lana Turner will come in. They used to, but don't anymore.

In Paris, we stay at a small Left-Bank place called Le Relais Christine. It used to be a monastery and each of its fifty-one rooms is different. The Claridge in London is special. They tolerate Americans but don't really like them. When I'm in San Diego, I stay at the grand old Hotel Del Coronado. In 1978, I was on the top floor during an AARP convention. (I was hiding with a camera crew trying to question the president, Leonard Davis—the insurance salesman who invented the AARP as a sales tool for his Colonial Penn Insurance Co.)

I like hotels but do have some complaints. Nothing, with the possible exception of movie tickets, has gone up in price more and faster than hotel rooms. In 1955, I stayed in a good hotel in New York for $4 a night. The same room today costs $230.

I wish they wouldn't put so many pillows on the bed. Sometimes they're piled so high that you can't see the clock on the table.

I wish there were an industry standard for shower controls in hotel rooms. It's easy to get burned or frozen in a strange shower.

Call me cheap, but I prefer to bring my suitcase to the room myself, not have it brought up by a bellboy. That was the only good thing about the Rossiya. They didn't have bellhops.

THE RAIN IN SPAIN AND HERE

It has never been determined whether human beings thrived on the planet Earth because conditions of atmosphere and weather were suited to their continued existence or whether, over thousands of years, humans went through some evolutionary process and adapted themselves to the conditions. For example, we sweat to cool our bodies. The process of evaporation uses energy—heat—which it takes from the body. The mechanism is all too complicated to comprehend and most people give in and just call it God.

Sometimes it seems like a close call whether we're going to survive with the weather we have. It is often perilously close to being too hot for us to live or too cold. We've been smart at countering the effect of weather on our lives. We no longer live in cold caves. We live in houses we heat and cool.

The trouble with these man-made weather deflectors is that they depend on electricity. When we lose our power, we're helpless. To keep from freezing to death we can heap on more clothes and survive, but there's no hiding from heat if the air conditioning is out.

There are occasional aberrations in our weather patterns that have a major effect on where Americans live. The hurricanes that hit Florida have a permanent effect on that state. A great many older people, living in other parts of the country, who were planning to retire to Florida, are going to rethink that plan. Florida has been hit too often by hurricanes over the years for anyone to think of it as the idyllic place for retirement. The real estate market in Florida may be depressed for years because of the memory of these hurricanes.

The real estate industry in California has suffered some of the same setbacks that Florida's has. People look favorably on the generally sunny weather in California, but then every few years there's a catastrophic fire, flood or earthquake that makes it seem something less than the ideal place to live. Surprisingly enough, California holds the one-day snowfall record. One mountainous area in the eastern part of the state got sixty inches of snow in one day years ago.

My choice for the spot with our country's worst weather is Washington, D.C., even though it ruins my theory that the most work gets done in places with bad weather. Washington gets the worst of northern cold weather and the worst of southern hot weather. If terrorists wanted to bring this nation to its knees, they wouldn't need to resort to nuclear or biological weapons. They could just pray to Allah for a few feet of snow in our capital. Half an inch brings Washington to a halt. They send people home and close government offices when it's cloudy.

New York, Massachusetts, Maine, New Hampshire and Vermont are not known for their good weather but their extremes are predictable. Arizona and Nevada are the new fad states. Their populations are growing faster than any other states'. Maybe it's because they don't have snowstorms or hurricanes, but what both need and don't have is rain. They get only about eight inches of rain a year so they could use a sprinkler system in the sky. There's nothing I like better than a good, drenching rain. I enjoy both a raincoat and an umbrella. They give me the same good feeling I had as a kid in a tent in our back yard.

New York has a fairly consistent rainfall of about forty-two inches a year. Maine gets about forty-five inches but a lot of that comes down as snow. Ten inches of snow is the equivalent of one inch of rain.

You don't think of Arkansas as wet, but three years ago Little Rock got seventy inches of rain. Mobile, Ala., also gets a lot of rain.

Most of us prefer the weather we have wherever we are—bad as it may be.

RING A DING DING

There's nothing civil about the way Democrats and Republicans are be-having. It should be called "The Uncivil War." It isn't just politicians, ei-ther. It's their supporters, as well, and I'm having nothing to do with all of them until it's over. I got a new toy yesterday that took my mind off the election.

Having recently lost my third cellphone, I acquired another. I write "acquired" instead of "bought" because the companies that make phones are so interested in having us buy their service that they're often willing to give us the instrument if we sign up. You know right away when they offer you anything free that they're going to get you later.

The people designing portable telephones in India or China or wherever they are, ought to take some time off. We don't need any new developments in their technology. We do not want our telephones to do the things they are designing them to do. All I want is an instrument that allows me to call home or the office. I don't want to see anyone on the screen. I don't want to "add to your database." I don't know what my database is or what data it contains.

If there are young computer geeks who are amused by telephones that do a hundred things other than what a telephone was invented to do, good. Make a phone for them but make one for the rest of us that sticks to the basic job that Alexander Graham Bell had in mind when he called Watson.

My new phone plays what its designers must have thought was a cute tune when I turn it on or off. I'm not only disinterested in cute noises that alert me to the status of my phone, I'm damned irritated by them. When I leave my new phone on to get incoming calls, it gives forth a loud beep every four minutes to let me know it's on. I know it's on. I turned it on and I don't want to be annoyed by any damned beeping de-signed to inform me of something I already know.

The noises my new phone makes got me thinking about all the sounds used to alert us to a wide variety of occurrences. I'm always im-pressed, when I travel to another country, by how different their sounds are. In London, ambulances and fire engines have a distinctive sound that I find more compelling and alarming than the sirens our ambulances and fire trucks use.

The family always enters our house through the kitchen door. The front door is for strangers, people selling something or kids at Halloween. There is a doorbell, but there's also a grand, heavy brass knocker on the door. I've noticed, over the years, that I like the people who use the knocker better than I like the bell-ringers. Brass knockers have gone out of style as sounding devices designed to alert the house's occupants to visitors. Too bad. There's something firm and deliberate about a knock on the door that a shrill bell doesn't have. Many old homes have both a bell and a knocker like ours, but I suppose some cost-conscious nitpicker decided both were unnecessary and chose to eliminate the knocker on new homes.

For some reason, we take our public and private noises without comment or complaint. We don't do that with anything else so dominant in our lives. We ought to complain and have some of them changed. I'd start by having them change the noises this new, free phone of mine makes.

Why couldn't one of the geniuses who keep changing cellphones come up with a different sound? Instead of what they call a ring— which isn't a ring at all, of course—they might have the phone emit the pleasing sound of a solid brass knocker on a solid wooden door.

EASY PASS FOR AIRLINES

A lot of the traveling people used to do by plane was frivolous. They went someplace for the sake of going, not because they had to get there for any good reason. The airlines depended on casual tourists like this because they filled their planes by outnumbering business travelers.

Even business travel was often unnecessary. Businessmen and women traveled to conferences because of the favorable impression this made on the people at the meeting. If they came a long way it lent importance to the occasion. Too often it was not important that they got there at all, and they're no longer going as often.

In 1985, a company vice president I knew was always going to meetings in far away cities. He loved to say, "I have to go to the Coast Wednesday." One New York tabloid even ran a daily column listing the prominent people who were going to Hollywood or returning from it to N.Y.

A friend of mine went to the airport one morning to catch an 8 A.M. flight to Los Angeles, where he was scheduled to attend an "important" meeting at 2 P.M. With the three-hour time difference, he figured he had plenty of time. The flight was delayed several hours while they repaired a windshield wiper and there was further delay on the runway. They encountered headwinds on the trip west and my friend didn't arrive at LAX until the meeting was over. He went back to the airline counter and caught the next flight back to New York.

He told me about this as though it had been frustrating but I never believed he missed anything important by not being at the meeting. A lot of travel used to be like that, but such trips are not being scheduled anymore.

I don't like to see an airline go bankrupt, but a lot of airlines are going out of business because of the intrusive and time-consuming security measures the government insists on. They are never going to catch one single terrorist intent on blowing up a plane, but they are going to deter millions of people from taking the kind of unnecessary trips airlines depend on for business. No one wants to undergo an hour-long strip search of body and luggage to take a pleasure trip. I do have a suggestion for airlines. It will probably be dismissed as elitist, but I like a little elitism.

It's my premise that most people, quite obviously, are not going to blow up an airplane or commit any kind of terrorist act. I know we're supposed to oppose profiling of any kind, but my profile is so benign they could safely issue me, and millions of other travelers, some kind of permanent, non-transferable ID card allowing us instant access to our seats on any plane.

I see no reason why most Americans couldn't apply for and receive such cards, permitting them to board a plane, with their baggage, as soon as they arrived at the airport.

While such a system might prove unfair to people unable to get a card, it would solve a lot of problems for the airlines. If there were such a pass, and if I had one, I would have flown six times in the past three months. Without it, I stayed home. Going wasn't worth the hassle.

If it was more foolproof than a card, they could use some kind of fingerprint identification system. Anyone who'd been cleared could walk up to the gate at the airport, press his thumb on a plate and an ALL CLEAR sign would light up as the device read the fingerprint.

THE AGONY OF FLIGHT

I have just taken a memorable trip I'd like to forget.

Because I was going to be in Los Angeles for only two days, I drove from my office in New York to Kennedy Airport so I'd have my car when I returned and could drive home to Connecticut. The parking area is just a minute's walk across the road from American Airlines.

When I arrived at the airport for a 9 A.M. flight at 7:30, I thought I had plenty of time. Sure. The short-term parking lot was closed for repair. I was directed to a lot two miles from the terminal. By the time I found it, parked and waited for the bus to take me to the terminal, it was 8:17. The baggage attendants outside told me my flight was "closed" and I could no longer check bags. Inside, I waited in line to check my bag anyway. By the time I got to the gate (all flights leave from the most remote gate), it was 8:40 and they were closing the door.

First class for the round trip flight cost $2,762.90. Business class cost $1,858.90. A coach seat was $517.90. I flew coach. Airlines make coach so uncomfortable that even people who can't afford it pay the "business" rate.

In flight, the pilot kept announcing that we were ahead of schedule. We landed nine minutes early, and after being told to keep our seats, we waited . . . and waited . . . and waited. Then came the inevitable: "There is a plane parked at our gate which should be moving out shortly. Please remain in your seats. Thank you for your patience." Which we were not.

Flight times should be recorded from the time they close the door for takeoff to the time they open the door to let passengers off. The advertised time of my flight was five hours and fifty-seven minutes. From the time we had to be on board to the time we were allowed off, it was seven hours and twelve minutes.

At baggage claim, the carousel went round and round. My bag never came 'round. At the lost baggage office, I waited in line. They were doing a booming business. I finally got to talk to a woman behind the desk, who said my bag would be arriving on the next flight. I opted to have the bag sent to my hotel.

In Beverly Hills, I went to the hotel I've stayed in a hundred times. It's also expensive but I could stay there for weeks for what first class costs on American.

In my room, I called American baggage service at 12:30 and was told my bag had been found and would be delivered "within six hours." I once worked at MGM, so I drove around some old familiar places, including Malibu Beach, wasting time waiting for my bag. I needed things in it to dress for dinner with friends. When I got back to the hotel, I called American again and got the "six hour" announcement again. It had now been five.

There was a huge window over the bathtub in the hotel room and by pressing a button next to the light switch, you could open a curtain that allowed you to look out on a palm frond garden.

I took a shower more to waste time than from necessity—I wasn't that dirty—and dried off with a thick towel that was six feet long. It made the bath towels at home seem puny.

After the shower, I read the paper and waited for my bag, which didn't come. It was delivered sometime after midnight, so I went out to dinner in khaki pants and slept in a terrycloth robe.

Sunday night, I ate dinner in my room because I wanted to watch *60 Minutes*. Mike Wallace interviewed Putin. Morley Safer's report on West Point was good. I could have done without Steve Kroft's chat with Ray Romano, but I watched it almost to the end. Almost. Next thing I knew, I woke up and they were showing the *60 Minutes* credits. I had missed the best part of the show.

I'll tell you about my trip home another time. It wasn't as good as the trip out.

GOING NOWHERE FAST

I've been thinking about airplanes since they grounded the Concordes because they were too expensive. It was sad. I flew twice in a Concorde. CBS paid for it and I forget how I convinced them I was that important and in so much of a hurry. I don't remember what it cost, but the fare on the last trip for one person from New York to London and back was $10,000.

There's some basic law of nature being violated—although I can't put my finger on what it is—when we are able to invent something so expensive we can't afford it.

Most people remember their first airplane ride or some memorable flight they've taken. I always get wondering how those little wings on a passenger plane can keep 200 passengers, all their luggage and 5,000 gallons of gas up in the air.

I flew a lot in what may be the greatest airplane ever built, the DC-3. It wasn't glamorous like the Concorde but it was the workhorse of World War II—top speed of 230 mph. The Air Force called it the C-47 and bought 10,000 of them from Douglas. It didn't fight any battles but it carried several million American soldiers all over the world and I was one of them. Dozens of DC-3s are still flying in South America sixty-five years after they were built.

They tried to improve the C-47 with the C-46 and it was a dud. I flew in one from India to China and it didn't make me easy knowing they'd lost many of them flying over the Himalayan Mountains, known as "The Hump." Some joker had scribbled on the wall behind my bucket seat: THIS IS A THING YOU DON'T SEE OFTEN— TWO ENGINES MOUNTED ON A COFFIN.

If anything compares with the DC-3 in longevity, durability and safety, it's the reliable little Piper Cub. It wasn't the Cub's fault that my school friend Charley Wood, the class poet, an artillery spotter, was killed when he was shot down in one in Normandy.

The last airplane so distinctive that I never forgot it was the four-engine 747. A pilot told me it was the best airplane ever built but it was also too expensive to fly.

There was a stairway to an upstairs lounge in the 747 and I was up there on a flight with Jimmy Durante and Jack Nicholson. You don't forget that flight, although Nicholson had a personality I'd like to forget.

I've lost track of airplanes since the 747. They're all the same. The biggest changes were to make the aisles narrower and the seats closer together. Passenger planes used to have aisles wide enough so you could get by the food carts to go to the bathroom.

During World War II, I flew in a B-17 as a reporter on the second 8th AF raid on Germany. My plane, the Banshee, was hit and I was scared stiff but it made a good story.

The British Spitfire was one of the all-time great airplanes. It helped save the British Isles from invasion.

Our best fighter plane then was the P-47s Thunderbolt. It wasn't as maneuverable as the Spit but much more powerful. An American who had been a Spitfire pilot and switched to the P-47 told me it was like the difference between riding a circus pony and straddling a tiger.

I wasn't being shot at during the most dangerous flight I ever took. I spent twenty-nine days in a helicopter flying across the United States taking pictures for a documentary film called "A Bird's-Eye View of America." The Sikorsky had two engines and two pilots . . . the best helicopter ever built, but they've never really finished inventing the helicopter. One of our two pilots was killed in a crash shortly after our trip.

Too bad about the Concorde. Like a lot of good things, we could afford it if we didn't waste so much on useless weapons like tanks, battleships, submarines and fighter planes.

Our latest fighter, the F-22 Raptor, costs approximately $133 million—and none of us will ever get a ride in one of those.

TAKE A STAY HOME VACATION

Some American companies have names that are so strongly associated with good, dependable products that we unconsciously think well of them when we see the names. We like car companies like Ford or General Motors. They make dependably good products. We trust the cereals made by Kellogg's. We know we'll get an honest deal in stores like Macy's or Saks.

The sound of airline names often evokes the opposite reaction. Many of these names are so strongly associated in our minds with cancelled flights, late arrivals, crowded seating, unpredictable fares and ruined vacations that we have sworn never to buy a ticket on one of them again.

Sometimes you can't avoid flying on an airline you dislike. When a flight attendant thanks everyone on board "for choosing Delta," "choosing American" or "choosing United," it rings hollow in the ears of passengers. They didn't choose one airline over the other because they liked it. They chose the airline based on cost or because it was the only one with a flight to the city they had to get to. I clearly remember the excitement of flight just after World War II. It was an adventure, but travel has long since lost its appeal. (It takes much longer to buy a ticket at an airline counter now that they have computers than it did when everything was done manually.)

I wish there was money for someone to mount an advertising campaign to get people to travel less. I'd like to write headlines for don't-travel ads:

THERE'S NO PLACE LIKE HOME—AND YOU DON'T HAVE TO FLY TO GET THERE!

IT'S NEVER BETTER SOMEWHERE ELSE! YOUR BAGGAGE WON'T GET LOST IF YOU LEAVE IT IN YOUR CLOSET!

BEFORE YOU PLAN A TRIP, REMEMBER WHAT A TERRIBLE TIME YOU HAD ON THE LAST TRIP!

FRENCH FOOD IS GREAT. EAT IT IN A FRENCH RESTAURANT IN THE UNITED STATES!

THANK YOU FOR NOT FLYING DELTA!

AMERICAN—THE DEPENDABLE AIRLINE. YOU CAN DEPEND ON IT BEING LATE.

It's hard to understand why so many people so often go to the trouble of getting to places when getting there is almost always an expensive and unpleasant experience.

The Christmas holidays of hundreds of thousands of people are ruined every year because they were trying to go someplace other than home for the holidays. US Airways changed its name from US Air a few years ago but it hasn't changed its ways.

The pilots, flight attendants and mechanics are mostly capable people. I've known a few airline executives and found them to be capable. So why are our airlines terrible? Maybe what they try to do is too difficult to accomplish. Just to begin with, they have to defy the laws of gravity to get the airplanes off the ground loaded with a few hundred people and baggage.

Whatever the reason, I am convinced that more Americans should stay home. Call it a people's strike against the airlines if you want to, but traveling for fun, if travel involves flight, is an oxymoron. We ought to get over this urge we all have to be somewhere else. There is not a city in the U.S. that has been explored by its residents the way those same people would explore a city in a foreign country. A trip of a few hundred miles by car can take any of us into a new and strange world, and those places ought to be our travel destinations rather than Rome or Paris.

THE PERFECT PAT DOWN PERSON

While I have no intention of giving up my day job, I wouldn't mind picking up some extra money. I'm thinking of applying for work as an airport security guard.

My desire is to help President Bush make this nation safe from terrorists. The way I want to help is by patting people down. Up and down, actually. It's apparent that the government feels the principal danger to our nation lies in the lines of Americans waiting to get on airplanes.

Last week, I came through airport security on a trip from New York to Boston. I quickly realized that gray-haired old geezers like me who need help lifting a briefcase up onto the conveyor belt that takes potential weapons through the X-ray machine are high on the security guards' list of suspects.

I could tell right away that the inspectors thought I was trying to sneak something like an atomic bomb on board the plane. They didn't find it with the screening machine but they persisted because they knew I must have it hidden somewhere, so they told me to remove my shoes. I was surprised they considered me so dangerous in view of the fact that two of them said, "Hello, Andy. Love your show," to me. They must have thought that for me to pose as a person who appears on television would be the perfect cover for a terrorist.

Ahead of me in the line was an attractive, well-dressed young woman. I already had noticed her although it wasn't because she looked suspicious. The security guard gave her special attention, too. She was asked to remove her coat and her jacket, which left her in a nice silk blouse. The security guard, a woman, ran her hand all over the woman. I was impressed with how thorough she was with this suspect.

As I stood by the checkpoint for a few minutes after I was found not guilty of weapons possession it became clear to me that no one but women security guards ever patted down women suspects. This is when I became determined to get a job as a security guard myself. More than that, I am determined to break down this sexist hiring practice. Am I any less capable of detecting a dangerous device hidden on the person of an attractive woman passenger than a same sex-security guard?

We men have got to face the fact that sex discrimination is a two-way street and too often, we are the victims. We should stop taking it lying down. There are no organizations demanding equal rights for men. Why? For what reason are men not allowed to do the job of patting down women in public places?

But seriously:

As I've said before, all frequent travelers who pass a test that indicates that they are not now and never will be terrorists, should be issued cards bearing their picture and fingerprints. These cards would allow them easy passage through security checkpoints and access to the aircraft loading area without having to go through the ridiculous and humiliating pat down process. The airlines have already established this as a possibility by allowing their crews easier access.

Air travel has become such a tedious and unpleasant experience that Americans are going to start staying home.

Since searches began, airport personnel have probably searched 50 million without finding one single terrorist. It is my sense that they never will find one because if someone wants to blow up an airplane, they'll find a way to circumvent the pat down procedure.

TECHNOLOGICALLY ILLITERATE

I'm treading the ragged edge of ineptitude. I may have to step back and watch the world go by because I'm too dumb to be part of it. On every hand, I have machines I don't know how to work, gadgets that are smarter than I am, tools that are more complex than the job I want to do with them.

In a box under my desk I have cords, cables and connectors for dozens of pieces of electronic equipment that I have long since replaced with newer models that use different cords, cables or connectors. It's apparent they are too important to throw away. And they don't go to anything anyone else owns. Their computer is the same make as mine but it's a different model. It is apparent the makers of computers redesign their products every few days.

I have a new, digital camera, but I never know whether I've taken a picture or not because it doesn't click when I press the button the way my old film camera did. I used to take the film to the drugstore in the morning and went back to get the pictures in the afternoon. Now I don't know what to do with the images in my camera.

Four months ago, I bought a new car. I still don't know how to turn the air conditioner on, off, up or down. I just keep pressing buttons until I get a desirable result. Evidence of the fact that change and progress have outpaced sales and service in cars became evident to me last week when I finally took the manual out of the glove compartment.

I spent fifteen minutes trying to match the pictures in it with the dials and buttons on the dashboard. I finally realized it was for the past model. The manufacturer had changed the dashboard without updating the manual.

This week, I'm going through a traumatic experience in my life as a writer.

Ten years ago, I made the difficult but successful transition from the typewriter to the computer, and I reluctantly concede that the computer is a better tool for a writer than the typewriter ever was.

I was introduced to the program called WordPerfect for DOS and became familiar with the keystrokes involved in writing using it.

A lot of people are now using a word processing program called Word. Word for Windows is a more complicated, user-unfriendly program that seems to have been developed by the Bill Gates organization as a way of forcing WordPerfect for DOS users to convert to a program compatible with Bill Gates' operating system. Word is, on all counts, not as good or as easy to use as WordPerfect. (I notice that the New York Bar Association has officially stuck with WordPerfect in preference to Word.)

The name of the old musical rings in my ears: "Stop the World, I Want to Get Off."

NO-SHOW REPAIR PEOPLE

When I read statistics about the number of unemployed people in the United States, I never feel very bad about it.

It always seems to me that, in most cases, they aren't working for some reason other than that they can't find work.

There's so much work that needs to be done that anyone out of work ought to be able to find the work that needs to be done if they really want to work.

The problem, of course, is that a lot of people who are capable of doing one job, cannot do another.

I'd like to see someone start a college that taught young people nothing but how to fix things.

Of the 3,463,000 times Americans have called repairmen (my estimate) and made a date for them to come to the house, only nine of those millions of repairmen came when they said they would.

The rest of the time, we waited in vain all day for them to show up.

We have two telephone lines in our house in the country so I can leave our private line available to friends who want to call when I'm working online writing something. Last Wednesday, the line I use for my computer was dead.

I called the telephone repair service and the person who books the repair work told me they'd come on Thursday between 8 A.M. and 6 P.M.

On Friday morning, I called Verizon repair again in the Albany area. The woman taking calls said that the repair crew had been too busy to come Thursday.

"Do they have a telephone with them?" I asked. "Couldn't they have called when it became apparent that they weren't going to make it, so I didn't have to waste a whole day waiting?"

"When will they come?" I asked. She assured me they would be at our house Friday or Saturday sometime between 8 A.M. and 6 P.M. They did not come Friday or Saturday.

When I called Verizon telephone repair again, I told the woman who answered that I was recording our conversation. She immediately put me on hold. Three minutes later, she came back on and told me her supervisor had advised her that it was illegal for me to record our conversation without her permission and she was not giving it.

I'd like to print a verbatim transcript of that conversation. If the phone company decided to sue me, I wouldn't worry. They probably wouldn't show up in court that day.

A NAME IS A BRAND WE'RE GIVEN

Most of us like our names. We can't imagine being called anything else. I'm ambivalent about my name. I like "Andrew," but only a few close friends and family members call me "Andrew." To everyone else, I'm "Andy." While I don't want to be called "Andrew" by everyone, I never warmed up to myself as "Andy." It always sounds to me like someone else. It's a name I use for commercial purposes. A few good old friends call me "Roon."

Most first names like Andrew are replaced in casual relationships with a nickname. It seems friendlier, I guess. William becomes "Bill," John is "Jack," "Hal" for Harold, "Ed" for Edward, "Joe" for Joseph, "Mike" for Michael. There are dozens of them. Occasionally, someone who takes himself seriously objects.

There are fewer nicknames for girls, I think. Elizabeth gets to be "Betty" and Katherine "Kate," but you can't do much with Helen, Joan, Mary, Doris, Mabel, Ruth or Anna. I don't know how some nicknames come about. Why is Sarah "Sally," or Elizabeth "Betty"?

The ten most popular boys names chosen by parents in recent years, according to Social Security records, have been Jacob, Michael, Joshua, Matthew, Andrew, Joseph, Ethan, Daniel, Christopher and Anthony.

The ten most common girls names now are Emily, Emma, Madison, Hannah, Olivia, Abigail, Alexis, Ashley, Elizabeth and Samantha. I'm suspicious of this list. I've never known a girl named "Madison."

President George W. Bush was lucky his parents gave him the middle initial "W," standing for "Walker." It inhibits anyone from calling him "Junior." A President shouldn't be called "Junior." As a matter of fact, no one should be called "Junior." It has always seemed to me to be wrong for parents to give a boy his father's name and tack "Junior" onto it. A kid deserves his own name. He shouldn't be burdened with his father's. For all his life there is confusion between the two men and there is something demeaning about "Junior," anyway. In order to differentiate between father and son, the kid is often called by some silly name or, perhaps worse, he's called "Junior."

Girls are not so often given their mother's names and, even though the word is not gender-specific, no one ever calls a girl "Junior."

Sometimes a nickname seems totally wrong. You wouldn't dream of calling some actors by a nickname. How could you call Robert Redford "Bob"? Richard Burton was never called "Dick." It would seem strange to call Sir Laurence Olivier "Larry." And imagine calling Ernest Hemingway "Ernie," William Shakespeare "Bill," or Edgar Allen Poe, "Ed Poe."

I envy people with three names. It makes them sound important. As a kid, I read Hans Christian Anderson and Louisa May Alcott. Then

there's Johann Sebastian Bach, Edgar Rice Burroughs, James Earl
Jones, Henry Wadsworth Longfellow, Joyce Carol Oates, George
Bernard Shaw and Martin Luther King Jr., of course. If I were really
important, I'd be Andrew Aitken Rooney. "Aitken" came from Scottish
great-grandparents.

We are victims of our parents when it comes to the names we're
given. They give it to us and, like it or not, we're stuck with it. The only
way out is a nickname and nicknames are not something we give ourselves. They come about naturally because that's who we seem like to
the people who call us that. I'm uneasy about seeming like "Andy." I
take myself more seriously than "Andy."

SNOWY THOUGHTS IN SUMMER

It's easy to think you prefer summer to winter when it's 10 below zero
and the wind is howling, and it's easy to think you prefer winter to summer when it's 94 in the shade, but I've set aside those factors that alter
our ability to think straight while we're enduring them. I've decided
that under any conditions, I prefer zero to 100.

It hasn't been 100 yet where I write, but it's been too close for comfort and I hate it. There's no limit to the clothes you can bundle up in
when it's cold outside, but there is a limit to how many clothes you can
take off to stay cool. Naked doesn't help. Even sleeping without pajamas
is no comfort. No pajamas only makes things worse; you stick to yourself instead of to them.

Air-conditioning was a great invention and a relatively new one. (I
think of anything that came along in my lifetime as recent.) We never
had it when I was growing up, and even now, there's no central
air-conditioning in our good old house. We make out with a few
unattractive air-conditioning machines hanging out the windows,
whirring away all night. The furnace that warms the house is a far

more satisfactory piece of equipment than the air conditioners. Air conditioners are intrusive. You're always aware of their presence. Radiators don't make a sound or blow anything at you; they quietly exude warmth.

I even recall with affection some of the cold weather clothes I had as a kid. My mother bought me a three-quarter-length sheepskin coat that kept me warm for five years, and I had a wool hat with flaps that covered my ears when they buttoned under my chin. I don't remember anything special I wore in hot weather.

On these hot days of summer, I find myself driving somewhere that I don't really have to go because the air-conditioning in my car is concentrated and a relief to be in. The system works well because the interior of the car is a small, closed space that cools readily.

One of the great pleasures of cold weather is a fireplace. Not many fireplaces are being built into new homes, and most of those are more decorative than functional. A gas-burning fireplace is not a real fireplace but a real one is a lot of work.

Swimming pools, lakes and ocean beaches are pleasant places in summer, but no warm weather pleasure compares to the healthy fun kids can have playing in the snow. I've always felt sorry for people who raise children in the parts of our country that don't get any. I'd rather have snow than oranges.

Nothing brings a community together like a heavy snow. You're all in it together, and a bonding takes place. The "good mornings" exchanged are more genuine after a snowstorm. On hot days, the "good mornings" are what I'd call desultory.

I've never wanted summer to end because I've always been on vacation, but I wish there was some way I could have my summer vacation with some snow instead of oppressive heat.

It occurs to me, I don't even write well when it's hot.

SIZING THINGS UP

The size of something is of first importance to whatever it is. Some things are too big and others are too small. It's a pleasure to get something that's just the right size, but it doesn't happen often.

Size is a big problem when it comes to clothes and shoes. I have trouble with shoes because I have wide feet. It's easy to get the right length, but few companies that make men's shoes give you a choice of width. There must be a lot of people walking around in shoes that don't fit. Women's shoes bear no resemblance to the size of their feet.

Some of the manufacturers who make socks have given up on sizes. Socks that say, "Fits size five to twelve" are too long for a size 8 and too short for a size 10. A lot of them say, "One size fits all," but it has been my experience that if the label says, "One size fits all," whatever the size is, the socks don't really fit anyone.

Most hats don't fit my head, so I don't wear hats. I have a big neck but short arms, so shirts that fit are hard to find. The shirts with big necks have the longest sleeves.

I'm always irritated with sizes in a grocery store when I buy eggs. The eggs in the boxes that say "medium" are small. Those marked "large" are medium, and the ones marked "jumbo" are large, if you're lucky.

When I decided to buy a new car several months ago, I went to the dealer who'd sold me my last one. I liked that car and was ready to buy a new model. I drive a lot in New York City, where space is at a premium. The new model was six inches longer than my old one. That was enough to turn me off and head me toward purchasing another car. My new car is three inches shorter than my old one. These days, it's difficult to get anything that's smaller than the model you already have. In New York, three inches in the length of a car can make the difference between getting or not getting a parking space.

Books are difficult to deal with because their sizes vary so much that they don't all fit in the same bookcase. Publishers ought to get together and decide to issue books in just two or three sizes. The books on my shelves vary from small ones, 4-by-6 inches, to fat volumes that measure

20-by-14 inches. The bigger ones are called "coffee table books" because they don't fit anywhere else.

The newspaper I spend at least an hour reading every day is an inconvenient size. I don't know how they started printing a paper that when opened to an inside page, is twenty-eight inches across and twenty-two inches from top to bottom. There is simply no way to handle it comfortably, and I end up folding it all sorts of different ways. Just as I get the page how I want it, I come to the end of a story and it says, "Continued on page 22," so I have to start folding again.

I realize this is sort of a ridiculous subject, but I started thinking about sizes and couldn't stop. What got me started was a copy of the new *TV Guide*. The editors (or maybe the sales manager) of *TV Guide* decided that the handy, *Readers Digest*–sized *TV Guide* was too small and they came out with a traditional magazine-sized magazine.

Next thing, I suppose *Reader's Digest* will be putting out a magazine the size of *Fortune* or *Esquire*.

MERRY CHRISTMAS FOR ALL

Please don't greet me at this time of year by saying "Happy Holidays." "Merry Christmas" has the sound I like. I associate it not with anyone's birthday, but with all the great December 25ths I've spent in my life with my family. "Happy Holidays" is a wishy-washy, politically neutral substitute that avoids any religious connotation but doesn't have any of the warmth and intimations of joy that "Merry Christmas" holds.

I don't mind those who think of Christmas as the birthday of Jesus Christ but I am not one of them. "Merry Christmas" long ago left behind any religious implications it ever had. It has a meaning all its own that exceeds any specific association you could attach to it. We all know what we mean when we say "Merry Christmas," even though it would be hard to spell out.

I don't dislike anyone on Christmas. I'm with my family and sometimes a few friends. I love the togetherness of it. I've never been lonely
on Christmas. I know I'm lucky and even that makes me feel good.

In the early days in New England, Puritans opposed the idea of
Christmas. They called Christmas "a Roman corruption of a heathen
practice." I don't know what the Puritans' hang-up was over Christmas.
Of course, there were a lot of crazy Puritans.

Christmas is celebrated in most European countries and we've
adopted some of their traditions here. The Christmas tree came from
Germany, along with stollen, their traditional Christmas fruit cake.
Aunt Anna made ours.

There's a difference of opinion about where "Santa Claus" came
from. The most common story is that he was originally a fourth-cen-
tury bishop from the area that's now Turkey. He was very generous, always giving things to kids, and the Christmas gift tradition started with
him. When I read that, I wondered if he ever got anything for someone
that he didn't like.

Christmas is older than I realized before I started reading about it.
The Roman Bishop Liberius is said to have chosen Dec. 25 as the birth-
day of Jesus in about 350 A.D. Dates like this are staggering to my brain.
That was 350 years after Christ was born and 1,656 years before 2006.
When you think about how hard it is to get a story right in the news the
day it happened, you wonder how accurate such an old story can be.

I don't think our great Christmas carols represent actual history either, but they're beautiful.

You won't hear "Bah, Humbug! or "Happy Holidays" from me.

"Merry Christmas!" is my greeting for the day and it should be used
by Christians, Muslims, Jews and atheists.

SORTING WELL-AGED FROM OLD

Some things—and people—age well. Some things—and people—just get old.

It's not easy to say exactly what makes one old chest of drawers a valuable antique and what makes another a piece of junk.

One of my favorite chores is going to the dump in my hometown on Saturday morning. Throwing stuff away that is cluttering up your house or your garage is a cathartic experience that feels good—but in addition to that, it's always interesting to see what other people throw away.

I don't like to have anyone see me do it, but I sometimes come home with more in the back of my Jeep than I took to the dump. Last week, the man in the car next to me was throwing out a piece of furniture that I couldn't identify. While he took one piece of it to the discard pile, I inspected another piece still in the back of his car. It was the top of some kind of table made of a single pine board almost forty inches square. Any board forty inches wide came from a huge tree probably 100 years old and the table itself was probably almost 100. When the man returned to get it to throw away, I asked if I could have it. I now have a beautiful old pine board that will have a new life because I will refinish it and turn it into something else. I feel good about saving it from being incinerated.

What started me thinking about this subject of old or used things was nothing as attractive as an old board. It was a banana peel I saw that someone had thrown in the street near where I park. Considering how attractive a banana looks sitting in a bowl of fruit along with some oranges, apples, pears and peaches, it's interesting that it turns instantly into so disgusting a piece of garbage once the edible part is removed. There is absolutely nothing aesthetically attractive about a banana peel.

Some of the used or secondhand cars you see for sale in lots with prices written on their windshields aren't much better-looking than a banana peel. On the other hand, I drove past an old-car show a few weeks ago and they had some antique beauties that were better-looking than the day they were made. What makes one old car junk and another collectible?

The clothes in my closet fall in two categories. A few of my good old tweed jackets made from material woven in Scotland or England have gained charm and character with age. They don't look seedy; they look well worn.

On the other hand, a lot of my old clothes ought to go. I'm running out of hangers and some of the suits hanging from them were mistakes when they were new and they've aged badly. I'd throw them out, but it hurts too much when I remember what I paid for them.

Some of my old books are ragged from the number of times I've thumbed through them looking for favorite passages. I've written remarks and notes in the margins and on the blank pages at the beginning and end. They're a mess, but they look beautifully familiar to me and I wouldn't trade them for brand new copies with pristine dust jackets. I don't know why it is, but old and new both seem more interesting than middle age. I have five pairs of middle-age shoes I'll never wear and never throw out.

THE SOUND OF SILENCE

There's no telling what wakes you on those nights you can't sleep. Last night, I awoke at 2:20. It was the sound of falling snow that did it. I knew it was snow because there was not a single, solitary sound. The silence of falling snow is deafening.

I lay there for several minutes, trying to breathe quietly so as not to obliterate the soundlessness. Finally, I couldn't handle my doubt any longer. I got up (I'm fighting off "arose"), pulled back the curtain and looked out on the backyard. Sure enough, there it was—gently falling snow hitting the ground silently, covering the little slate walk and clinging, half an inch thick, to tiny branches which are themselves no more than half an inch thick. It perched on top of the points of the picket fence in a beautifully symmetrical peak that no human hand could fashion. They say no two snowflakes have ever been the same but we don't know, do we? I saw two that looked very much alike.

There are all kinds of sounds in nature that are better than noise. Some sounds are good or bad depending on where you are and what you're doing when you hear them. Nothing is worse than a downpour of rain when you're caught out in it without a coat or umbrella. But inside, the sound of the same downpour is a pleasure that makes you appreciate your shelter.

Of all the sounds combining weather with nature, none is so persistently loud and impossible to turn off as the roar of the sea rolling up onto a broad, sandy beach. I envy people who live on expensive property near the ocean. There's the roar as thousands of tons of water advance on a broad front along the width of the beach, or the crash when the waves hit the immovable rocks that cup the shoreline at either end of a sandy crescent. There is the soft, seething sound as the water recedes. It pauses briefly out at sea, gathering strength for its next attack. A beach confounds angry waters by accepting them and defeating their destructive intentions, waiting patiently for the waves to go back where they came from, out to sea.

The heat of summer is as silent as snow but it's an oppressive silence. There is no pleasurable relief from heat comparable to the great feeling of pulling up the extra blanket on a cold night. Air conditioning is a modern marvel but it is loud, heartless and mechanical, with no charm. I don't like it but I don't know how we ever lived without it.

Wind is nature's most unpredictable sound. You never know for sure what it's doing, where it's coming from, or where it's going when it leaves. It's going somewhere but while it blows, it seems to stand still. The trees in front of my house are miraculously strong standing up to the wrath of a gale. The trunks creak, the branches crack, but the big maple has stood through hundreds of storms since it was a slip of a tree whipping in the wind fifty years ago. The tree will, in all probability, survive many more years.

My perfect day would be to awaken to a cool and sunny day with a sun that shone in the kitchen window while I ate breakfast. I'd take my own shower under circumstances that improve on nature's showers by allowing me to control the force and temperature of the spray with the twist of a dial.

By the time I sat down at my typewriter, which is not a typewriter at all any longer, my ideal day would be cloudy with a threat of rain that discouraged my considering even grocery store travel and encouraged this kind of overwriting.

DON'T MESS WITH MY GRASS

I have what I think is bad news for people who own a home that has a lawn.

James Hagedorn, the president of Scotts Miracle-Gro, says that his company has developed a new, slower-growing, genetically engineered grass that hardly ever has to be mowed.

I'm for progress in most areas, but grass is one thing that doesn't need to be improved. I don't want my lawn to be genetically engineered. What makes Mr. Miracle-Gro himself think I'll be any happier if I only have to mow the lawn twice a year? If he's so smart, how come he leaves the "w" off "grow" in the name of his company? He thinks "Miracle-Gro" is clever?

The fact is, Mr. Hagedorn, people like to mow their lawns. It's like shoveling the snow off the sidewalk. There are just a few simple chores left that are easy and satisfying for the homeowner, and those are two of them. If someone has a sidewalk too big to shovel or a lawn too exten-sive to mow, they must be rich enough to pay someone to do it for them. Cutting the grass is not a job we hate. It's easy, satisfying and it makes the place look better. So leave our grass alone, Mr. Hagedorn. We like it the way it is. Nothing makes people feel prouder than mowing their lawn . . . unless it's shoveling their sidewalk.

There are women who enjoy ironing because they find ironing relaxing. For the few minutes it takes them to do it, they know exactly what they're doing. That's the way it is with a man shoveling a sidewalk or mowing a lawn.

If Mr. Hagedorn wants to help homeowners, he ought to give some attention to the jobs we really hate. How about coming up with a machine that would clean out the attic, tidy up the basement, or make more room in the garage, Mr. Hagedorn? Could you redesign a lawnmower to do that? If you could, you'd be doing something for us. We'd all like to be able to get two cars in our two-car garages. Could you arrange that?

As a matter of fact, you've got some work to do redesigning the lawnmower before you redesign grass. Forget about not mowing lawns. Figure out a place where we can put that damn lawnmower when we're done with it. A lawnmower doesn't fit anywhere. We use it seven times a year, and the rest of the time it's just in the way. Give us a lawnmower that folds. The lawnmower takes up too much room that we need for other things like shovels, rakes, bicycles, gas cans. There isn't a mower of lawns among us who likes the design.

When I mow the lawn, I make a satisfying executive decision. The question is always whether to mow up and down, up and down, or across and across, across and across. Sometimes, I alternate the pattern of my mowing. I'll just keep going around and around in a diminishing oblong pattern until the patch in the middle gets small enough so that the mower's wheels span the strip of grass left and I can get it with one satisfying pass.

I'll bet Mr. Hagedorn thinks you ought to rake up the grass you've cut, too. I don't rake. I take the position that the clippings have all the nutrients the grass took up out of the earth while it grew. It's better to leave them and let them gradually leach back into the soil. I also think the clippings protect the roots of the grass from the hot sun.

I've often raked together a little pile of grass I've cut and stared at it. So nice. It seems as if it ought to be good to eat. If horses and cows find grass so delicious, why is it that humans never eat it? Fried in a little butter with salt and pepper, maybe? If grass turned out to be a delicacy, Mr. Hagedorn would regret the day he developed a lawn that hardly grew at all.

Next time I mow the lawn, I may cook a few cups and have the neighbors over for grass.

NOTES ON THE NEWS

- A recent survey concluded that half of all working Americans don't like their jobs. That's a sad statistic but I wonder if it's true. I'm always surprised at how interested people are in what seems like dull work to me. I don't meet a lot of people who are unhappy with what they do. My father worked for a company that sold products to the papermaking industry. I always thought Dad did the dullest work I ever heard of but he liked it so much he always hoped I'd follow him into the business. I wonder if the people who did that survey like surveying.

- The mayor of New York has proposed raising the tax on a pack of cigarettes by 50 cents. Smokers already pay $3 tax on a pack. A pack costs $6.90 in most stores. That means one cigarette costs about 34 cents. No one dares complain when they raise the tax on cigarettes, but there's some question whether governments that raise cigarette taxes are trying to make money or reduce smoking. It's wrong if their object is to make money. Why don't they make smoking cigarettes illegal? Marijuana is illegal and I wouldn't be surprised if tobacco was worse for people than grass. We might find a legal way to provide tobacco to people who were hopelessly hooked on it. They could be exempt from the no-smoking tobacco law for a limited period while they found a way to kick the habit.

- Daniel Dennett, a professor at Tufts University in Boston, says in an interview: "Certainly, the idea of a God that can answer prayers and whom you can talk with, and who intervenes in the world—that's a hopeless idea. There is no such thing."

- I hope you'll think I'm doing the wise thing by having no comment to make on Professor Dennett's statement.

- I keep reading airline ads offering special, low-cost deals on certain flights. I have a suggestion for something they ought to include in their lower fares offer. They ought to charge less for anyone who has to sit in a middle seat. Maybe they ought to build thinner airplanes without any three across seating. There would be no middle seat.

- The report that Ford is closing fourteen plants and laying off 30,000 workers is terrible news for all America, not just for those 30,000 workers. If Ford is in trouble, America is in trouble.

- I have a press ticket for the Super Bowl and it's a good thing. Stubhub, the online ticket agency, has posted ticket prices for the game. Two tickets together on the 20-yard line in row 17 are $2,858 each. If you want to sit in a suite on the 20-yard line, one ticket will cost you $176,475. It makes saying, "I don't wanna go anyway" very easy.

- A man would have to need money pretty bad to take a job as a coal miner. I've never heard of a woman coal miner. Maybe they're too smart to take the job.

- A U.S. Army interrogator got off scot-free after an Iraqi general he was questioning died of suffocation. I hate it when I'm embarrassed to be an American.

- I read where some real estate agents are betting that more and more older Americans are going to start retiring to Mexico instead of Florida. Maybe, but I'd be surprised. It has its problems, but "Florida" still sounds better to most Americans than "Mexico."

- It doesn't matter what time of year it is, when I look through the newspaper, fur coats are always on sale. Does anyone ever buy a fur coat that isn't "half off"?

PART TWO

Feeling Philosophical

No, I'm not committed to being open-minded. You can carry being broad-minded too far. By this time in my life, I know what I know and I know what I think and it's very damned unlikely that I'm going to change.

THE EVIL THAT MEN DO

Seldom do we get public figures so clearly evil as Osama bin Laden, Kenneth Lay and John Walker Lindh. Writing something negative about any one of them is so easy it's almost unfair. Writers often get in trouble expressing unpopular opinions about people who are admired by some and disliked by others, but there's nothing so bad you can say about these three that would evoke a pile of angry letters.

I wish it was always that easy to assess the character of a public figure. I was talking to a good friend about a politician I'd met the other day and I said, "He's a good guy."

Well, I'd never met the guy before and didn't really know much about him. My opinion was based on something I'd heard him say that I agreed with. For all I know, he takes money under the table from company executives he helps get government contracts and beats his wife when he comes home at night. It was ridiculous for me to pronounce judgment on him.

We do a lot of that. We make snap decisions about people based on insufficient evidence. We certainly do it with politicians. We decide whom to vote for based on what someone looks like or because of some insignificant comment we heard the person make on television. Appearance influences our opinion more than substance.

We do the same thing with sports figures; we see them as either all good or all bad. I decided I disliked the St. Louis Rams quarterback, Kurt Warner, and it was a big help to me watching the Super Bowl that year. I knew I wanted the New England Patriots to win because I'd heard that before every game Warner prays to God that his team will win.

We often decide we like—or dislike—someone for no good reason. It's unfair, but if we waited until we knew everything about everything before we made up our mind or decided whether we liked someone or not, we'd never make a decision. Inevitably, we make some wrong decisions about people and issues.

The confusing thing about deciding whom to like and whom to dislike, whether they're politicians or people we meet during an average day, is the great number of contradictory characteristics we all have. A domineering Mafia boss may take money for protection from all the dry cleaners in town and arrange for the murder of a dozen people—but still love his wife, dandle his grandchildren on his knee at night and hate violence on television.

Some of the brave firemen who died trying to save others in the World Trade Center were very likely the same guys who, in the weeks before the disaster, cheated on their overtime.

We were all faced with this dilemma about character when Bill Clinton was President. Here was a bright, capable, charming guy with the moral standards of an alley cat. If you ignored his ability and concentrated on his shortcomings, he was one of the least admirable Presidents of modern times. If you judged him on his ability as a leader alone, he was one of the best.

I've read that Thomas Edison was impossible to get along with. Thomas Jefferson, Franklin D. Roosevelt and John F. Kennedy all had secrets which would not have increased their popularity if the facts had been made public.

We have to face the truth that we can't judge a great scientist, an inventor, a novelist, a politician or an athlete by the sum total of his personality. We should only judge them on what they did in one area of their lives that was better than the rest of us could have done.

No matter what virtues may exist in the characters of Osama bin Laden, Ken Lay or John Walker Lindh, I think we'll still judge them for their worst behavior because it dominated their characters.

It's very satisfying for all of us to have three people so clearly and undeniably bad. That makes it easy for us.

THE TERROR GOBLIN

"Geoffrey draws on his boots to go through the woods, that his feet might be safer from the bite of snakes; Aaron never thinks of such a peril. In many years neither is harmed by such an accident. Yet it seems to me, that, with every precaution you take against such an evil, you put yourself into the power of the evil."

Ralph Waldo Emerson wrote that more than 150 years ago. I first read it 10 years ago and I've been thinking about it ever since our government began warning us about the probability of another terrorist attack. Are we being careful, or have we put ourselves "into the power of the evil"?

If you've bought an airline ticket and tried to fly to another city, you certainly might think you were in someone else's power—someone evil. Airline security is not going to do any more to inhibit terrorism than Geoffrey's boots did to prevent snake bites. No terrorist is going to be caught trying to board a plane with a bomb or weapon in his briefcase.

On grounds that it might compromise our ability to gather intelligence from sources they suggest are secret, agencies like the FBI and CIA say they can't reveal where they got the information that another terrorist attack was imminent. I strongly suspect that if we'd known what the information was and where the government got it, we would have been less fearful.

Now that the time when the attack was supposed to have taken place has passed, wouldn't it be OK if they told us why they thought it was coming? I hope they notice that they've been wrong so far and should not trust the same sources of information next time. They wouldn't have made this up just to keep the Geoffreys among us pulling on their boots, would they?

People obviously fall into different character groups. The modern version of Emerson's Geoffrey Group built bomb shelters in their back yards in the 1950s and stored canned food, water and toilet paper for a six-month stay—or until any nuclear cloud dissipated in the atmosphere.

They felt it would be safe then to come out to view the desolation and the dead bodies of their Aaron Group neighbors who hadn't pulled on their boots.

Some measurements are too difficult to make and some statistics too complicated to set down in numbers. The loss that the terrorist attack has inflicted on the airline industry might be judged within a few hundred billion dollars with some wild guesses. But the changes we've been forced to make in our way of life following the attacks are so complicated and multitudinous that they could never be measured numerically.

What figure do you assign to the loss of happiness a grandmother suffered because she did not dare travel from Boston to San Diego at Christmas to see three grandchildren?

I am clearly in Aaron's camp. I've spent little time in my life being cautious because it's almost always a waste of time. Either the danger never materializes or, if it does, the preventive measures don't prevent anything.

PRO- AND ANTI-SEMITISM

There's a lingering vestige of social anti-Semitism in the United States but it is limited to a small number of small minds. There are no longer mainstream clubs or organizations in every community that routinely exclude Jews. Anti-Semitism is out of fashion.

Jews have made a contribution to progress in every area of our civilization in the United States that's out of proportion to their numbers. Many—maybe even most—of our greatest inventors, writers, musicians, entertainers, mathematicians, scientists, doctors and judges have been Jewish. There are a great many Jewish politicians (nobody's perfect).

It is, in part at least, our conscious determination not to be anti-Semitic that keeps most Americans who think so from saying that the Jewish leadership of Israel is behaving badly. (We do not include Arabs in our desire to avoid being anti-Semitic, even though they are as Semitic as

Israelis.) While terrorism on the part of Palestinians is barbaric, since September 2000, many more Palestinians have been killed than Israelis.

If Yasser Arafat had not been so easy to dislike and distrust, the Israelis might have had to make concessions to the Palestinians years ago. Ariel Sharon or Benjamin Netanyahu could hardly have chosen a Palestinian leader better for their own purposes than Arafat. He was eminently dislikable, and to Americans, he even looked like the bad guy. To the extent that he refused a reasonable plan for peace toward the end of Bill Clinton's administration Arafat, as much as anyone, was responsible for the mindless slaughter carried out by both sides.

The facts are that in 1947 the United Nations voted to partition Palestine, creating the new Jewish state of Israel in 1948. Desperate Jews in Europe needed a place to call home and we were all agreed that giving them part of Palestine was the right thing to do. Well, not everyone agreed. The Palestinians didn't like the plan even then because it was their land the UN was so generously giving away.

In 1967, Israel took more land for itself when, over the objections of the international community, they occupied the West Bank and Gaza, taking what rightfully belonged to the Palestinians. Now, after thrity-five years of Israeli occupation, about three and a half million Palestinians still live as disenfranchised vagrants in their own land under Israeli domination. They feel like they are not free in their own country.

The Israelis have been able to move military units in and out of Palestinian territory with impunity. They kept Yasser Arafat under virtual house arrest for two months because they had the military strength to wipe out his housing complex if he had ignored their order to stay put. They have the most modern weapons because we, the United States, give them the weapons and $3 billion in aid every year. This is by far the most we give any country in the world.

Without the money it gets from the United States, Israel would collapse. We underwrite every action they take even when we disagree with the action.

This is an idiotic and unfair war between the Palestinians and the Israelis. No one is going to invade Israel because we won't let them.

Israelis wouldn't even have to defend themselves; we would defend them. We could also stop Israeli aggression by cutting off the cash and sophisticated weapons we give Israel.

Anti-Semitism is a cancer and it is irresponsible of Israel to encourage its reemergence.

ANTI-ISRAEL, NOT ANTI-SEMITIC

It's difficult to write anything of substance about anything without offending someone. And then, sometimes I'm wrong, too.

It is not my intention to offend anyone—that would be foolish of any writer who wants to be read—but too many people refuse to face the truth about something they're close to. I may sometimes be ill-informed, but I'm not biased. On issues, I know where the middle of the road is and usually take it.

I occasionally have been called anti-Semitic. It is a charge that should not be made lightly. I've been on the side of the Jews too long for that. I don't recall seeing any of my critics there on April 12, 1945, when I entered Buchenwald with the U.S. Army. I know something about anti-Semitism that someone who wasn't there will never know. No one entering Buchenwald that day could ever be anti-Semitic.

Although most Israelis are Jews, most Jews are not Israelis. I do not use these words interchangeably, as many of my cities do. They refuse to accept the fact that it's possible to be occasionally anti-Israeli, which I am, without ever being anti-Semitic.

There are people who are unwilling to accept that the Palestinians being killed, mostly by American weapons, are human beings who wail when their sons die and weep when their homes are destroyed. They won't admit Palestinians have a right to a homeland of their own.

I do not resort to the some-of-my-best-friends-are-Jews defense. Not some. Most of my best friends are Jews. When we argue, I often re-

mind the ones with a sense of humor about their Jewishness, of Ogden
Nash's couplet:

> How odd
> Of God
> To choose
> The Jews.

I don't pretend to be a Middle East scholar, nor am I much interested
in becoming one. The events of long ago in that area have been so often
retold, rewritten, translated, embroidered and fictionalized that it seems
unlikely they bear much relationship to what actually happened. Forget
200 B.C. You can't even be sure of today's report of something that happened yesterday. Nor does it matter. We have to deal with the world we
have today.

WHO? ME WORRY?

If you're worried about your own problems, one of the good ways to stop
worrying about them is to start worrying about the world's problems.

There are plenty of them big enough to make anyone forget worrying about money, marriage, the job, the kids, the dent in the car or a
leaky faucet.

The first story big enough to worry about is the possibility of our being attacked with biological or nuclear weapons. If I were in the State
Department, I'd be on the alert if large numbers of suspicious-looking
people started leaving the country. This might mean they know something we don't know.

Before the destruction of the World Trade Center, New York City
seemed impervious. Not any longer. The core of New York is the island
of Manhattan, just twelve miles long and three miles wide at its fattest

point. It must look like a bull's eye to any enemy looking for a target. The bomb we dropped on Hiroshima would reduce New York City and all the 9 million people in it to ashes in a flash.

If an enemy didn't have nuclear weapons, it might choose to wipe us out with biological weapons by fogging the city with clouds of deadly bacteria that would kill us all in hours. Thoughts like this make me wonder why everyone doesn't move out of New York. That makes me worry about the decline of New York because I love New York.

Many areas of the nation are suffering from drought. Drought worries me more than torrents of water, even though flood pictures of houses being washed away and dogs in rowboats are more dramatic. In my worried little mind, the earth is more apt to dry out than drown.

Drought is a time-consuming worry that can take your mind off your own petty concerns for a long while because of the daily reports about global warming. There are stories of huge icebergs (the size of Rhode Island, they usually say) breaking away and floating out to sea where they melt. I worry a lot about icebergs melting.

One of the things that worries me is the report that as the icebergs melt, the seas rise. How can that be? If you put ice cubes in a glass and then fill the glass to the brim with water, the ice cubes float above the rim. When the ice cubes melt, the glass should overflow but it does not. Why then, I worry, do melting icebergs cause the oceans' level to rise? There must be a physical principle here that I don't understand.

One of the reasons we're drying out, in spite of the melting icebergs, is because we've depleted the ozone layer that acts as a protective screen from the direct and damaging rays of the sun.

Earthquakes are something anyone in California can worry about as a diversion.

If we survive these potentially catastrophic, civilization-ending disasters and the world doesn't come to an end, I'll be able to concentrate on worrying about cloning. The tinkering that scientists are doing with the genes of sheep is child's play compared with what they're going to be able to do with humans. And nothing's going to stop them from cloning a person.

The best we can hope for to end all our worries is that science will isolate the best genes and produce the perfect human being. Dishonesty will be eliminated from the human character. There will be no thieves, no evil corporate executives, no Adolf Hitlers or Saddam Husseins.

Meanwhile, though, there's a lot to worry about.

NOT A LOVERS' QUARREL

Most of us don't change our minds about anything important after the age of twenty. We get set in our ways early. One of the earliest mind-sets to form is about religion. Kids baptized as Catholics and sent to a Catholic church when they're too young to understand religion usually end up as church-going Catholics for life. No young child says to a parent, "I don't want to be a Catholic. I think I'll be a Baptist." Or vice versa.

The training or indoctrination of young people can be good or bad but whatever it is, it usually sticks for life. In the 1930s, Adolf Hitler, playing on the resentment some Germans felt toward the Jews, formed youth groups that taught hate. It was those young people who became Nazis. They weren't born Nazis.

If all the children in Peoria, Ill. (a city I pick at random), had been brought up as Muslims instead of Catholics and Protestants, they would be Muslims now. There wouldn't have been a lot of ten-year-olds stomping their feet saying, "I don't want to be a Muslim. I want to be a Presbyterian."

One of the greatest dangers to the survival of a civilization is the rise of hatred within the culture. There have been recent pictures and articles about the extent of the training exercises in the Middle East that combine a philosophy of hate with education in murder. Young Muslims taking courses in terrorism are not going to grow up trying to win the Nobel Peace Prize. They will have been convinced in their youth that Americans are evil and that the right thing for them to do is kill as many of us as they can. There's no hatred like the hatred based on religion.

It's not easy to understand why the races on earth are so different and so unable to get along. We don't know whether there was always some basic, genetic difference between Eskimos and Africans, Asians and Europeans, or whether racial characteristics developed as a result of the differences in the environments in which humans with originally similar characteristics flourished over the centuries. However it happened, there's no doubt that now there are fundamental differences among races. Our philosophies of government, our personalities, goals, religions and even our beliefs in old wives tales differ. And those aren't going away.

It's hard to know what the United States should do about all this hatred. Spending more on weapons doesn't seem like the best way to eliminate the crisis in the Middle East. A thousand nuclear bombs are no deterrent to a few containers of anthrax.

I remember a college course in which I read a dialogue between two philosophers. One philosopher expressed dismay over the possible end of civilization as a result of the invention of gun powder.

I'm a little old to worry about it myself, but I'm not so selfish that I'm ready to have this great world end with a biological or nuclear bang just because I'm not going to be around to see it.

THE HISTORY OF HISTORY

Last week, I attended a ceremony at the school I went to growing up for the dedication of several large brass plaques bearing the names of graduates who served in the military during this country's twentieth-century wars.

The emphasis was on the World War II plaque because it bore the most names. Many of us who had served were there. Someone pointed out how curious it was that the school had waited sixty years before honoring its World War II heroes. (The word "heroes" is used with increasing abandon as the years between the action and the present expand.)

We're all more interested in our own world, our own history than in anyone else's. For years now I've been surprised and pleased by the attention being paid to WW II because it was my war. The interest in WW II was already growing before Tom Brokaw wrote *The Greatest Generation*. The movie *Saving Private Ryan* enhanced the memory of WW II. My own book on the topic, *My War*, has sold 175,000 copies and I'm acutely aware of how lucky I am to have had the cathartic experience of writing it.

I say "lucky" because there aren't many people who experienced WW II who haven't thought of writing a book about it. I get fifty letters a year from veterans who want to write a book, or have started writing a book, or who've finished a rough manuscript about their wartime experiences. They ask for advice on how to get their work published. It's sad for me because most of those efforts are sincere but seriously short of literary merit or any general interest.

The question in my mind about both world wars has always been why my children, born after World War II ended, know so much more about it than I ever knew about World War I. That conflict ended the year I was born. It is not just our children, either. Everyone's children know more about WW II than they know about WW I, and the only possible answer is that the methods of preserving historical information are better than they were after WW I.

Our knowledge of ancient events is based on flimsy evidence, and often myth substitutes for history. Little was written down in ancient times and no visual or oral recordings were made to provide a record of events. What historical information we have from ancient times is based on twice-told tales handed down by word of mouth until paper was invented.

There were some crude motion pictures taken of some of the events of World War I, but photography was still young and most of the sound-recording devices we have now were unknown.

It's easy to be pessimistic about civilization, but looking at the progress we've made in the past 100 years in our ability to preserve historical data is encouraging. If knowing history prevents our having to repeat it, then our ability to record the present for future generations is good.

My memories of the history courses I took are of wars and the evil deeds of modern and ancient kings, dictators and presidents. Wars, crimes and disasters are always the biggest part of recorded history. Historians don't pass down long narrative accounts of peaceful years because they're dull and no one would read them.

It's a pretty good world Americans have had to live in for the past sixty years. I hope that when future generations are exposed to the history of our era they get something besides Iraq, Watergate and Monica Lewinsky.

FAITH IN SCIENCE

We've got such a good thing going for ourselves here on Earth, it would be too bad if future generations missed out on it, but things don't look good. Biological and nuclear warfare, global warming, the AIDS pandemic are ominous.

There's no doubt the world is endangered and no doubt that the future of civilization rests on the work that science can do to save it. It's only fairly recently, within the last 100 years, that human beings have understood the importance of science. Before that, they were impressed by scientific discoveries but unaware of the significance of science in the Big Picture.

The existence of humans is brand new given the millions of years the earth has existed. Other life forms that once dominated the planet, like the dinosaurs, have disappeared. We think of ourselves as permanent but there's no written guarantee. There are threats to human life on Earth that could end this whole ballgame we're playing.

There are three basic areas in which science can work for our benefit. Astronomy is crucial. We've got to keep studying the universe so the earth doesn't end up getting too hot or too cold to support life.

Second, science has to keep plugging away on health issues and finding cures and preventive measures against things like cancer, diabetes, heart disease and AIDS.

The third area in which we need immediate help from science is with our environment. There's a war going on between business and science. If we're going to survive, we have to concede the power of deciding what to do to science, not to industry. Scientists look for solid data; industry is guessing and trying to make money.

If we admit that it is our best hope, the next question is how to use science. Right there you have a problem because as soon as you say "use science," there's trouble. Science, at its best, isn't used. Scientists should go off on their own and poke around in their labs until they find something. Pure science isn't trying to save the world or make anything useful; it's just being scientific.

We've tried to use science by having government direct scientific study toward improving life for humans. Things seldom work out when government gets involved and tries to direct science to solve a specific problem. The first thing a government agency does is lay out a set of standards by which a department will work. Science doesn't work within a set of standards. Discovery is outside the boundaries of standards and, if you force scientists to work within boundaries, they seldom make discoveries.

When government gets its hands on science, it wants practical results. This practice can attract an inferior group of scientists and, first thing you know, government has science making weapons.

The other problem with science and government is that, inevitably, the scientists are subservient to the politicians. The interests of the two groups are different, and if politicians' interests are forced on scientists, it doesn't work.

Scientists ought to be given the money they need and left in a corner by themselves to work without interference or direction from anyone.

They should not be given an agenda they're expected to follow. Given a free hand, scientists will usually do the right thing.

VOUCHERS FOR ATHEISTS, TOO

With the new Supreme Court–approved voucher system that will pay tuition to private schools, there will be a proliferation of new institutions starting up to get in on the tax money being handed out to religious schools.

While the majority of existing parochial schools are Catholic, a good number are Jewish and Islamic. The religion of the Muslims is the fastest growing in the United States. It is likely that the new schools will be associated with less well known religions or the growing ones interested in having government help to promote their creeds.

I met a man with the name of Charles Ausseldorfer who told me he's opening a school for the children of atheists. He doesn't call the children atheists because he says they're too young to know what they believe.

Mr. Ausseldorfer told me his school will be called the Atheist Academy and he looks forward to the help he'll be getting from American taxpayers.

Mr. Ausseldorfer, 54, a former stock market analyst who became disenchanted with Wall Street—but not until he'd made a lot of money—said he'd bought an abandoned factory on the outskirts of a Midwestern city. I told him I'd like to take a camera crew out to get pictures of the school, but he asked that the exact location of the Atheist Academy not be revealed yet. Contractors are dividing the old brick building into twelve classrooms and one larger meeting room with a stage for lectures, he said.

Tuition for the Atheist Academy will be $5,000, approximately half of which will come from tax money provided through the school voucher program. The school's motto will be Tom Paine's famous statement: "My country is the world, my religion is to do good and all men are my brothers."

Mr. Ausseldorfer was a charming conversationalist but I told him I object as much to having my tax money go to a school teaching atheism as to one teaching Catholicism, Islam or Buddhism.

"Each school day," he told me, "will begin with students reciting the Pledge of Allegiance without the words 'under God.'" We'll make it clear to our students that God is none of the government's business and the government is none of God's business."

Mr. Ausseldorfer said he hopes to have an athletic program.

"We'll play schools with whom we can compete . . . smaller schools representing some of the fringe religions like the Latter Day Saints and the Unitarians.

"It will be an interesting experiment," Mr. Ausseldorfer said, "to see if our football team can beat any of the teams whose players pray to God to win."

I asked whether school attendance will be restricted to atheists or the children of atheists.

"Absolutely not," Mr. Ausseldorfer said. "We'll take agnostic kids, Jewish kids, Baptists, Muslims, Buddhists, Presbyterians. Like the Catholic schools, we'll try to get children to see things our way. With those tax dollars, we're going to promote logic, reason and good sense. We will teach courses in all the religions of the world, as well as courses in the Bible and the Koran. We hope that studying them will expose them."

I questioned him about whether atheism would qualify as a religion.

"The voucher system is not restricted to religious schools, even though 97 percent of the schools getting the money are (religious)," he said. "It will be no different than the government paying tuition for a Catholic, a Jewish or a Muslim school."

I asked Mr. Ausseldorfer if he thought many church-going Americans would object to paying to support a school whose mission was to promote the idea among children that there is no God.

"They may object," Mr. Ausseldorfer admitted, "but no more than atheists object to having tax money pay for a Catholic or a Muslim school."

You understand of course, that Charley Ausseldorfer is fictitious.

WAR IS HEAVEN

Just when it seemed as though the people who make war had invented every possible device with which to kill people, we're faced with a strange new weapon that is not a device but a method—terrorism.

We thought we'd found the ultimate way to kill with the nuclear bomb. Now we've come up with an even more terrible form of warfare. Terrorism is a new way to kill. There have been isolated incidents in the past 20 years but the newness of it is the willingness of terrorists to die for their cause. Before, the enemy was as interested in survival as its victims. There were things each side knew the other would not do in combat because of some immutable law of self-preservation. The only time that unwritten law had been broken was when Japanese kamikaze pilots willingly died for their God and their country.

Soldiers have been finding new ways to kill each other since the beginning of recorded history. They were probably finding ways before that, too. The early wars between armies in ancient Greece were clumsy battles. The front line of an attacking force was made up of men in horse-drawn, armored chariots. As the two forces clashed, hand-to-hand battles were fought by soldiers behind the chariots who carried the latest tools of war-battle axes, swords, shields, spears, dart throwers and bows. Those weapons must have evoked the same fear terrorism evokes in us today.

Somewhere around 1200, the evil Mongolian Genghis Khan put his troops on horseback. This enabled him to conquer the entire known world.

When Genghis Khan got to China, he was temporarily slowed by Chinese fortifications and soldiers who were more intelligent than his troops. To defeat them, Khan adopted a new tactic that made use of the Chinese soldiers' reverence for family. He captured thousands of women, children and old men, and then, when his troops advanced, Khan forced the captives to walk in front of his soldiers. This provided a phalanx that could only be penetrated if the Chinese chose to kill their own.

Around the same time, the Chinese invented gunpowder but used it more for firecrackers than in weapons. They were ineffective against Khan's ruthless advance and as many as 18 million Chinese, a substantial percentage of the number of people living then, were killed.

There was relatively little progress made in ways to kill people for hundreds of years after explosion-propelled missiles were invented. The Civil War wasn't fought with weapons much different from anything invented hundreds of years before.

In World War I, the armored tank struck fear into the hearts of infantrymen, but the tank turned out to be a paper tiger, as often a crematorium for its crew as an offensive aid to the infantry.

The Germans were the first to use a chemical weapon when they released mustard gas in World War I in front of a wind that wafted it toward French lines. The gas sickened some French soldiers but its course was so unpredictable that it was ineffective. It could drift in the wrong direction.

Aircraft were used in combat for the first time in World War I. A German plane and one zeppelin dropped small bombs on England but neither was capable of carrying anything large enough to do serious damage. Air action was limited to the romantic dogfights between men like the Luftwaffe's legendary Red Baron Von Richthofen and American ace Eddie Rickenbacker.

War came of age in World War II, when aircraft capable of carrying tons of bombs could destroy whole cities. Even high-explosive bombs turned out to be a relatively inefficient method of mass destruction once the United States developed nuclear weapons and dropped two on Japan.

When men were reluctant to die in the process of killing, it was possible to understand war. The newest threat to civilization—terrorism— is as frightening as any of its predecessors. And it won't be the last.

HUMAN AND INHUMAN NATURE

When you have an enemy, as we have in the Muslim terrorists, who would gladly wipe you off the face of the earth, it's difficult to continue believing that all men are created equal. Not the same, certainly.

It would appear to us as though there was something basically evil about this enemy, but you can bet the terrorists don't think of themselves as evil. They're certain that they are serving God. Religion does amazing things to people.

It is my not totally baked opinion that almost no one does something bad knowing and believing that they are bad for doing it. The petty thief rationalizes his thievery by thinking that the person from whom he's stealing has plenty of money and probably didn't make it honestly anyway. Not that long ago in this country, slavery was accepted by tens of thousands of decent Southerners who were able to make themselves believe they were doing their black servants a favor by providing them with food and shelter.

One of the questions that comes to my mind most often is whether human character has improved as much as civilization has progressed technologically. Inventions have enabled those of us alive today to live vastly more comfortable lives than our ancestors. We're able to carry heavy loads, farm the fields and travel now that we have wheels and the engines to make them roll. Has there been a similar improvement in our ability to reason and think?

I'm inclined to say yes, but then something happens that makes me doubt that conclusion. The people of Massachusetts today would not stand for hanging women accused of witchcraft, but how do we explain the thinking and actions of the terrorists who killed nearly 3,000 people with one, deliberate act? They're part of our same human race.

Is it possible that people in some parts of the world have progressed less than the people in other parts? Darwin is lurking here somewhere. He said that each living thing has to compete and owes its place in life to where it falls in competition with other individuals of its species. That must be as true of nations as of individuals—and the Arab world has not fared well in the competition. Because Americans have done so much better in providing ourselves with the good things of life than they have, some Arab nations resent us. "Resent" isn't strong enough. They hate us.

It seems probable that people in one part of the world grow up with forces on their character that change them in basic ways that people living elsewhere do not experience. Eskimos, who grow up in a cold, sometimes dark place, inevitably develop, over the generations, into a people somewhat different from humans who spend their lives on a warm Pacific island or in a large city.

The people of the Middle East have not done nearly as much for themselves as people living on other parts of the earth have done for themselves. They don't make much of anything. They don't grow much. They don't produce any substantial amount of art or literature good enough to be recognized by the rest of the world. Economists have a theory that they have been spoiled by a glut of easy-money oil. However, if that were true, Americans, with our vast country, rich in so many natural resources, would be lazy, too.

A great deal of the early progress made by mankind in such intellectual areas as language, astronomy and mathematics was made in the Middle East, and it's difficult to understand how the people of the region regressed from there to where they are today.

My old college roommate, Bob Ruthman, called me last week. He had just read something I had written. He says I'm not as funny as I used to be.

NO WOMEN ALLOWED

Tom Wyman, a former president of CBS whom I knew more as a boss than as a friend, dropped his membership in the Augusta National Golf Club because the club has persisted in refusing to admit women as members.

The chairman of the club, Hootie Johnson, has been dumb and pig-headed about this. He says they do not admit women and they are not going to change that policy. Wanna bet, Hootie?

The word "club" suggests exclusivity and the reasons for any club excluding people for one reason or another are often valid. When I was young, there were Boy Scouts and Girl Scouts, a YMCA and a YWCA. The Knights of Columbus probably wouldn't want a lot of Presbyterians, Jews or Muslims applying because it's a Catholic organization. That's defensible. NOW, the National Organization for Women, has only about 10 percent men as members.

A group of men together has a different character about it than one that includes women. There is an undeniable camaraderie among a collection of men in a locker room that would not exist if there were women present. It isn't just a matter of getting caught with their towels down.

Men behave differently in the presence of each other than they do when women are there. I could not begin to say why, even if I knew. It's not only different, but the atmosphere, for that brief time, is often better. I should think the same thing is true about a group of women who gather for bridge or to elect a candidate to office. I can't speak about a women's locker room.

There are good things about exclusive clubs. However, the advantages are outweighed by the necessity of doing something about the bad deal women have gotten over the years as a result of men's discriminatory treatment. One of the things that can be done is to break down the barriers for entry into previously all-male organizations.

There are thousands of social organizations that help form the fabric of our society and many of them are exclusive for some reason or another.

We prefer to mingle and we're happiest mingling with our own. "Our own" can refer to national origin, religious affiliation, or something like having served in a war, or bowling with the same people every Tuesday night. We join bridge clubs, sewing groups and political organizations.

They all provide a place for us to exchange and express opinions with people basically like ourselves.

I belong to a club in New York City that was all male for the first 125 years of its existence. Around 1988, after a bitter battle among members, women were admitted. Many enlightened members who didn't like the idea of letting women in nonetheless voted in favor of it because they thought it was the right thing to do. The club is undeniably different but not worse.

ARCHITECTURE AS ART

New York City wrestled with the problem of what to do about replacing the destroyed World Trade Center with another building or group of buildings.

It isn't often that putting up a building involves so many practical, emotional and artistic considerations as this does. Usually, when steel, stone and cement or wood are laid out, squared, rounded smoothed and fitted together into various shapes, it is to make working or living space for people. Decisions about the final appearance of a building by people who look up at it as they pass by on the street, are incidental to how it will be used. This accounts for why there are so many ugly office buildings, apartment houses and homes in the world.

Because of the trauma associated with the deaths of 2,800 people in the World Trade Center, no one is satisfied with the idea of erecting just another office complex. They want it to be a beautiful monument, a practical working space and a work of art, too. That's some order for an architect.

When we use the word "art," we're usually referring to a painting, so I was surprised just now to look up the word in my dictionary and note that the words "painting" or "picture" aren't even mentioned. "Architecture" isn't mentioned as an art, either, but that didn't surprise me.

Under "Art," the dictionary says: "Human effort to imitate, supplement, alter or counteract the work of Nature; 2) The conscious production or arrangement of sounds, colors, forms, movements or other elements in a manner that affects the sense of beauty . . ." Architecture seems to fit in there.

The trouble is that architecture has to serve too many practical purposes to be routinely called art. There is nothing artistic about most buildings, but some of the world's great structures certainly are art: the Taj Mahal, Chartres Cathedral, Notre Dame, the Pyramids, the George Washington and Golden Gate bridges, the Capitol in Washington, the Arc de Triomphe, the Parthenon and the Colosseum, the Alhambra in Granada, the Tower of London, the Duomo in Florence. One of the best buildings erected in recent years is the CBS headquarters building in New York, known affectionately as "Black Rock" because of the great color of its fired granite exterior.

It was unfortunate when some long-forgotten writer started calling tall buildings "skyscrapers." The word sounds like a small joke and has none of the majesty or grace about it that some of our best tall buildings have. In their own modern way, much like the Chrysler Building, the Empire State Building and Rockefeller Center, the World Trade Center's twin spires were art, too, even though, as in the case of the other three buildings, ultimate decisions about their construction were dominated, not by how they would look to the eye but by what their function would be.

At the bottom end of architectural art are the homes we live in. Most of them have been put up by carpenters of modest ability and no aesthetic sense. Over the years, as families grew, homes have been enlarged with additions that were tacked on with no consideration given to their appearance. Even worse than the homes built without the direction of an architect are those mass-produced houses in residential "developments." An architect draws plans for a basic house and makes small changes to alter its appearance, so that every fifth structure is identical to a previous one just down the street.

I hope some architectural genius designed a new World Trade Center that will meet all the specifications of work space, memory and art.

IS IT MUSIC OR NOISE?

Nothing divides one generation from another so definitely as its popular music. Those who grew up listening to the Beatles are either not interested in, or actively dislike, the sound of rap, hip-hop or heavy metal.

One night I had a lot of time to think about music while I forced myself to stay up through four hours of Grammy Awards. I don't want to be left out of what's going on even if what's going on doesn't appeal to me.

The music of the youth of people my age was jazz and you'd have a hard time convincing any of us that Eminem, Bono or even the appealing multiple-Grammy-winner Norah Jones can match the musical talent of the great jazz musicians. It seems certain to us that people like Louis Armstrong, Dave Brubeck, Benny Goodman, Artie Shaw, Ella Fitzgerald, Dizzy Gillespie or Charlie Parker have a better chance of achieving a permanent place in the history of music than the Dixie Chicks. To prove I'm fair, I wouldn't give much chance to the other music of my youth known as "swing," played by the forgettable Guy Lombardo.

Only occasionally does a musician's popularity span several generations. Frank Sinatra's did and so does that of Tony Bennett. (In spite of his limited talent, I'm soft on Tony because more than forty years ago I wrote a television show he did.)

The appreciation of music doesn't come naturally to me. My hearing is perfect. My shortcoming is listening. I hear better than I listen. My brain doesn't have whatever faculty it needs to understand carefully arranged sound. I want music to mean something that can be expressed with words and music doesn't do that. It's hard for me to believe there are any ideas expressed in the music of the Grammy Awards—or even in Beethoven's Ninth Symphony, for that matter. Maybe I'm asking something of music it isn't meant to provide. I accept that, but I don't accept the suggestion that there is something profound in the cater-wauling of a rock group. Some of the appeal of music is the predictability and anticipation of rhythm and too much modern popular music doesn't even have that.

If art of any kind doesn't have an idea behind it, I'm not interested. I can do without artificially induced emotion. It accounts for my apathy toward the paintings of so many modern artists. I don't understand their work and if there isn't anything there to understand, I don't want to waste my time looking at it.

I remember reading once that Beethoven said music is a higher revelation than philosophy. I don't doubt Beethoven's genius with music but I don't agree with that.

The intellectual pleasure of listening to a symphony concert or an opera escapes me and, while I recognize this as my shortcoming, not the music's, it doesn't make it any easier for me to sit through a concert. My ability to appreciate music is limited to my recognition that consonance is soothing and dissonance is irritating. My idea of a good evening of music is a virtuoso performance by one talented singer or player of an instrument like a piano, guitar, saxophone, trombone or violin. There's something about the solitary sound that appeals to me more than a blend of many sounds from a hundred instruments. I keep trying to isolate one sound and cannot so it's cacophony to my ears, the audio entry to my brain.

It isn't clear how the brain makes sense of music so there's no way we're ever going to explain why some of us like some music that others do not like.

I do know one thing. Next year, when the Grammys are on television, for entertainment I'll just go to bed early.

TOO TRUE TO BE GOOD

Some time ago (actually quite a while), I read a story about a homeless man who struck it rich with a winning lottery ticket. It annoyed me because it was the kind of story that encourages idiocy.

The homeless or unemployed have no business buying lottery tickets, and if they do, they're only going to win about once every 5 million times. Because I was more irritated than amused, I amused myself by writing several news stories that are closer to the way things are more likely to happen.

First story:

Homeless Man Buys Lottery Ticket with Last Dollar

A man known to the people who pass him everyday simply as "Big John" has been homeless for six years. Last week, Big John took the nickels and dimes he'd begged from passers-by and bought a $2 lottery ticket.

Yesterday, he was sleeping over a warm sidewalk grate when a wind-blown newspaper caught on his foot.

John looked at the headline announcing the winning lottery number, reached into his pocket, and with bleary eyes, read his lottery ticket. He didn't have the winning number, of course, and he went back to sleep, $2 poorer.

Next story:

Twin Sisters apart for 40 Years

Elizabeth and Esther Murray, twin daughters of Ralph and Mary Murray, were six when their parents divorced. It was agreed that the father would raise Elizabeth and the mother would raise Esther. Ralph Murray's job took him to Paris, where Elizabeth graduated from the Sorbonne and started a successful business designing and selling women's shoes. Back in the U.S., Esther dropped out of high school and was fired from several jobs. Hearing of a new French company opening an expensive women's shoe store in town, Esther got an interview with the manager, a woman who had recently arrived from Paris.

When Esther was shown into the luxuriously furnished office, she saw a well-dressed woman seated behind the desk and her heart stopped. It wasn't her sister, Elizabeth, though, and she didn't get the job.

Last story:

Family Moves West without Pet Retriever

The Santleys had lived for years on a quiet street in Nutley, N.J., with their beloved golden retriever, Dirk. John Santley's company decided to move to Seattle and if he wanted to keep his job, he had to move there.

The Santleys packed their worldly possessions and prepared to leave.

When movers arrived, Dirk was nowhere to be found. The Santleys delayed their trip for two days, but Dirk never returned home. Heartbroken, they left without him.

On their third day in Seattle, 2,900 miles from Nutley, the Santleys sat despondently over a second cup of coffee in their new kitchen, when they heard a scratching at the front door and the soft, pleading whine of a dog. Mr. Santley raced to the door, threw it open and there sat a small white poodle that looked nothing like Dirk.

The moral to all these stories is this:

If it sounds too good to be true, the chances are, it isn't true.

FOR IT AND AGAINST IT

Every time someone makes a statement about abortion, capital punishment, affirmative action, Iraq, Hillary Clinton, George W. Bush, Pepsi-Cola or Coca-Cola, I disagree no matter which side the person is on.

Sometimes I don't know what to think, and if I do think it, I don't dare say it. It's not that I'm afraid of what people will think of me.

We didn't find the weapons of mass destruction that were supposed to be the reason we attacked Iraq. Should we blame the Bush administration for lying to us to justify the action it took for some other, more devious reason? Gee, I don't know.

And, if we attacked Iraq because they had weapons of mass destruction, should we attack every nation that has them? Having such weapons isn't always bad, is it? We have them and we aren't bad. The British have them and they're our friends. The French have them. North Korea has them. China has them. Where do we start, where do we stop?

The Supreme Court decided that the University of Michigan can give black applicants for admission preference over white applicants with the same qualifications. I approve. If we're ever going to have racial equality we have to take positive steps to make the races equal.

Wait a minute, though. Does that mean it's OK to take race into consideration when we decide things? I thought it was always wrong. If you consider race in college admissions, you're admitting that it's OK to accept or reject a person because of his or her race. That's not right.

The question is too hard for me.

What about capital punishment? Is it ever right for a government to take the life of a person as punishment? It seems wrong to me. The United States is one of the few countries left in the civilized world that still puts people to death. Killing a prisoner reduces those who do it and all the citizens who approve of it, to the level of the criminal.

So then, I disapprove of the death penalty—Well, sort of. I do and I don't. Every time they decide to execute some particularly vicious murderer, I notice I'm willing to make an exception to my opposition to the death penalty. Why should we spend $60,000 a year providing food, housing and medical care for someone the world would be better off without? Is there any reason not to dispatch the creep David Westerfield, who sexually attacked, then murdered seven-year-old Danielle van Dam?

And then, there's abortion. Once again, I disendear myself to both sides by being on the fence, although I'm more often in agreement about other issues with the "pro-choice" people. "Pro-choice" is the loaded name they've assumed for themselves in the propaganda war against those who call themselves "pro-life," an equally loaded term.

But then, confronted with the demand for an answer to the question, "Don't you think a woman has the right to choose what to do with her own body?" one answer comes to my mind that "pro-choice" people don't like. That answer is: "She already made the choice of what to do with her body when she had sex with a man knowing it could result in the conception of a new human being."

At what point a fetus becomes a human being is impossible to decide. Anyone who has enjoyed life would hate to have been thought of as too young to matter any time after being conceived . . . even if it was only ten minutes.

WHAT GOETH BEFORE FALLING

We're all proud of being American, which is good if we don't make fools of ourselves and irritate the rest of the world by forcing it on them. A little pride goes a long way. Having the biggest flag doesn't mean you're the most patriotic.

We like being proud of a lot of different things that don't justify it. It's strange sometimes. For example, people often display pride in ignorance. You hear people say, "I'm not good with numbers." I always think they mean to leave the impression that they're good with everything else. Or they say they can't remember names. That's trying to make something good out of being rude or not paying attention. It's nothing to be proud of.

I hear bright kids whose favorite phrase these days is, "I have no idea," or "I don't have a clue." They delight in not knowing.

It makes sense to be proud of some things. We take pride in ownership. A lot of car sales are based on the pride people take in being successful enough to own a new one. The old car is still serviceable but it has

84,000 miles on it and a 2007 model looks better in the driveway. You don't put a Hummer in the garage where people passing by can't see it.

There's a kind of reverse car-pride, too . . . people who are proud of keeping a car past its prime. I have an old friend from high school who visited us last summer. He and his wife drove up in a battered 1974 Chevy. It was so rusted out from years driving on salted roads in the winter that the floor under the brake and clutch pedals was rusted out. You could look down from the driver's seat and see the road. My friend is a successful surgeon who was proud of driving this old heap instead of spending a small fraction of what he makes on a new one.

Sometimes, people are even proud of their infirmities. They'll tell you, "I have flat feet," "I can't hear high notes," or, "I'm colorblind." They are extraordinarily proud of being colorblind. Walter Cronkite is normally a modest man but he never misses an opportunity to say, proudly, that he can't tell one color from another.

Strangers often come up to me to say they don't watch television. Somehow they seem to think that not watching television makes them smarter than the rest of us who do. When someone tells me they don't watch television, I always say, "You must be very intellectual."

I confess to occasionally displaying false pride myself. Recently, the Dave Matthews Band attracted 80,000 people to Central Park in New York. I found myself being proud of telling people I'd never heard of Dave Matthews—or his band. I should think Dave Matthews probably would be proud to tell people he never heard of Andy Rooney, either.

I'm always telling people I don't go to the movies. There are lots of good movies. Why in the world would I think not going was something to brag about?

There are food snobs. They're proud of things they won't eat, or think they can't because of some rare allergy. "I can't eat broccoli." "Chocolate makes my nose red." "I only eat white meat chicken."

My friend Ralph Martin told me he'd canceled his subscription and wasn't reading the morning newspaper anymore because it took too long. He was proud of it.

As with cars, a lot of people are proud of the new clothes they wear but there are others just as pleased with themselves for wearing years-old shoes or tattered clothing. A torn shirt is worn like a medal of honor. Some are proud of how much they spend on clothes, others proud of how little.

Most of us take pride in our signature. An illegible scribble suggests others ought to know who we are even if they can't read the letters in our handwritten name.

It's surprising more of us don't fall if that's what pride goeth before.

LEAVE NO WAR BEHIND

No amount of high-minded argument to the contrary could convince me that we're all born equal. There simply is no question in my mind that some of us are more equal than others. Just as surely as some are born with genes that make them six feet tall, some are born with brains that enable them to think better than others. I'm aware of being smarter than some people but not so nearly aware of that as I am aware of being dumber than a lot of others.

This differential is a problem teachers have that I'm glad I don't have to face. Our system of education has to assume, as an institution, that we are all equally educable, and we are not. In school and college, I tried to assimilate Latin, chemistry, physics and some mathematics higher than algebra and simply could not. They'd say I wasn't applying myself. They'd say I wasn't doing my homework. They'd say I was more interested in football than studying. But they wouldn't face the fact that my brain was different and in some ways not as good as many of my classmates.

I'm able to live with my mental insufficiency based on my belief that my brain has other facets that make up for its shortcomings. It's capable of some tricks of thought that might escape the Latin scholar, the scientist, the mathematician or the chemist—I like to think.

Our educational system, from grade school through graduate school, operates on the false assumption that every student has the same ability to learn. If we're going to get the best out of the brightest, schools have to be allowed to ignore that idea and give the best students as much as they can take without giving poor students less than they can take.

Whatever the solution is to this problem—or there may not be a solution—it seems obvious that we aren't spending enough on education. Both the smartest and the dumbest among us should be getting all the education they can take, and that isn't happening. We aren't maximizing this country's potential to accomplish things with its economic wealth because too many young people are being left behind or left out when it comes to education.

Is there any doubt we're shortchanging education? We're spending something like $455 billion on weapons, vehicles and pay to soldiers and sailors. At the same time, President Bush is asking for a record $53 billion for education. Some record compared with $455 billion. Does it seem right to spend more than eight times as much on war as on education?

You can't necessarily judge efforts to improve education by the amount we spend but that's the only measuring stick we have.

We all believe—I think we all believe it, anyway—that education promotes progress and happiness. People who have maximized their ability to take in and store information—educated people—are happier because they get things done.

There's no written guarantee that life on earth will never end. As Americans, we have more of the good things than we have wisdom about how to assure our survival. We need a better educational system, not more nuclear weapons or infantry divisions. President Bush's promise to "leave no child behind" had a nice ring to it, but children are being left behind.

width:1039px; height:1650px;

TO CATCH A THIEF

It was a shock to read that there are now 2,100,000 Americans in prison. That means one out of every seventy men is behind bars. The worst thought I have about it is that there are probably twice as many criminals who ought to be in prison and are not. A few who are prisoners ought not to be because they didn't do it.

The statistic was a shock because I think of people as being honest. Most of us hedge a little in speaking the whole and absolute truth at all times but that's usually in the interest of civility; we tell people who don't look good how good they look. This doesn't call for a prison term. We wouldn't dream of taking something that wasn't ours.

Prison is a relatively new institution in the history of the world. Before the 1800s, accused criminals were flogged, stoned, put in stocks in public places or hung without trial.

Now we put people in prison for two reasons. We lock them up to keep them from hurting the rest of us and we put them away to punish them for having committed a crime. We make it unpleasant for them while they're in there so that when they get out, they'll think twice before doing anything that might put them back in.

I think of the burglar, the embezzler, the murderer, the rapist as the rare exception in our society. Am I kidding myself when I think 9,999 Americans out of 10,000 are honest? I'm unaware of ever having known anyone who would steal even if it was easy and he was sure he (or she) wouldn't be caught. That number of Americans in prison makes me wonder if I'm right. I'm questioning a lot of things since we learned what happened in the Abu Ghraib prison in Baghdad. I didn't think Americans did that sort of thing, either.

"To be virtuous is to take pleasure in noble actions," Aristotle said. I thought that's what Americans liked to do—act nobly.

Another interesting aspect of the prison figure is the disparity in the proportion of incarcerated men to women. Of the 2,100,000 inmates, only a hundred thousand are women. Are men really 20 times more dishonest or inclined to commit crimes than women? Are women better people? If they want equality, women should demand that they be equally represented in our prisons.

While I believe most of us are honest on a personal level, I do think there's a lot of dishonesty in business. It's impersonal theft. Most white-collar crime is the work of people who wouldn't think of stealing from a neighbor who left the door open. In business, though, they don't call it stealing. They call it free enterprise.

After reading the prison story, I was driving near a grade school. When I stopped for a light, I watched more than seventy kids cross the street. They looked so good, so innocent, but I couldn't help wondering which of those seventy kids would be the one who ended up in prison. Not one of the girls, probably.

We don't know where mankind is going or where the inevitable process of change will take us, but the biological evolution of man brought about by change in our culture, differences in our environment and differences in the food we'll be eating will certainly make us different humans in 3004 from what we are in 2004.

If scientists are allowed to tinker with human nature—and in spite of all the opposition they're going to do it whether we like it or not—they will certainly try to improve it by eliminating whatever genes some of us have that make us dishonest. Imagine what an honest world would be like. We'd have no locks on our doors, no keys to our cars, no bank vaults or hiding places.

We wouldn't have to pay for millions of convicts in prison because we wouldn't need prisons.

USING THE FLAG

During his acceptance speech at the Democratic Convention in 2004, John Kerry said, "I don't wear my religion on my sleeve."

The suggestion was, of course, that the sleeve is where President Bush wears his religion.

At almost every vote-raiser, Kerry wore an American flag in his lapel. My question was this, John: If you don't wear your religion on your sleeve, why did you wear your patriotism in your lapel?

President Bush and Dick Cheney wear American flag pins in their lapels. Condoleezza Rice doesn't wear one and I have wondered whether it's because she's not patriotic or because she's always well-dressed and doesn't think the flag looks good on the expensive clothes she wears.

It's my opinion, and probably not a popular one—I'm not running for office—that no one should push their religion, their politics or their patriotism on the rest of us by displaying some indication of it. They may wear symbols on their clothing or put signs on their cars or their kitchen windows. A devout Roman Catholic woman often wears a crucifix as jewelry around her neck. It seems wrong to me to turn this cruel symbol of one of the most barbaric acts in history into a decorative bauble. The cross often hangs deep into the cleavage of a low-cut dress.

I saw a diamond-encrusted cross in a jewelry store on Madison Avenue in New York with a $7,500 price tag. Will that make a favorable impression, for the woman who wears it, in the eyes of God? Religion is a private matter and we ought not be propagandized in favor of one over another by public displays of an individual's affiliation. It's interesting that no male candidate I've ever seen wears a crucifix around his neck or in his lapel to pronounce himself Catholic. That may be because being Catholic is not so widely approved as being a patriotic American.

When someone hangs an American flag out in front of their house, there's something about it that suggests to me that these people are saying they are more American than I am. A common practice among New York cab drivers who are recent immigrants, not yet citizens and a little uneasy that someone might accuse them of being less than 100 percent patriotic, is to display American flags somewhere on their taxis. The American flag on a New York cab is an almost certain indication that the driver is new to this country and seeking approval.

I don't like flags used as bumper stickers any better than I like them as lapel pins. The American flag is one of the best, most meaningful pa-

triotic symbols the world has ever known. It not only looks great flutter-
ing in the breeze from the top of a flagpole but its stars standing for the
fifty states and the stripes representing the thirteen original states, have
real meaning.

It should not be used as decoration or as just another vote-getting
gimmick by candidates for office.

BROKAW: ANCHOR AWAY

Few people have the good sense and resolve to retire while they're still
doing their job as well or better than they ever did, and as well or better
than anyone else is doing the same job. Even fewer retire while they're
still physically able to pursue other pleasures denied them because of
the time it took them to do their work. Of course, I'm not one to talk.

Tom Brokaw is the remarkable exception. He has all his marbles
and most of his muscles. He is as good or better in retirement as he
ever was as an anchorman and reporter. Seven years ago, I was sitting
at my desk, fiddling with an idea when Brokaw called and explained
that he was writing a book to be titled *The Greatest Generation*. He
had read the book I wrote called *My War* and wanted some comments
on his proposition that mine was a generation superior in character to
previous or subsequent generations because we fought and won World
War II.

Because my role in life seems to be as a critic and naysayer, I said
"nay" and thus became a chapter in Tom's book. I told him I was proud
of how members of my generation fought WWII but did not believe
that it was a sign that we were in any way "greater." I pointed out that
the present generation has not distinguished itself with bravery in winning World War III because they have not fought it. If the present generation had been faced with Adolf Hitler, it would have pulled itself
together, risen to the occasion and fought the war as mine did.

The rise of Greek civilization was unique. There had been civilization in Egypt but nothing like what developed in ancient Greece in art, literature and mathematics. The Greeks who lived around 500 B.C. were their country's "Greatest Generation."

But then what happened? Future generations did not build on the great start those early Greeks gave them. There were centuries when things fell apart and civilization deteriorated.

The question of human progress—or lack of progress—has occurred to me 10,000 times over the years. Are we better people than people were one hundred, one thousand or even ten thousand years ago? I always think of the Romans who fed Christians to the lions. Are we better to each other than they were? If we are, how did Abu Ghraib happen? Does accomplishing more and making more of the good things of life contribute to the betterment of the human race? Are we better or just happier because we have cars, airplanes, television, computers? I can't decide. We have more mechanical aids to help us do things so we get more done and go more places than generations past but are we better people because of them?

There's a terrible and inexplicable disparity in the state of civilization in different parts of the world. The people of many countries are living in the Dark Ages by our standards. They have none of the appurtenances of modern civilization in the United States, Europe, the Far East or even much of the Middle East. They need a greatest generation of their own.

I'd like to ask Tom Brokaw one question. If my generation was greater than yours and greater than this present generation and also greater than past generations, how do you account for the fluctuation in quality? If you said mine was simply better than past generations, we could conclude that progress had been made, but if you argue that my generation was superior to past generations and also superior to the present generation, you suggest that civilization has regressed.

The Greatest Generation was a good title. But I question your proposition that mine was a greater generation than either my dad's or your own.

NOT ABOUT THE POPE

I will not be writing about the Pope. More than half of you don't want to hear another word about him. I can't say what Catholics, who can't get enough about the Pope, want to read. I will say that as a matter of writing style, I believe the word "Pope" should be capitalized when it is referring to the one man who has the job but all the newspapers spell it "pope."

About 75 percent of Americans call themselves Christian. About 25 percent of them are Catholic. That's the largest number of Americans belonging to one church. Protestants still outnumber Catholics by three to one, but Protestants are divided into a lot of different denominations, each of which is smaller than the unified body of Catholics.

After Catholics, the most Americans are Baptists. There are a lot of Baptists but they're divided among half a dozen different church bodies. Baptists ought to get together and choose one leader like a Pope. Methodists are the third largest Christian group. There are dozens of others like Lutherans, Presbyterians, Episcopalians, Jehovah's Witnesses and members of the United Church of Christ and the Church of God. They could all use a Pope.

If three Americans were stranded on a desert island, it seems likely the one thing they wouldn't agree on is religion. They'd each believe something different. Even within one church, individual members usually hold their own beliefs. Church members are often very loyal to their denomination. However, a loyal Baptist would have a hard time explaining the difference between what he believes and what the Presbyterians, Methodists and Episcopalians in town believe.

Worldwide, there are something like 2 billion Christians and more than 1 billion Muslims. There are almost 800 million Hindus and 325 million Buddhists. After those big four, the numbers drop off sharply. For example, there are about 20 million Sikhs and 14 million Jews.

The percentage of people in the United States who say they are Protestant has dropped in the last twenty years from about 63 percent to

51 percent. Statisticians say the drop has more to do with people who no longer claim they are affiliated with any religion than because of the influx of Catholic immigrants. Islam is the fastest growing major faith in the U.S., but Muslims still make up only about 4 percent of our population. It will be interesting when the Muslim population in a big city reaches the level that adherents want to put up a plaque in a public school with excerpts from the Koran.

Most Americans know that Muslims accept the Koran as the word of God the way Christians accept the Bible. They know nothing at all about any Buddhist, Sikh or Confucian holy books. I certainly don't.

Over the years, religions have adapted themselves to the people who believe in them more than people have changed their lives to conform to their churches' rules. When I was young, the Catholic boys I played with wouldn't eat a hamburger on Friday, and the Jewish kids in school wouldn't eat a ham sandwich on any day of the week. Things change. These days Catholics who practice birth control, get divorced, and eat meat on Friday no longer worry about going to hell.

TOO MANY CHURCHES

Any time the subject is religion, there's a good chance that anything anyone says will offend someone.

They closed 300 Catholic churches in Ireland in 2006 because of the number of priests who've been accused of molesting young boys, but I'm going to ignore the issue of young boys and Catholic priests and say something else that might be offensive to most churchgoers. There are too many churches.

I think it might strengthen all churches if they closed half of them, tore down the buildings and sold the property for money they could use for other purposes. They might sell the property to someone who would put up a useful residential or business building on the site.

There are about 300,000 houses of worship in the United States. Many occupy huge pieces of real estate in prime locations in every major city in the country. They pay no taxes. On many Sundays, even during the main service, the pews at thousands of churches are at far below capacity.

Many of the clergy, ministers or priests address their prayers and remarks Sunday after Sunday to a few dozen people in buildings that could hold several hundred. For the rest of Sunday, and for all twenty-four hours of the other six days of the week, many churches are deserted. It seems like such a waste, and while we don't think of it when we see empty churches, they cost every one of us a lot of money over the years.

There are some beautiful churches in every city that should be preserved, but there are even more ugly, empty churches that should be torn down. You don't have to be an atheist to believe that.

I'm not knowledgeable enough about the differences in the beliefs of a Southern Baptist and a Presbyterian to know for sure, but it seems to me the various Christian sects have enough in common that they could worship as well together in one building as apart in several.

Even if they didn't want to convene at the same hour, there would be plenty of time for each group to meet separately with just its members. Is there something members of one of these churches believe that would offend members of any of the others? Why can't they pray together in one building?

I grew up in a city with a population of 125,000. I still visit there occasionally, and the population is about the same. In the phone book, there are 775 listings for churches.

This excludes a lot of church-related listings.

If these figures are accurate, my old hometown has one church for every 167 people. If half the population went to church, it would be one church for every 84 people. If one quarter of the 125,000 attended services, which seems like a more realistic number, there would be one church for every 42 people.

When I lived in town, there was a Baptist church across the street, a Catholic church on the corner, and my mother sent me to the Presbyterian church a block and a half away.

We were never short of churches.

Today, I live in New York City within a block of a church that's doing what all churches should be doing. It's called a United Methodist Church, but the building is also home to Congregation B'nai Jeshurun and the Iglesia Cristo Vivo.

On Sunday morning, the Methodist pastor speaks to about 200 of the church's 400 members in a room that holds 1,100.

On most week nights, the room is used for meetings by a wide variety of neighborhood groups for (or against) an equally wide variety of issues.

The church has a huge kitchen in its basement that provides meals for hundreds of homeless people who come there from all over the city. It is an unusual church.

There are estimates that about a hundred million Americans attend church regularly.

That figure seems high and was probably made by some church organization but even if the figure is true it means there are 333 churchgoers for each of the 300,000 churches.

The fact of the matter is, very few churches in America have 300 parishioners who attend regularly and most churches are less than 25 percent occupied on Sundays.

They could all use business managers to work out their problems, which would almost certainly involve some real estate deals and consolidation.

THE KORAN IS THEIR BIBLE

I've been reading the Koran. The word "Koran," or "Qur'an," is from an Arabic word meaning "reading" or "recitation." Most Americans do not readily accept any religion other than Christianity, but there are more than 1 billion Muslims in the world and they take Islam so seriously that we should get to know more about their religion.

Muslims believe the Koran contains the words given or revealed to Muhammad by God, Allah. Muhammad was born in 570 A.D. and had a difficult early life because both his parents and grandparents died when he was young. His life improved when he went to work for a wealthy widow named Khadijah. She was impressed with how well he was handling her affairs and, although she was fifteen years older than Muhammad, they were married and lived happily together for many years. They had seven children.

Muslims believe that Muhammad was a contemplative man who often went off alone to meditate in a cave. It was there that he said he heard the voice of Allah telling him that he, Muhammad, was the messenger, or Apostle of God. The voice of Allah is said to have given Muhammad words of wisdom. It told him to spread those words. Muhammad passed these sayings on to others and developed a following. Their beliefs formed the religion Islam.

In case you've never read the Koran, I've chosen a few samples to give you an idea of its style and content. There are 114 sections called "surahs." The first ones in the Koran are short and they become gradually longer. Like the Bible, every translation of the Koran is different and, also like the Bible, some of the Koran is not readily comprehensible to an ordinary person.

Serious Muslims say the only legitimate Koran is the Koran written and read in its original Arabic. Its rhythmic beauty cannot be replicated in any other language. These excerpts I've chosen are from three versions I have:

There are some similarities between Christianity and Islam but many differences. The Koran, for example, says:

"Never has God begotten a son nor is there any God beside him."

The Koran has its own ideas about marriage and divorce:

"If a man divorces his wife, he cannot remarry her until she has married another man and been divorced by him; in which case it will be no offense for either of them to return to the other if they think they can keep within the bounds set by God."

The Koran is hard on those who don't believe in it, condemning them to burn eternally in hell. It speaks of unbelievers frequently. For example:

"The unbelievers say, 'Pay no heed to this Koran. Cut short its recital with booing and laughter so that you may gain the upper hand.'"

In another translation of the Koran, that same paragraph reads, "Those who disbelieve say, 'Heed not this Koran and drown the hearing of it; haply ye may conquer.'"

Allah is all-knowing to Muslims. Of those who pretend to believe but don't really, he is quoted as saying, "They utter with their mouths a thing which is not in their hearts. Allah is best aware of what they hide."

There are many passages that explain the willingness of Muslims to touch off bombs tied to their backs if they believe they are dying for Allah.

"If you are slain in the way of Allah or you die, certainly forgiveness and mercy from Allah is better than the worldly goods they amass."

Muslims, like the worshippers of any faith, are not open-minded about religion. The Koran admonishes: "Believers in Islam, take neither Jews nor Christians for your friends. They are friends with one another."

MURDER MOST VILE

Where do all the murderers come from? I don't know any. You can't pick up a newspaper or watch a news broadcast without having the details of a murder in your face. I don't ever remember a time when there were so many nasty crimes:

After killing his grandfather and a woman friend at home in Minnesota, a sixteen-year-old boy went to his school, where he killed five students, a teacher and a security guard. Then the boy killed himself.

In Wichita, Kan., Dennis Rader was arrested and charged as the so-called BTK killer. Rader was accused of picking victims at random, binding them, torturing them and then killing at least ten of them.

In California, Scott Peterson was convicted of killing his pregnant wife, Laci, and dumping her body, along with the unborn infant, into San Francisco Bay. At the trial, Laci's brother, Brent Rocha, said he'd bought a gun with which to kill Scott but decided he'd rather see him go through the agony of being found guilty and executed.

A previously convicted forty-six-year-old sex offender, John Evander Couey, is said to have confessed to kidnapping nine-year-old Jessica Lunsford, raping and killing her in Homosassa, Fla. Couey allegedly told four people that he had killed the girl but they didn't report him to police.

Brian Nichols was being taken into a court in Atlanta to be tried for rape. Authorities allege Nichols grabbed the gun of a deputy and shot her in the face, then shot and killed the judge, Rowland Barnes. As Nichols ran from the courtroom, he allegedly killed another deputy, hit a reporter with his gun and took the reporter's car.

In Chicago, an unemployed electrician who had unsuccessfully sued just about everyone, killed the husband and mother of a judge who dismissed one of his lawsuits.

I don't know whether there are more bad people, or whether newspapers are just covering more murders, but you can't escape them.

I hear people saying, "There's so much bad news that I don't read the newspapers anymore," or "I never watch television news." Well, real-life crime gets my attention. I find these stories interesting and educational. It's not just the crimes but the consideration of the motives of the people who committed them. Ten years ago, I was fascinated by the details of the O. J. Simpson trial. It was interesting because it proved you can get away with murder. The not guilty verdict in the case charging Robert Blake with murdering his wife confirmed that opinion for me. Reading the paper alone, I do not have to be fair and unbiased.

Half of these murders were committed by people with some kind of mental disorder. If someone murders another person and then takes his own life, chances are the murderer was not really sane. (Fewer than 10 percent of murders in the United States last year were committed by women.) In reading about crime, I'm harder on the chairman of the board of a company who steals $200 million than I am on a sixteen-year-old boy who grew up in a dysfunctional family and ends up a sick kid who murders his classmates. The chairman thought it all out and decided to be dishonest. The boy was, in part, a victim.

There's no way to tell whether our murder rate is lower now, in 2006, than it was in 1706. Statistics indicate the murder rate has gone down recently but you wouldn't think so. In the United States last year, there were approximately 16,000 murders. In Japan, there were about 1,500 murders. Great Britain had about the same number as Japan. Are we kidding ourselves when we think we're the most civilized nation on earth?

FOOD FOR THOUGHT

When world leaders met in Scotland for the G-8 Summit, several years ago they decided to double the amount of money they're giving to desperately poor African countries.

President Bush did not approve of the increase and neither do I, but for a different reason. Most aid money goes for food, clothing and housing. I'd like to see more of it spent on reducing the number of Africans we're trying to feed. Their biggest problem is not a shortage of food, but a proliferation of people.

The annual birthrate in the U.S. is 14 per 1,000 adults. France, Belgium, Norway and Great Britain have birthrates around 12 per thousand. Scotland is 11 per thousand. Last year, Russia was 9.8 per thousand.

I didn't know the rate for African countries until I looked it up. In Nigeria, a country of 130 million people, the birthrate is 40 per 1,000. In Zambia, it's 41 per 1,000. Ghana is practically progressive at a mere 24 per 1,000. The birthrate in Africa is a disgrace, and birth control information and condoms should be handed out before the food.

The rest of the world feels sorry for Africans and has a genuine desire to help. In 1985, a lot of popular musicians got together for the Live Aid concert. It raised millions of dollars "to stamp out African poverty." It was a noble effort, but you could hardly say it "stamped out poverty in Africa."

Too many Africans are behaving as if they don't know or don't care what produces babies. They ought to be told with literature accompanying every pound of food we give them. Unfortunately, some of the organizations trying to win Africans to their own cause oppose birth control in any form.

The African states are often called "developing nations," but they are not developing. Many Africans are poorly educated and are having more children than they can feed or take care of. Children are often considered an asset in poor countries. They go to work at an early age and contribute to supporting their parents. The average African family has more than five children, and a lot of them have fifteen.

The organizations doing good work in Africa are divided on birth control. President Bush has decided to cut off our contributions to the United Nations Population Fund because of his opposition to birth control.

God is quoted in Genesis as having said, "Be fruitful and multiply." Were the Lord to look around our planet today and see the problems in Africa, I think He'd revise that and say, "Enough already!"

PART THREE

On Food and Drink

Milk without fat is like non-alcoholic Scotch.

WAR ON A FULL STOMACH

There are things about your life it seems as though you ought to remember but cannot. I spent four years in the Army but don't recall much about Army food. This comes to me now because when I see pictures of U.S. soldiers, I wonder what they have to eat.

In almost a year with the 17th Field Artillery Battalion before I was reassigned to the Army newspaper, the *Stars and Stripes*, I must have eaten close to 1,000 meals and I don't remember a single one of them. It's probably because the food was forgettable.

I remember being seated at the end of a table in a mess hall one day when other soldiers were in line with their trays, waiting to get to the steam table where the food was laid out. No matter what they were serving, they always gave you either coffee, tea or cocoa for a hot drink. You filled your pint-sized canteen cup with whatever it was that day. One of the men standing in line looked down into the cup of the soldier sitting next to me and asked, "What do they have today—coffee, tea or cocoa?"

My friend looked down into his cup, which was almost empty, then looked up at the questioner and said, "I don't know. They didn't say."

And that's the way the food was, too. One dish tasted pretty much like another.

After I was shipped to England and transferred to the newspaper, I no longer ate Army food on a regular basis. I got what was known as "per diem." It amounted to about $30 a week and with that I paid for my rent in a London apartment and food. I often ate in an Indian or Chinese restaurant because I preferred what they served to British food. An average meal cost me the equivalent of about $1.35.

Because I regularly visited the air bases outside London to report on what the 8th Air Force had bombed that day, I often saved money by eating in the mess hall at the base. As a correspondent, I ate in the officers' mess even though I was a sergeant. The food was much better than in the enlisted men's mess hall.

After the D-Day invasion, I ate the food provided by the First Army press camp. It was like the food in the officers' mess. However, we had one creative mess sergeant who often swapped Army staples like sugar, flour, bacon and, of course, cigarettes, with local farmers in Normandy, for fresh eggs, milk, cream and vegetables.

When I was up front with soldiers fighting the war, I ate what they ate. The food they got depended on how intense the fighting was. If things were relatively quiet, the company mess sergeant could set up a mobile kitchen and do some basic cooking in huge pots over propane stoves with what was the best Army field ration, called the ten-in-one. It was a heavy carton of food about 20-inches-by–12-inches-by-6 inches. I forget whether it was meant to feed ten men for one day, or one man for ten days but it had good stuff in it.

If an infantry division was at the front, with the enemy behind hedgerows 100 yards across an open field, they ate K-rations. Each heavily waxed container was about the size of a Cracker Jack box, if I remember correctly, and contained a small can of hash, tuna fish or a portion of some dense, cooked egg mixture. There were a couple of graham biscuits, several envelopes of sugar, powdered coffee or lemonade and a fruit bar. The packages differed. Sometimes they had cheese, a chocolate bar that wouldn't melt, bouillon cubes, matches, four cigarettes and toilet paper. They always contained chewing gum because the K-ration was packaged by Wrigley.

VIVE LA FRENCH FOOD

Call me disloyal, say I'm unpatriotic, charge me with being a turncoat: I feel about the French the way we all feel about difficult members of our family: They are infuriating but we love them anyway.

Following are some notes I made—mostly about French food:

Whatever else you think about the French, they are incomparably better with food than the people of any other country. They enjoy it more. They savor each morsel and make an event of the simplest meal. Americans gulp it down on the run.

At noon, you see people everywhere walking home in France for lunch with long sticks of crusty bread under their arms. French bread is so much better than ours we should be ashamed of ourselves for eating Wonder Bread.

Their cheese and their fruit are served soft and ripe. Too often our fruit is green and our cheese hard.

We ate in Alain Ducasse's restaurant in the Plaza Athénée Hotel, considered by some to be the best restaurant in the world. It was a wonderful experience.

Wine costs more in a restaurant where the waiter leaves it on its side in one of those wine servers than it does if he stands the bottle in the middle of your table. A French waiter puts less wine in a glass than a waiter does in a New York restaurant so a bottle seems to last longer.

Several restaurants we ate in served both sweet and salted butter. That's classy.

The charm of truffles escapes me.

Dinner in any good restaurant in Paris costs almost twice as much as it would in New York. I don't know how Parisians afford to live in Paris. Everything costs more. I priced men's shirts in a store on the Rue du Faubourg Saint-Honore and they were 120 Euros each. One Euro, the money system that has replaced francs and other European currency, cost $1.19 when we were there. I didn't buy a shirt.

I went to the French Open one day. Out back, I had an ice cream bar for $6.00.

Ice cream is the only food better here than in France. Theirs is more like frozen custard.

One restaurant served "Curdled ewe milk, caramel-parfait honey ice cream." Vanilla will be fine, thanks.

I wanted to see the prices of basic groceries like sugar, flour, meat and vegetables so I asked the people at the desk in the hotel where I could find a supermarket nearby. The two men looked at each other and shook their heads. There are no supermarkets in Paris. To some extent, this is true of New York, too. The markets in the suburbs are much more super than those in the city. New Yorkers, like Parisians, often shop at the little store around the corner on their block.

I made dinner reservations for 8 P.M. every night and we were always the first ones in the restaurant. They gradually filled up by 10 P.M. I don't understand what time people get up and go to work if they don't finish dinner until midnight.

French food is better than French plumbing—but I don't want to go into the details.

Restaurants include a tip on the check for "service"—usually 18 percent. It makes it easier for those of us who are never sure how much to tip. I think that's almost everyone.

I am alternately charmed and infuriated by the French, but I like to go to a foreign country once in a while to make sure I still like it better here. I only go to countries I've been to before and I spent a year of my life in France during World War II. You don't get over spending a year in France when you were twenty-three.

FOOD FOR THOUGHTLESS

Few writers who've written a book can resist going into a bookstore to see where they have it displayed. Usually the author finds it hidden away in the back of the store where no one's going to find it. I always thought some store manager decided which books to put in the window and in the front of the store, and was disappointed to learn that publishers pay bookstores to display a book in a prominent position.

There were dozens of diet books in one store I visited, and a short distance away there must have been 100 cookbooks. *The Joy of Cooking* and *Fanny Farmer* are still going strong. It's ironic that the bestselling books anywhere are No. 1, cookbooks—books on eating—and No. 2, diet books—books on not eating.

I was surprised to see they're still selling the Atkins and Pritikin diet books and Dr. Herman Tarnower's Scarsdale diet book. The first Atkins book was publishing in 1972. Since then, millions of copies have been sold. He allows a lot of fats but few carbohydrates. Pritikin advises eating a lot of carbohydrates.

Both Atkins and Tarnower died badly. Tarnower was murdered by Jean Harris, and Atkins fell on an icy sidewalk in New York and died of a head injury. I met Tarnower at dinner on several occasions because Jean Harris was headmistress of a girls' school where Margie taught math. I remember being nervous about my eating habits in the presence of the eminent diet doctor.

There have never been any surveys done on what long-term effect diet books have on overweight people. Not much, I suspect.

Cutting down on the amount of food you eat takes more willpower than most of us can muster for any length of time. It also seems apparent that genes have as much to do with a person's weight as his or her eating habits. If your father or mother was fat, chances are you're going to be fat. It isn't so much the inclination your body has to be fat as it is your brain's inclination to goad you into eating too much.

There's a lot of flimflam in most diet books. The actual text of *The South Beach Diet* is very short—fewer than 100 pages. The rest of the book comprises fillers like recipes and lists of recommended and prohibited foods. The author, Dr. Arthur Agatston, also includes testimonials from eleven anonymous patients of his listed as "Paul L.," "Kate A.," "Daniel S." and "Judith W." The most interesting thing about the segments Dr. Agatston claims his patients wrote is how much they all sound like Dr. Agatston. The writing style, phrasing and punctuation are all similar to his. I asked the publisher if Dr. Agatston would provide me with the full names of those people and was hardly surprised when he would not.

I think I'll just avoid diet books.

BETRAYED BY AN APPETITE

Our shape is always a matter of concern to us. We're confronted with what we look like naked every time we take a shower. There aren't many of us who are satisfied with what we've got in the way of a body. We have too much of it here, not enough there. Clothing is for more than warmth.

I am moderately overweight and have been since I was a small boy. My mother, who never had a negative word to say about me, used a collection of euphemisms to describe me. She'd say I was "stocky," "heavyset" or "big boned." "Fat" she never called me. I played football in high school and college and at 5-foot-9 and 185 pounds, I was hardly tall and thin, but I was in good shape. Unfortunately, the muscles I had then are long gone or much diminished so, like everyone, I've occasionally considered "going on a diet." My firm belief that diets are nonsense and don't help has saved me going on any of them.

There have been half a dozen diets over the years that have been wildly popular. One of the earliest was called "Fletcherization." A man named Fletcher had the theory that if you chewed your food for a long time before swallowing it, you'd lose weight.

My theory is that diets work—if they work at all—not because of what they tell you to eat or not to eat but because they get you thinking about the food you're taking in. That's the secret in any diet.

If you're going to lose weight, you can't do it sensibly the way sensible doctors recommend that you should. They tell you to simply eat less of everything. Easy for them to say. If I sat down to write a diet book to make money, I'd push my theory that you can't lose weight sensibly. You have to adopt some crazy plan like the South Beach or the Atkins Diet, so I'd make up a new but crazy diet. It doesn't matter what diet you decide on, it has to be something you can be proud of yourself for following. I suspect that if you ate nothing but Hershey Bars, nothing but bread and butter, nothing but beets or potatoes or eggs, you'd end up losing weight.

When you consider how fine-tuned the body is in many ways, it's surprising that it's so dumb about what it tells us to eat. You would think that our appetites would direct us to the foods that fulfilled our individual needs for nutrition and vitamins. Why does our appetite so often misdirect us and make us want something that isn't good for us? I don't understand that. If we get a speck of dust in an eye, the eye waters to wash it out. If our body needs fluids, the sensation of thirst comes to us. Why then, do we have a desire to eat more than is good for us? Why are foods that are not what our body needs often so appetizing?

When I have a small, simple lunch in my office, I often start back to work with the feeling I've done the right thing. Then, within minutes, I find myself overcome with the desire for a cookie, a piece of candy or a dish of ice cream. My body can't need whatever the ingredients are in anything I want and I'm already overweight so why would my brain play such a dirty trick on me as to create the sensation that I want something more to eat?

It would be better for our bodies if eating wasn't so much fun.

COOKING'S THE THING
WHEN VACATION COMES AROUND

When I am at work, I write. When I am on vacation, I cook. I hope I write better than I cook, but I've done a lot of both. (It bothers me, in observing myself, to note that I eat more than I read.) Over the years, I have learned more about cooking from eating in good restaurants than I have learned from cookbooks. Every city has a couple of good restaurants, and New York has hundreds. It is now the best restaurant city in the world.

Paris has some of the best, but the best in Paris are all French. New York has a great diversity. One of the interesting things that has happened in this country is the growing number of Japanese restaurants and the diminishing number of Chinese restaurants. Monosodium glutamate was the beginning of the Chinese decline.

When you're cooking, it's fun to borrow a little from the cooking styles of other countries. You can take a little French and mix it with what you know of Japanese or Chinese. No one borrows in the kitchen from the Germans or the British, although there are some uniquely good German dishes.

I often buy one of those little pork tenderloins. They're deceptive because they're solid meat with no waste, so they're bigger than they look. Mine was a pound and a third, more than enough for four people. I cut it into cubes and stir fried it briefly and made a semi-Chinese dish with rice, onions, mushrooms and teriyaki sauce.

I use rice more than potatoes, and pasta about as often as potatoes. I buy Basmati rice in twenty-pound bags because it's so good and, while it costs more, the price of rice doesn't have much influence on what dinner costs. I don't follow the instructions anyone gives for cooking rice because they all tell you to use too much water. If you're cooking one cup of rice, a cup and a quarter of water is enough. Add maybe half a teaspoon of salt. I like to cook rice in a broad-bottomed frying pan with a tight cover.

Bring the water with the rice to a boil, then turn down the heat and leave it for six or seven minutes. Turn it off and forget it. Don't remove the cover to look at it! Leave it for fifteen minutes and, anytime you're ready, take off the cover and shuffle it off the bottom with a spatula. I add a little butter.

When I cook potatoes, I either bake them until the skins are hard or cut them into half-inch cubes and put them in the oven on a sprayed cookie sheet at about 400 until they're brown. You have to shake them up once in a while. In a separate pan, I cook a chopped-up onion in butter and mix it with the browned potatoes. If I bake the potatoes, I cut them in half lengthwise when they're done. Then I scoop the potato into a bowl, mix it with butter and sour cream, salt and pepper and put it back in just half the skin so it's heaped up. A little paprika on top doesn't taste like much but it looks as though the cook cared.

Blue cheese is good in either a salad or baked potatoes. Blue cheese is American and pretty good. Stilton cheese is from England and is better. Gorgonzola, from Italy, is excellent, and French Roquefort is much the best, but we got into a fight with the French about something and put such a high tariff on Roquefort that you can't afford to buy it.

Lettuce is better than it used to be, but tomatoes are worse. Like melons, you hardly ever get a ripe one. For years, I used nothing but romaine but now there are a lot of different kinds of greens that are good. I used to use mayonnaise in my dressing but now I just use olive oil and vinegar. Expensive olive oil is like a good bottle of wine but cheaper and worth it. Fancy vinegar is a waste of money. Sometimes I chop up a small red onion and put that in.

Last night, two grandchildren were here for dinner, and I made ice cream from a quart of cherries Cecile bought.

Today, I'm making bread. Making bread is one of the most satisfying little jobs anyone can do—better even than washing your car in the driveway. Rising bread could make an atheist believe in God. It's like magic. My bread has been a disappointment over the years, though, and I've decided I've been trying to do it too quickly. So I'm letting this batch rise four or five times. What I'm after is sourdough. I hit the dough mixture in the bowl with no stick spray before covering it with plastic so the top doesn't dry out.

Maybe you'd like to come over for dinner some night.

THE KITCHEN SINK IN COOKIES

A lot of people enjoy cooking because it's a creative hobby that can turn the chore of getting dinner for the family into a good time for everyone.

I cook on weekends and miss once in a while because I don't use a cookbook. If you need a cookbook, you may produce some good meals but you probably aren't a real good cook.

We have half a dozen cookbooks on the shelf in the kitchen and I'm puzzled by the fact that none of the recipes in the cookbooks use the ingredients they put in so many of the things we all buy in the grocery store.

Look at the ingredients listed on a box of any popular cookie, Fig Newtons, for example. I have a box in my hand. Nabisco, the company that makes them, doesn't have to worry that they'll be driven out of business by people who make their own Fig Newtons. No kitchen I know has the stuff they put in them.

Here are the ingredients listed on the Fig Newton box: "Flour, niacin, reduced iron (I could probably get some iron but I wouldn't know how to reduce it so I could put it in my cookies), thiamine, mononitrate, riboflavin, folic acid." We don't have any of those in our kitchen. (Everything seems to have those same ingredients, even though I can't find a reference to any of them in the cookbooks of Fanny Farmer, Julia Child or Martha Stewart.)

The ingredients are listed, by law I think, in the order of their volume. Nabisco proudly announces on the Fig Newton package that the cookies are "Made with REAL FRUIT." In other words, no fake figs. "Figs preserved with sulfur dioxide" are listed among the ingredients in Fig Newtons. Apparently some of the fruit is not fig.

The cookies are artificially flavored. Does artificial flavor come in a bottle or a box? It must be cheaper than real flavor but what's it made of? Fig Newtons also contain partially hydrogenated soybean oil, calcium lactate, malic acid and soy lecithin.

I also looked at the ingredients in a typical loaf of white bread in the supermarket. It's terrible bread but it must be what people like. I often make bread, and all you need is flour, yeast, a little salt, a very little sugar and milk or water. A lot of the taste depends on letting the yeast and flour mixture mature together for a while, but look what was in the supermarket loaf: "Flour, iron, niacin, thiamine, riboflavin" . . . that same old list again. My dictionary says riboflavin is "the principle growth-promoting factor in vitamin B."

I bought a box of Famous Chocolate Wafers. They are thin, crispy and good. Sometimes, for a party dessert, I whip heavy cream, add a tablespoon of sugar and a little vanilla, and then "butter" the cookies with the whipped cream. I stand the cookies in a row, the way they were in their box, on a long plate, and cover them with more whipped cream.

These cookies are totally different from Fig Newtons, but they seem to have been made from a lot of the same ingredients.

A box of Kellogg's Frosted Flakes contains, in addition to corn flakes, niacinamide, reduced iron, pyridoxine hydrochloride, which they identify as "vitamin B6," "riboflavin" and many of the other things that are in Fig Newtons and Famous Wafers.

A jar of peanut butter also has "partially hydrogenated oil" in it. I looked up "hydrogenate." It means, "to infuse with hydrogen." So I looked up hydrogen and it says, "A colorless, highly flammable gaseous element."

Why in the world would Skippy put a colorless, highly flammable gaseous element in its peanut butter?

SOME THOUGHTS ABOUT DRINKING

In the middle of the night when I can't sleep, it seems to me I do my best thinking. The thoughts that seemed so bright and good in the middle of the night never seem so good the next morning. Often I can't even remember some of the most brilliant ones I had.

At 4:30 A.M. yesterday, I got thinking about all the things I'd had to drink in my life. I would have written that "all the things I had drunk," but "drunk" isn't a friendly word to use, socially or grammatically.

As a boy, I drank milk that was delivered to our house by a farmer who owned a small herd of Jersey cows. They're the brown-and-white ones. Holstein cows are black and white. Holsteins produce more milk that isn't as good as that produced by Jersey or Guernsey cows, so naturally, the way the world works, almost no one sells milk from those cows anymore. Farmers complain that people aren't drinking as much milk. People aren't drinking milk because milk isn't as good as it used to be.

In a supermarket, it's hard to find a bottle of whole milk. Everything is "reduced fat," "non fat" or "2 percent fat." Milk without butterfat is like non-alcoholic Scotch. The nation's children have become fat drinking nonfat milk.

The only drink in more trouble than milk is water. When I'm staying in a hotel room and want to take an aspirin, it's frequently impossible to swallow it with water from the tap in the bathroom. There are not many cities left that have water free of chlorine. If I want decent water in a hotel room, I have to open a pint bottle of water from their little refrigerator that shows up as $2.75 on my bill. If it was gas, I'd be paying $22 a gallon. I try to go to a store near the hotel to buy a few bottles of water because I also use it to make coffee in the morning. You have to have good water to make good coffee. We have fouled our nest here on Earth and ruined the drinking water in the process. We have a well 430 feet deep that provides the water for a country house we own. That's how deep you have to drill to get away from the mess civilization has made with the surface of the earth.

My hard drink is bourbon. I enjoy the civilized custom of two drinks every evening before dinner while I watch the news. However, I'm angry with people who give drinking a bad name by doing too much of it. On the other hand, I was pleased with the recent story saying that moderate drinking is good for us.

My most frequent soft drink is a carbonated spring water from France. In most stores, it sells in a green bottle for $1.19 a liter, a sip more than a quart.

One of the strangest success stories in American business is Coca-Cola. It's strange because no one who drinks it knows what's in it. It won the legal right to be called by its nickname "Coke" years ago when it was sued by Pepsi-Cola.

The best idea the Coca-Cola Company ever had was that small, original, green-tinted pinched-waist bottle. In the Army in North Carolina, I was exposed to Dr Pepper and Moxie but I never took to them. On several trips to Russia, I drank the Russian equivalent of Coke, called Kvas. It tasted like Moxie and the soft drink trucks selling it on the Moscow streets only had one glass and everyone who bought Kvas drank from that glass.

This must have been about when I stopped thinking about drinking and went back to sleep.

WE AREN'T WHAT WE EAT

A trip to the supermarket is one of the pleasures of my Saturdays. It's satisfying to have worked all week to make enough money to be able to spend some of it on Saturday for things you see in a store. I buy things I don't need. It seems uncaring to say in a world where so many people are starving, but shopping, for many Americans, is entertainment.

I am dismayed lately by the fact that two of my favorite things to eat, oranges and tomatoes, are either so expensive or of such poor quality that I wouldn't think of buying any of either. I'm used to melons being hard, green, expensive and inedible when I buy them anywhere in the eastern part of the United States. This is because they are grown in places like Arizona and New Mexico and are picked before they're ripe. They are then shipped green, arrive green and are sold green. Some melons do not ripen once they're picked. They reach the stores in New York where I foolishly buy one occasionally and they are always rock hard and inedible. One of my New Year's resolutions is not to buy another cantaloupe.

Tomatoes have deteriorated over the past twenty years because of genetic alterations made to their seed by scientists in the business of horticulture. Tomatoes are harder and not so red and juicy as they used to be. It makes them easier to ship and reduces the loss due to rotting in transit. I don't know what these scientists have done to tomatoes but they've done something and it isn't good for those of us who eat tomatoes.

It seems likely that wholesale buyers of tomatoes like McDonald's, Burger King and Wendy's probably prefer these rock hard, pale pink, genetically altered tomatoes because they keep longer and are easier for their short-order cooks to slice and handle. As long as they look sort of red in a sandwich, they don't care that they are hard and tasteless.

Up until this year, oranges have been dependably good and affordable. There's no better and more satisfying taste than a tall, cool glass of fresh-squeezed orange juice, and I miss being able to have one. The so-called "freshly-squeezed" product that comes in plastic milk bottles is good but no match for genuinely fresh-squeezed juice. California oranges are still available, but you shouldn't squeeze a California orange. You peel and eat their navel oranges. They have more meat and less juice than a Florida juice orange. You squeeze a Florida orange— except this year. Yesterday, in my supermarket, the sign over a bin of small Florida oranges said, "Three for $1.99." It would probably take four of those little oranges to make an acceptable glass of six or eight ounces of juice, and $2.65 for a drink of orange juice is out of my price range.

I am unsympathetic to the tomato growers because they brought on some of the deterioration of their product themselves. However, both orange and tomato growers were victims this year of bad weather. Hurricanes did in their crops and the shortage and consequent soaring prices are not all their fault.

When I'm in a store thinking about getting dinner, I often end up with chicken. I like steak, but I'm uneasy about the animals we kill to get it. I don't have the same feeling about chicken or fish. I have occasionally worried over whether a fish suffers much when it is caught and dies out of water. Is it like drowning for a human?

THE MORE YOU EAT

What follows is a list of the ten best tastes.

No. 1: SUGAR. This sweetener is at the top of the taste list even though too much of it is cloying and unpleasant. It's the most important ingredient in many things we eat—even things we don't consider sweet. When I make bread with six cups of flour I put a full tablespoon of sugar in the flour because of what sugar does for the yeast.

No. 2: SALT. Without salt, anything is tasteless. I like a little too much salt; a tablespoon in the bread.

(Too much sugar or too much salt is bad for us, but one of the things we all recognize is the direct relationship between how good something tastes and how bad it is for us. The better it tastes, the worse it is for us. There is some eternal equation.)

No. 3: BUTTER. Nothing improves the taste of anything as much as butter. Fake butter was an unfortunate invention and it isn't much cheaper or any better for you than the real thing.

No. 4: BREAD. It is with some hesitation that I put bread on the list because commercial bread in the United States is terrible. How it ever happened that the French eat such great bread every day and Americans eat such bad bread is a mystery.

A great bread-maker in the Bronx, named Terranova, makes a round loaf so hard you can drum on it with your fingers. When I asked him what he put in his bread to make it so good, he said, "It's what I *don't* put in it that makes it good."

In spite of the waxed-paper-wrapped mush in the supermarkets, almost every city or town has a good bakery where you can get real bread. You can tell a good restaurant before you eat your meal by the bread it serves.

No. 5: CHOCOLATE. Clearly one of the ten best tastes, chocolate is another thing Europeans make better than we do. A chocolate bar from Belgium, Germany, Switzerland or even England is better than one made here. Vanilla is a good taste but not as important as chocolate. Chocolate is important.

No. 6: CHICKEN. Chicken not only tastes good but it's also cheap and can be cooked in a thousand different ways. It can be baked, fried, deep-fried, stewed or broiled. It's the best leftover you can have in your refrigerator.

No. 7: STEAK: I'm embarrassed to have it on the list but can't leave it off.

No. 8: POTATO. The taste of potato isn't good or bad until you do something with it. You can bake potatoes, mash them, boil them, fry or deep fry them. You can scallop them and if you're good in the kitchen, souffle them.

No. 9: PASTA. If you have a variety of pastas in the cupboard, you never have to worry about dinner. You can find something in the refrigerator or in the pantry to go with whatever pasta you have on hand. Just don't overcook it.

No. 10: RICE. Rice is on my personal ten best foods list. Basmati rice is best.

No. 11: ONION and GARLIC. I know I said ten, but I can't leave either of these out.

Maybe this was a bad idea. I'm up to eleven and I haven't mentioned the tastes of orange, lemon, tomato, strawberries, peanuts or eggs. I haven't even mentioned two of the world's great tastes: vanilla ice cream with chocolate sauce, or a bacon, lettuce and tomato sandwich—without chocolate sauce.

PART FOUR

At Work and in the Newsroom

My problem is that having opinions is what I do for a living. If I didn't have opinions, many of them uninformed, I wouldn't have anything to write about.

IT'S TIME TO REARRANGE TIME

More as a matter of habit than plan, we divide our days, weeks and years into parts that don't make sense. We're locked in by the fact that the Earth revolves around the sun "once every 24 hours," but that figure 24 is arbitrary. Cro-Magnon man should have worked out some decimal system for both time and distance. It might have made more sense to divide the day into 10 equal hours instead of 24. Each hour would be subdivided into 100 minutes and one minute into 100 seconds.

It has always seemed wrong to me that we sleep for seven or eight hours out of every twenty-four but apparently the body needs it. I don't know how eight hours became the standard workday, either. It seems probable that a few hundred years ago most work was manual labor and eight hours was about all of that the body could take. Daylight hours had something to do with it, but we're no longer dependent on the sun for light. Eight hours seems like a short day to me, but I'm not lifting anything heavy.

It's a surprise to Americans traveling abroad to find that in most European countries the workday is shorter than ours. In Germany, many people are working six- or seven-hour days and four-day work weeks with six-week vacations. I feel sorry for people who find work onerous. Emerson wrote, "The high prize of life . . . is to be born with a bias toward some pursuit, which finds him in employment and happiness."

We all look forward to our weekends. Shopping is a favorite pastime so a lot of it is done weekends, even though many communities still have what are known as "blue laws" (origin unknown), meaning never-on-a-Sunday. Closing stores on Sunday is a custom based on the Biblical warning in Exodus, "Six days may work be done but on the seventh day it will become something holy . . . a day of complete rest . . . ."

Most Christians are selective about what they take from the Bible to live by. The most devout who approve of keeping stores closed on Sundays would stop short of the next line in Exodus which reads: "Anybody doing work on the Sabbath will be put to death."

We ought to rethink who works which days and what hours. Traffic at 8 A.M. and 5 P.M. has become a major waste of time for too many of us and a terrible source of pollution. We should not all go to work or come home at the same time. We've got to start using more parts of the day and more parts of the week. That would involve more of us working Saturday and Sunday and some of us taking our "weekend" on Monday and Tuesday. We could get used to that.

Pleasant though it is, it's wrong that so many of us take off every Saturday and Sunday. For example, 95 percent of all doctors are out of their offices every weekend. The weekend is when most of us have time to see a doctor and more doctors ought to accommodate patients by taking their two-day break on days other than Saturday and Sunday. Doctors have us where they want us, though. There are more of us who need medical attention than there are doctors to treat us. No other business stacks people up in "the waiting room," and makes it hard for them to get any service if they get sick on Saturday or Sunday or before 9 A.M. or after 5 P.M. weekdays.

Maybe what we need is a new Cabinet position. The President would appoint a Secretary of Time.

READING TIME

It makes me feel as if I'm off to a bad start in the morning when I don't read everything in the newspaper. Yesterday, I resolved to do that, so I made some calculations.

I estimated the number of words in a column, counted the columns and multiplied that number by the number of words. I then divided the number of words in the paper by the number of words I read in a minute. My arithmetic indicated that if I read yesterday's paper at my speed for ten hours a day, I wouldn't have finished it until next Tuesday—by which time four more papers would be out in my driveway.

The fact is, there is more in a newspaper than any busy person has time to read. You have to approach a newspaper like a buffet. Pass by the table once without a plate to see what they have, then go back and start at the beginning. Don't take more than you can eat. Look through the headlines of the paper and decide what you want to read. Skip the rest. Don't read the obituaries of people younger than you.

Newspapers are better than they used to be. Television news is worse. Newspapers are better for a lot of reasons. Reporters and editors are better educated than they used to be. They take their work more seriously than people in other businesses. They don't think of it as a business. They wish they made more money but they didn't get into the business to make money.

Integrity is a lunchtime topic of conversation among journalists. A group of newspaper people at a social occasion are more apt to talk about ethical considerations in their business than a collection of insurance agents are apt to talk about ethics in their business. Newspaper editors and reporters are obsessed with themselves but it works out best for readers.

There are other reasons for the improvement. Nothing has been more improved by technology than our ability to communicate information and ideas, and no business has benefited more from this than newspapers. During World War II, American reporters covering the air war against Germany from London had to limit their dispatches to what words they could read in three minutes on the only transatlantic telephone line. One enterprising newspaper, the *New York Herald Tribune*, hired a vaudeville performer whose act was speed reading. He could speak 750 words a minute. He talked so fast that no one could understand him. However, his words from London were recorded on a tape machine in New York and then played back at a slow speed which could be transcribed by a stenographer. Reporters for the paper were able to transmit stories with three or four times as much information in them as their competitors.

Today, information pours into newsrooms from all over the world every day. More of this information gets into newspapers than on television. Television news, working on the advice of analysts who tell producers what people want to hear, largely ignores foreign stories in favor of the latest medical report on the treatment of carpal tunnel syndrome or some other less than deadly affliction.

If local and national television news broadcasts had to pay for the basic reporting of events that they routinely lift from newspapers, they'd go out of business. On any given night on any of the three network news broadcasts, half of what they report has been generated, not by their own sparse staff of reporters but by newspaper reporters. Television news is unconscionable in using newspaper reports without attribution. It is seldom that you read a newspaper story that appeared first on television.

We need a device that will play a half-hour television news show in fifteen minutes. I'll listen faster.

MY NAME'S BEEN STOLEN

Two years ago, someone broke my car window, took some things from the glove compartment and a suitcase I had left on the back seat. Twenty years ago, I had a motorbike stolen from my garage. In the Army, at Fort Bragg, someone went through my footlocker and took $20 I had saved for the day I could get a twenty-four-hour pass. These were the only brushes with crime I'd had in my life until recently. Now, several thieves have taken something of great value from me—my name.

More than a year ago, people started sending me copies of an e-mail that was appearing on computers all over the country. It was a list of about twenty comments, each one or two sentences long, under my byline. The piece was titled, "In Praise of Older Women—By Andy Rooney." It was sappy and obviously nothing I might have written, but harmless. While I didn't like the idea of someone using my name as his own, I didn't try to do anything about it.

Several months after I first saw the e-mail, a man named Frank Kaiser wrote asking why I had put my name on something he had written in 2000 for his syndicated column called "Suddenly Senior." I called Frank immediately and he accepted the fact that someone else had taken what he wrote and put my name on it.

There have been two other instances of someone distributing a list of opinions under my name. What would make someone write down a series of personal observations and distribute them using my name as the author? It mystifies me.

About a year ago, I became aware of a more serious theft of my name and it is so hurtful to my reputation that it calls for legal action against the thief. Hundreds of people have written asking if I really wrote the 20 detestable remarks made under my name that have had such wide circulation on the Internet.

The list of remarks begins: "I like big cars, big boats, big motorcycles, big houses and big campfires."

It continues:

"I believe the money I make belongs to me and my family, not some governmental stooge with a bad comb-over who wants to give it away to crack addicts for squirting babies."

"Guns do not make you a killer. I think killing makes you a killer."

"I have the right NOT to be tolerant of others because they are weird, different or tick me off."

Some of the remarks, which I will not repeat here, are viciously racist and the spirit of the whole thing is nasty, mean and totally inconsistent with my philosophy of life. It is apparent that the list of comments has been read by hundreds of thousands of Americans, many of whom must believe that it accurately represents opinions of mine that I don't dare express in my writings or on television. It is seriously damaging to my reputation.

The only good thing to come out of this incident is the dozens of letters I've received from people saying they know me well enough to know I didn't write the comments. There must be many more, however, who are ready to believe I did write them.

I have tracked the e-mail back to an address in Tucson and a Web site called CelebrityHypocrites.com, which is owned by a man named

Dave Mason. Mr. Mason lists as his address, 405 East Wetmore Road, No. 117 PMB 520, Tucson, AZ 85705. I was in Tucson recently and foolishly went to that address thinking it might be Mason's home or business. I'd like to know more about Mason, but the address was a commercial mailbox business and I didn't wait around for him to show up so I could confront him. If it is Dave Mason who has stolen my name, I demand that he put out a retraction that reaches as many people as his fraudulent e-mail did.

ON LIKING YOUR WORK

Over the years, I never cared much for some of the most popular television comedians. Milton Berle never got to me and I couldn't stand Jerry Lewis. Until I saw him in action firsthand, I had been lukewarm about Bob Hope.

Enthusiasm isn't listed as a virtue in the Bible but it's one of the most attractive attributes a person can have. An entertainer who loves to entertain has a big head start appealing to an audience, and no one ever loved being on stage more than Bob Hope. Every time he got up in front of a crowd, he had a good time and it was catching; his audience had a good time, too.

I met Bob Hope several times. For five years of my life, I wrote for Arthur Godfrey. In 1955, Godfrey was at the Blackstone Hotel in Chicago broadcasting his hour-and-a-half morning radio show. He heard that Hope was also staying there and told me to go to Hope's room and ask him if he'd come to Godfrey's suite and do the show with him.

I was uneasy about my mission because I couldn't imagine that Hope would want to spend an hour and a half doing a radio show for nothing, but I was wrong. When I told him that Arthur wanted to talk to him on the air, he didn't hesitate. "Sure," Hope said. "What room's he in?"

In the hotel room that day, it was apparent that it didn't matter to Bob Hope whether he was on television playing to 20 million people or in a small room with four. When he was on, he was happy.

Arthur greeted him and Hope sat down, took the microphone in his hand and immediately reached into his file-catalog brain for Chicago jokes, hotel room jokes and President Eisenhower jokes.

"I was in The White House last week. Ike misses the Army. He wants them to set up a tent in the Oval Office."

On hotel rooms:

"The house dick knocked on my door last night," Hope began. "He said, 'You got a woman in there?' I said, 'No, I got no woman in here,' and he said, 'Sissy!'"

Before Hope left Godfrey's room, he had rattled off, with machine-gun speed, dozens of jokes that had us all in stitches. We all had a great time listening to them because Bob Hope had such a great time telling them. He was his own best audience.

On the fiftieth anniversary of D-Day Margie and I sailed on the Queen Elizabeth to Normandy for the celebration. Bob Hope and his wife were aboard. I talked to them several times and was ashamed of myself for being surprised to find that Bob's wife, Dolores, was so charming, attractive and talented.

Although I think they might have been able to afford to pay for the trip, each of them performed in front of a small audience in the ship's first-class dining room. I assume they were singing for their supper—and stateroom.

With an orchestra in the background, Bob, then ninety walked to the middle of the swaying ship's floor and had a great time rattling off a hundred or so predictably funny jokes. He seemed to remember them without any trouble. The orchestra leader had worked with Bob a lot over the years and when I saw his lips moving twenty feet behind Bob, I was puzzled. It turned out that it wasn't music he was holding in front of him, it was pages of Hope jokes. Bob had a small radio receiver in his jacket pocket attached to an earpiece. The orchestra leader read a few lines of a joke, Bob remembered the rest of it and told it, just as if he was ad-libbing, to the roaring approval of the crowd.

Bob Hope got back as much as he gave in his performances to American troops around the world but he was one of the most genuinely entertaining entertainers who ever lived.

FREE SPEECH

It isn't good form for a writer to use what he puts down on paper to further his own interests but I want to make an exception. For more than two years I tried to collect money owed me by a speakers bureau called The Program Corporation of America in White Plains, N.Y.

I spoke at Indiana State University in Terre Haute. The embarrassing thing I have to reveal is that I was to be paid $20,000 plus expenses. That's more than I was paid for the whole first year in my first job.

It's fun to go to a college town and interesting to meet students and some of the faculty. I am amused to assess college presidents, too. They should be smarter than I am and I try to determine whether or not that's true. Sometimes it is but occasionally it isn't.

Instead of calling me directly to ask if I'd come there to speak, Indiana State officials made the mistake of going through the speakers bureau, headed by a man named Alan Walker.

To get to Terre Haute, I paid $386 for taxis and my airplane ticket, flew to Indianapolis and drove to Terre Haute, where I had an interesting lunch with twelve people at the president's home. Later, I spoke to a crowd of about 1,000 people. I'm not a great speaker, but I wasn't bad and it was a satisfying experience. Money was the last thing on my mind.

Five weeks later, I was paying the American Express bill for my plane ticket and it occurred to me I hadn't been paid. I felt it was beneath me to beg for money myself so Susan Bieber, who works with me, called the university. They had sent Alan Walker their check for

$30,000—not the $20,000 he had told me. I had not known that he was taking an outrageous $10,000 off the top. It wasn't smart of me or Indiana State University.

A month after my inquiry, I got this letter from Walker: "My accounting department is now processing the payment which will go out to you no later than June 2."

Over the next few months I received half a dozen letters or phone calls from Walker. He most frequently called at 7 or 8 P.M., after he was sure I'd left, and he'd leave a message that he had tried to contact me. On June 11, at 8 P.M., he said: "A check will hopefully be going out next week . . . certainly it will be no later than the week after . . . so keep a lookout for it.

"$2,500 will be issued to you in July and $2,500 in August. In September, we will send you the remaining amount to fulfill our financial obligation to you."

On Aug. 18, a letter signed, "Assistant to the President," sounded as if he wrote it himself. It said: "Mr. Walker is out of the country on a business trip to the Middle East and is scheduled to return at the end of the month. I have put a check on Mr. Walker's desk waiting for his signature to be sent to you . . . "

At a convention in Tucson, I met Mike Leonard of the *Bloomington Herald Times*. Mike wrote a column about my problem that went out on the Internet and I was besieged with phone calls from news people who were also owed money by Walker. Lynn Scherr from ABC News and Linda Ellerbee both called. Charlayne Hunter Gault of CNN had sued Walker for $78,000. Linda Greenhouse, who covers the Supreme Court supremely for the *New York Times*, had flown from Washington, D.C., to Washington State to speak and was never paid.

I drove to White Plains with a camera crew one day and parked outside Walker's house. I was going to do a Mike Wallace. There were five cars in the driveway. With the camera rolling, I knocked on his front door. I planned to say simply, "I came to get my $20,386."

No one came to the door and we left and drove to Walker's office. He wasn't there, either. I had failed my Mike Wallace confrontation test.

We were able to determine that the registration on several of the cars in the driveway had expired. So too, I'm afraid, have my chances of getting paid for my speech at Indiana State University. All I got for my work was that free lunch at the university president's house.

There was finally an end to the story in 2005. Alan Walker was convicted and sentenced to five years in prison.

NO NEWS IS BAD NEWS

It's dismaying that most Americans get their news of the world from television because television gives them so little of it. There has been a relentless chipping away of the quality and quantity of news broadcasts in general, and foreign news has suffered the most.

In the beginning of television—I'm old enough to have been in on it—news was offered almost as a public service. Men like William Paley at CBS, David Sarnoff at NBC and Leonard Goldenson at ABC, who founded their networks, were businessmen but they seemed to have a sense of obligation to give something back for what they were getting that doesn't exist among media moguls today. They gave the public news in exchange for their licenses to make hundreds of millions on their entertainment shows.

Time taken from the news content of broadcasts to make way for commercials and network promotions for other shows has doubled. The news broadcasts at every network and local station are minutes shorter than they were. Without the commercials and promos, *60 Minutes* is 41 minutes. The half-hour evening news broadcasts are really only 19 minutes long. Nineteen minutes is the time they have to tell us what has happened in the whole world. Is it any wonder that Americans are ignorant of what's going on?

Jim Lehrer's *NewsHour* on public television is good, but the broadcast has limited facilities and not many reporters of its own.

The networks all subscribe to services that tell them what news their audiences want to see and hear. This accounts for why there are more stories about miracle cures in the world of medicine, spurious though they may be, and fewer stories about what's happening in the world. It accounts for why the sick story of Michael Jackson and small boys dominated news broadcasts in 2004 on the day our President was making an important speech in the British Parliament. Americans tell the pollsters they aren't interested in foreign affairs so news broadcasters don't give it to them. At one time, CBS, NBC and ABC each had bureaus in a dozen foreign cities. The reporter in Moscow lived in Moscow and knew Russian. The correspondent in Berlin, Buenos Aires or Tokyo knew the country and knew the people. Now, all the foreign bureaus seem to be in London. The television correspondent flits to where the story is for the day, has his picture taken in front of some landmark that Americans associate with the country he's in while he says his piece. The reporter is more of an expert on travel than on Afghanistan, Seoul, or Taiwan.

The number of network reporters stationed in foreign cities has been sharply reduced because reporters and bureau offices are expensive. One network that had ninety-seven reporters twenty years ago, has fifty-one now and that includes some who are more news readers than reporters. Without their own reporters, network news broadcasts borrow shamelessly from newspapers that do their own foreign reporting.

Broadcast news should be separate from entertainment and separate from business. Information for the American public is too important to dismiss as an expensive sideline to the amusement from which the money flows in.

News is vital to a democracy if citizens are going to know what they're talking about when they talk, or what the issues are when they vote. There must be ways to pay for so essential a service without resorting to the stultifying commercials we get. I always return to the same thought: Broadcast companies using the public airwaves should be forced to provide news in exchange for the privilege they have of making millions on entertainment.

News might be paid for by a foundation established for that purpose by all of us. Pooling our money to pay for a service we need is not a new idea. Our postal network wasn't organized to make money for carriers. Our judicial system isn't designed to make judges rich. Our police forces aren't paid by the cases they solve. News organizations should also be free of the need to be profitable.

A REPORT ON REPORTING

A few weeks after I first appeared on *60 Minutes,* I got a call from a drug company selling aspirin. They asked if I would do a commercial for them because, they said, my voice sounded just right for someone with a headache.

This was the first time I ever realized I had a nasal, vaguely unpleasant-sounding voice. The money they offered was interesting but I told them I was a journalist and that journalists didn't do commercials.

Although I'd never dream of doing any commercial, I often make a sales pitch for journalism. I like the news business and intend to say good things about American journalism and the reporters and editors who work in it whether for broadcast or print. My desire to tell you how highly I regard reporters and editors is prompted by several negative stories that have appeared in recent years about dishonest reporting. The stories are dismaying to all of us who work in news. We know they reinforce the negative opinion many Americans have of us. We want to be loved and respected.

USA Today announced that, after a thorough investigation by a committee under the leadership of distinguished journalist John Siegenthaler, it had determined that one of *USA Today*'s star reporters, Jack Kelley, had invented many of his stories from war zones. He'd also borrowed information from other newspaper reporters and often added quotations he'd invented to make his stories livelier.

USA Today did the wrong thing when it kept Kelley on the job long after some of its own staff members suspected he was a fraud, but did the right thing when it had the matter investigated. I don't recall offhand any other company selling a product that paid to have an investigation conducted of some aspect of its own business and then made public the details of what it did wrong. The report said Kelley's stories had often been dishonest and that the editorial staff had been lax in not finding this out sooner. Half a dozen newspapers recently have fired reporters for dishonest or unethical reporting.

While *USA Today* has never been a paragon of editorial excellence, it has capably filled the gap left by good local newspapers in towns and small cities across the country that don't pretend to cover national and international events. Many people who buy *USA Today* buy two newspapers.

Believe it or don't, but I can tell you that newspaper or television reporters, working at *USA Today* or elsewhere, are more concerned about the ethical standards of their profession than the people in any other business. I don't think car dealers, manufacturers or clothing store operators worry much about the impact of their life's work on fellow Americans. Journalists think of themselves as belonging to an exclusive club and are proud of their membership.

The fact that news has become a profitable venture for large corporations has not always been good for people in the business. The disappointing fact is that a large part of the American public reads a newspaper and watches television news more for entertainment than information. This has contributed to the profit-driven companies' tendencies to deal less seriously with the truth in favor of entertainment. The truth is often less interesting than rumor or gossip and our good newspapers are to be congratulated for their imperfect resistance to being entertainers.

I've met hundreds of news people during my sixty years in the business. In World War II, I lived in a press camp with twenty-five and met my first bad apple reporter. He wrote for a news magazine and was ostracized by the others because he regularly put quotes in the mouths of anonymous soldiers he had not interviewed and described events he had not seen.

There's one in every crowd, but what I want to say in this commercial for journalism is this: Reporters are more honest and ethical than the people in any other line of work. It's just very difficult to get the whole truth and tell it accurately.

DON'T STOP THE PRESSES!

The American public is not so enthusiastic about either news or the people giving it to them these days. In 1988, 58 percent of the public didn't think television news reporters showed any political bias. In 2004, only 38 percent of viewers absolved them of that charge. Even fifty-eight percent isn't very good.

The use of doctored papers in a Dan Rather report to question George Bush's Air National Guard service was seriously wrong, but I hope the public gives CBS News management credit for having appointed an independent panel to look into what it did wrong and who did it.

The charge is that CBS was out to hurt the President and derail his re-election campaign. That reporters or anchormen have often made apparent their liberal political opinions is true, but it's interesting that there isn't any evidence that their liberal views had any influence on public opinion. If journalists are liberal and people are influenced by them, how do you account for President Bush's election and re-election?

Television viewers are ambivalent about those who write or tell them what the news is. They think of anchormen as special because, like authors and actors, they're celebrities. On the other hand, many people don't trust them. Dan Rather's fame exceeds his reputation.

The journalists I know—and I know a lot of them—are obsessed with being impartial in their reports and when they are not, it is a mistake in execution, not intention. That certainly is true of Rather. The public asks too much of news. People expect news organizations to supply them with the whole truth about everything and news can't do that. For one thing, there's too much of it. The other reason is, most important news isn't interesting. News companies have an obligation, as business enterprises, to make money. To do that, they have to attract a large audience. If editors and producers judge that their audience isn't interested in an important story, they don't use it. This accounts for why Americans are so uninformed about what goes on in the rest of the world. They don't want to know so they aren't told. If that's what the NBC anchor is telling them, they'll turn to CBS. If the World Bank raises interest rates, it may be of significant, long-term importance to the economy, but people won't read about it because it's dull compared to the bathtub murder of a blonde bimbo.

The battle in the newsroom of any good news operation every day is how much to give people of what they ought to know compared to what they want to read or see.

News outlets are important whether they're trusted or not. We all deal secondhand with most of the institutions in our lives. We don't know our banker because we bank by mail or he's over behind a window where we can't get at him. We don't know the farmer who grows what we eat because we buy food at the supermarket. We buy insurance after reading a sales pitch. We don't personally know our politicians. We depend on news reports to let us know who's cheating, who's good, who's bad and whom to elect.

People expect journalists to be better at their job than readers and viewers are at theirs. They expect them not to make mistakes when reporting something, but they do. Reporters make mistakes by accident or by observing something through eyes, which, like everyone else's, are sometimes clouded. Journalists make fewer mistakes than people in most businesses because they're being watched more closely and they know it. A journalist's mistakes are out in the open, where everyone can see them.

The public doesn't appreciate how infrequently news organizations violate their own high and self-imposed journalistic standards.

LIFE IS GOOD . . .
OR AT LEAST FAIRLY GOOD

Life is good, but it's a mess. Mine is, anyway.

Some days, I have so much to do I can't get anything done because I have something else I have to do first.

I've never been able to see my life as a whole and set out to do the right things in the right order by assigning degrees of importance to them. My hours, my days, my years are fragmented. I would certainly get more done if I could put my brain to work on my problems full time, but I cannot. I flit from here to there doing first one thing, then another without paying any attention to which is more important. Invariably, I start one thing, then go to a second before I've finished the first. And then I interrupt the second to start a third.

This morning, I started to read the newspaper, but the mail came so I put the newspaper down to read that. There were several bills I should have paid. I decided to write the checks to the phone company and to a store but couldn't find my checkbook.

It doesn't take much to put me off writing a check. The phone rang while I was looking and I got talking to Bob about the tennis match I saw last night at the U.S. Open. It was a terrible match, but Andy Roddick set a world's record by banging a ball at 153 mph, so I was pleased to have been in on that.

I got an ominous call from the American Express Fraud Unit while I was at my desk. They wanted to know if I had recently charged $4,000 worth of stuff to my account from several stores in Brooklyn. I had not. Clearing your account of $4,000 worth of bills you did not incur takes time.

I had a remarkably interesting week but all in small pieces. It was like a puzzle that was never put together. First, the producer of *60 Minutes* asked me to do something about the Republican National Convention, so I went to Madison Square Garden looking for an idea. After several hours, I left without ever coming up with an idea for a story.

The next morning, I sat at my typewriter and worried again about what to do for *60 Minutes*. I didn't want to go through the long process of getting past the crowd of cops surrounding Madison Square Garden again, so I read some stories about the convention. One story said New York officials thought the convention would bring $250 million into the city. Business is never any good during a political convention, so I decided to interview some store owners.

There were some things I had to do first, though. I needed a haircut before I did anything on camera, I had to take some clothes to the dry cleaners, the accountant who helps me with taxes needed some stuff I have in a box somewhere, I had a doctor's appointment because Tums gave me indigestion, I couldn't find the key to our back door, my car was 3,000 miles overdue for an oil change, and I still had to do that *60 Minutes* piece about the Republican National Convention for Sunday.

Have I made my point?

NOT THE RETIRING KIND

People ask me when I'm going to retire.

How about never. Would that be an acceptable answer?

I concede the possibility I might die someday, but I won't be retired when that happens unless someone retires me—over my dead body. It won't be an action I take and if I don't take it, the word isn't "retired." The word is "fired."

When I hear someone say they're just sticking around at their job for another two years until they can get Social Security, I feel both sorry for them and angry at them. It must be a terrible life for people who hate what they do for most of the hours of their days so much that they can't wait until they quit working.

There is nothing I could do retired that I don't do now, working. I make furniture as a hobby and enjoy that. Some weeks in the summer I spend as many as thirty-five hours in my shop. I enjoy it but if I had the opportunity to spend eight hours a day, five days a week in my shop making furniture instead of in my office writing, I wouldn't take it. You couldn't pay me not to work.

I like home, I like my family and I like the friends I have outside the news business but the thought of spending seven days a week, twenty-four hours a day resting and without any purpose in life scares me. I'm not tired. I am never happier than when I'm working. There is no question that it is more satisfying to make money than to have it. Having it is just a comfort.

There are about 35 million Americans at or over the age of sicty-five, which is generally considered the retirement age. Of that 35 million, only about 10 percent of the women are working and 18 percent of the men. That means there are almost 25 million people who have no known reason other than having to go to the bathroom to get up in the morning.

Being one myself, I don't mind being with old people but I dislike the great concentrations of them in retirement communities. Florida is not my dream state to live in. For their own sake and the sake of the rest of the community, retirees should be mixed in, somewhere close to their relationship in percentage, with the whole community. There should be an intermingling of children, young adults getting started and working men and women in a neighborhood with the old.

One argument put forth as a reason for retirement is that it opens up jobs for younger people. This argument presupposes that there is a finite amount of work to be done in the world and that it can be done by a fixed number of people. That's nonsense. There is more work to be done in the world than could ever be accomplished if everyone worked 100 hours a week. There is no end to work.

There are about 40 million people collecting Social Security and I am one of them. It has always seemed strange and somehow wrong that I am paid handsomely for writing and for doing my commentaries on *60 Minutes* and then also receive a subsistence allowance from the government of $28,992 a year. It is obvious that I wouldn't starve without my monthly Social Service stipend of $2,416 a month. I understand that it would be unfair not to give me back some of about half a million dollars that I've contributed over fifty-five years of employment and I also understand that if the government stopped paying Social Security to people who continued to work, it would greatly increase the number of people who retired. But there's still something wrong with it.

It's almost II P.M. now and I think I'll retire—but just for the night.

PART FIVE

The Nation at War

We are not all powerful and we ought to get used to it and stop acting as if we were. It's no longer possible for us to impose our idea of how people ought to govern themselves in a Muslim country—or any country, for that matter. There aren't weapons enough on earth for us to force everyone else to be like us.

THOUGHTS ON A PEACETIME WAR

One of the strange facts of life is that wars energize the people who fight them. People get more done when they're at war than when they're at peace. It doesn't seem as if it should be true but the most productive time in the whole history of the United States was the four years of World War II.

When people are at peace, they invent ways of simulating the intense competitive pressures of war that produce such good things in us as courage, invention, endurance, enterprise and bravery. In their own way, all the games we play are tiny wars designed to evoke some of those good elements in our character that only emerge during times of military conflict.

No war can ever be a good thing, but good things have come out of war. It always seems a terrible waste for us to spend $300 billion a year making weapons, supporting our Army, Navy and Air Force and doing weapons research. The fact is, though, most of the things developed for our fighting forces have had a great effect on our lives during peacetime. The technology we've developed for building warships, airplanes, helicopters, all-terrain vehicles and a variety of medical procedures have all been used more during peacetime than wartime.

Wars put our brains to the test, too. In a college history course I took, I recall the story about a pass through the Apennines Mountains of Southern Italy where the Roman Army trapped several thousand enemy soldiers. Cato, the Roman leader, couldn't decide whether to kill all of them to eliminate them as a threat or to let them go unharmed as a way of making friends.

My memory of that history course stops short of recalling what Cato decided to do, but the story of 3,500 former Taliban soldiers being held under cruel conditions by a notoriously sadistic Afghanistan tribal leader put the United States in Cato's position a few years ago. We could have allowed them to be killed by these unlikely allies or insist that they be treated humanely. Most Americans would have preferred the latter.

The enemy has to be the bad guy but not all Taliban soldiers were responsible for the terrorist attacks on us or even knew about them. They should be treated like human beings. They should be fed, clothed and, of course, interrogated. They should not have been slowly starved, frozen and tortured to death for information they probably did not have.

During World War II, German prisoners were generally—not always—treated humanely and the Germans generally—not always—treated American prisoners humanely. The best reason to treat prisoners according to the rules of war is that if the enemy knows it is going to be killed when captured, it will never surrender. In the process of fighting on after all hope is gone, an enemy kills a lot of the winning Army. If they know they'll be treated decently, they surrender and it saves lives on both sides.

"Taliban" is a relatively new word in our vocabulary and isn't in any of our dictionaries. Translated literally, it means "student." What its members are students of is an ignorant, militant way of life that they find justification for in some corrupt version of their religion that has nothing to do with the religion of the average Muslim.

The Taliban, in a monstrously uncivilized act, wantonly destroyed the treasured 2nd-century Buddhist statues in Afghanistan.

On the other hand, to the great displeasure of Afghan farmers, the Taliban banned the growing of poppies. As evidence of their dysfunctional leadership, they continued to allow the sale of the opium made from poppies.

It's apparent that wars weren't meant to be understood—just fought.

DIPLOMACY: LYING POLITELY

There are a hundred places in the world that need the help U.S. power and money can provide. But we have to ask, how much can we

do and how much do we have the will to do? How effective would
diplomacy be?

The dictionary says of "diplomat": "one skilled in diplomacy." Under
"diplomacy," it reads: "tact in dealing with people."

The dictionary doesn't say so, but being diplomatic also means not
always saying what you think. "Tact" can mean saying something
that's less than the whole truth in order to influence or avoid offending someone.

The diplomats don't dare tell us the whole truth because half the
time we wouldn't let them do what they think our country should do.
They may know best but we don't want to hear it.

We've had a lot of good secretaries of state over the years. Thomas
Jefferson was George Washington's secretary of state. John Quincy
Adams and Martin Van Buren were both secretaries of state before be-
coming president. Daniel Webster was a great one. Henry Stimson,
Dean Rusk, Cyrus Vance—a great American who died just recently—
were all better than good. Most people thought Madeleine Albright
was good at the job. Not everyone thought the same of Henry
Kissinger.

President Woodrow Wilson made a speech to Congress right after
World War I that became famous because it contained his "Fourteen
Points of Diplomacy."

One of them insisted on "Open covenants of peace, openly arrived at,
after which there shall be no private international understandings of any
kind, but diplomacy shall proceed always frankly and in public view."

Other points included "Absolute freedom of navigation on the sea,"
"Removal of all trade barriers" and "General Disarmament."

Americans aren't much interested in diplomacy because it usually
means dealing with foreign countries. If a vote were taken and the
choice for Americans was between never having any relationships with
any foreign country again, or doing everything within our power and
wealth for the poor people of the world, we'd vote to curl up and forget
everyone else. A great many Americans don't think we should concern
ourselves with the rest of the world's problems. It doesn't make our

government's job any easier that Americans are losing their enthusiasm for the Israeli cause.

There have always been a lot of Americans who are isolationists, and sometimes they've been right. It seems likely we should never have become involved in either Korea or Vietnam. We were embarrassed about being too slow to enter World War II, so we made up for it by moving too quickly in Korea and Vietnam. When Hitler moved into Poland and started to take over Europe, Americans generally were cool to the idea of going to help. Our policy was indifference. An organization called "America First" had a huge number of supporters who were isolationists.

It took the Japanese attack on Pearl Harbor to make us realize we were also residents of this Earth and what happened any place on it also happened to us.

UNINFORMED AND MISINFORMED

The restrictions put on reporters trying to tell the American people what's going on in any war we are involved in is wrong and un-American.

The American public often doesn't seem to realize it's not getting anything but government-approved information from the front—or from the back, for that matter. We have to depend on the almost-nightly press conference from the bright, engaging, sharp and fork-tongued Donald Rumsfeld for what little he chooses to tell us. Rumsfeld shares the generals' belief that it's easier to fight a war if the people you're fighting it for don't know what you're doing.

Someone said the Pentagon isn't telling us what its doing because it doesn't know what it's doing.

One of President Bush's best moments in his whole presidency came when he stepped in to close down the new "disinformation" agency. As part of the war on terrorism, the Office of Strategic Influence was apparently going to spread false information to influence opinion in foreign countries.

President Bush, in indicating he disapproved of the agency, hedged a little when he stated, "We will never misinform the American people." He left the door open for us to lie abroad.

There has always been animosity between journalists and generals. Generals don't like being watched. If they bomb the wrong target or alienate several million people in a foreign country by killing innocent citizens by mistake, they don't want anyone back home to know. They cover their mistakes by not allowing reporters where the action is.

The death of Daniel Pearl, the *Wall Street Journal* reporter, has helped the military. Every time a reporter is killed, injured, or captured it reinforces the Pentagon's claim that it's too dangerous to let such fact-finders go forward to where the facts are.

Journalists are no more or less brave or heroic than anyone else. There have always been reporters who risked their lives to get a story up front while other reporters waited behind the lines for a handout from the military. Sometimes the reporters went where it was dangerous, not based on any grand vision of informing the American public but to get a story no one else had. Even if it was glory the reporter was after, the story served the American public better than a Pentagon announcement of what happened. You won't read about any of our military disasters in the bulletins issued by a U.S Army public relations office.

Our current military leaders in the Pentagon would find the press operation in World War II hard to believe. In June of 1944, days after our invasion of France, I joined the First Army press camp. There were about twenty-five reporters there.

The motor pool for the press camp had fourteen jeeps and one Diamond T truck. We shared the jeeps and as the Army pressed forward across France, our tents were packed into the truck and the press camp was moved up nearer the action.

Every morning, reporters from different news organizations paired up in the jeeps and set out for the front lines. The *Time* magazine reporter avoided the jeep with *Newsweek*'s man. AP didn't share with UP. CBS didn't go with NBC.

The reporters in search of stories told no one where they were going. They didn't tell the fighting units they were coming. They asked permission of no one. They each went where they thought the story was and talked to the soldiers fighting the war. No one stopped us.

We had two censors, lieutenants, assigned to the camp. Their only job was to delete anything that might reveal troop locations. They were not charged with changing our copy to make it more favorable to Army commanders.

The American public learned first hand, in a day, more about the progress of World War II than it will learn in a year anywhere our military is in control of what the public is told.

THE ASHCROFT ISSUE

At my age, which is plenty, there aren't many things that happen to me for the first time anymore. Last week, something happened to me for the first time that I feel assures me of a place in history. I was attacked in an editorial in the *Wall Street Journal*.

The *Wall Street Journal* is a good newspaper, especially if your primary interest in life is money. Serious philatelists have a publication called *Stamp Collector*, which they wouldn't miss. Sports fans read *Sports Illustrated*. I look for the newest tools for my hobby in Fine *Woodworking*. Business executives, stock brokers and bankers read the *Wall Street Journal*.

If I didn't read anything but *Fine Woodworking*, I would have impaired vision of what's going on in our government. I feel the same about people who read no newspaper but the *Wall Street Journal*. Most of what's in the paper is related to the interests of money collectors.

The *Journal*'s complaint about me was for remarks I made in an interview with Larry King. I said that our government had made it difficult for reporters to ask difficult questions without being accused of being unpatriotic.

The fact is, I believe our government assumed, for government agencies like the CIA and the FBI, powers that were invasive of the privacy of individuals and are therefore un-American. If John Ashcroft had been an influential member of the Constitutional Convention that met in 1789 to correct some omissions in the original document, it seems likely the First Amendment would never have been passed. He does not trust the democratic system. Democracy is easy to mistrust because we are such idiots as individuals that it is hard to believe we're wise collectively.

It's difficult to argue for a continuation of our traditional American openness in the face of potential terrorist attacks. I am reluctantly ambivalent about some of the steps we've taken for our own security. It means they have won. I don't want Americans to die and I don't want our landmarks blown up. Therefore, I concede that maybe we have to give up the free life we have in this country and let the government invade our privacy.

It's easier to make a case for secrecy in government than for privacy. Government officials make the argument for not telling us much. We are getting little or no independently generated information about the war on terrorism because our government believes it's in the best interest of the American people for them not to know. It's for our own good that reporters are kept away from the action.

Who are we to say that is wrong? Do you want terrorists to blow up the Golden Gate Bridge, the White House, the New York subway system? If you don't want that to happen, our government doesn't think you should complain about secrecy in government.

When viewers of *60 Minutes* dislike something I've said and want to hurt me with a mean letter, they always say I should stick to my amusing little comments about the ingredients in a corn flake. The *Journal* used this style of attack, saying, ". . . the CBS humorist turned into a pundit. . . ." This is designed to put me in my place as someone who is funny but not smart enough to have a serious thought. The word "pundit" is most often used in a pejorative sense and people who are occasionally funny are not ever taken seriously. Adlai Stevenson never got to be President because he was too quick with a funny remark. I, on the other hand, was chastised by the *Wall Street Journal* for being too quick with a serious remark.

A WAR OF WORDS

The funny thing about this terrible time we're in—well, it isn't funny, it's strange—is that we don't have our dependable old enemies. We're practically best friends with the Russians, the Japanese, the Germans. We have billions of dollars worth of conventional weapons that are of no use anymore because the enemy has changed its tactics. Tanks don't work against an enemy we can't find. Stealth bombers don't help. At West Point, they make the cadets stand up straight for four years—and even that doesn't do anything for us.

When we were fighting the British during the American Revolution, their soldiers stood in strict formation during combat.

Today, our enemies behave differently. We can't see them, so we aren't "facing" them at all. "Face" is not the only word we're using loosely. The words "terrorist" and "terrorism" are not quite accurate and we only use them because we haven't come up with anything better. Americans are not terrorized. We're nervous and aware there may be another attack, but to suggest we are "terrorized" is not valid.

The dictionary says terrorism is "a systematic use of terror as a means of coercion." A terrorist is "one who coerces by intimidation." Well, we do not live in fear. We have been neither intimidated nor coerced.

We say that what we're in is a "war" but it's not a war. I don't know what to call it. President Bush has called the enemy "evildoers," and even evil is hard to define.

The hard line Muslims who made up the Taliban and followed Osama bin Laden didn't think of themselves as evil. The Taliban destroyed that ancient Buddhist shrine because they believed this would please their God. The Sept. 11 bombers thought that destroying as much of America as they could was what their God, Allah, wanted. They thought they were doing the right thing in the eyes of God. How do we fight that?

There has always been confusion about what is and is not evil. In Puritan times, several women were hanged, in the name of God, after being accused of witchcraft. The Puritans didn't consider themselves evil; they thought they were religious. Most of the world is religious, but there's no evidence that religious people are less evil than those who are not religious. Our prisons are filled with the devout.

We're clearer about virtue than we are about evil. Every school should have classes in virtue. The virtues can be named and explained better than evil. Children should have no doubt what constitutes virtue—they should be told. Sunday schools do some of the teaching, but the message is too often buried in Biblical stories that are not direct and clear.

Resisting our worst impulses is virtuous. Stopping to help someone across the street when we're in a hurry is virtuous. Entering a burning building to rescue someone at the risk of your own life, which you like very much, is virtuous. What constitutes bravery is shadowy, though. We call a Muslim fanatic evil when he dies crashing a plane into a building in the name of Allah, yet, among his own, he was "brave." We're in a war of words.

A GEOGRAPHY LESSON

There's so much going on in places I don't know anything about that I've been giving myself a geography lesson. In school, I was good at geography. Once, in the fourth grade, I had to list the capital of every one of the forty-eight states—there were only forty-eight when I was in fourth grade—and the only one I missed was the capital of Nebraska (Lincoln).

Most of my problems with geography now are in the Middle East, sometimes referred to as the Near East. I know the Middle East is not as far away as the Far East, but I'm not sure what the Middle East is in the middle of. We refer to a lot of the places there as "Arab countries," so I looked up the word "Arab" in my dictionary, and it says, "A native or inhabitant of Arabia."

I went to my world atlas and tried to find "Arabia," but there's no such country as "Arabia" anymore. There must have been an Arabia at one time because I clearly remember reading the book *Lawrence of Arabia.*

Another definition says an Arab is anyone from the Middle East who is Semitic. Israel is in the Middle East and Jews are Semitic, but there are not many Jewish Arabs. I have concluded, to my own satisfaction, that the word "Arab" refers more to cultural and linguistic distinctions than to geographic ones. I'm easily satisfied when the conclusion is my own and I am no longer using the word "Muslim" and "Arab" interchangeably.

For most Americans, the fact that Iran and Iraq sound so much alike is a problem. It was easier years ago when Iran was called "Persia" and Iraq was called "Mesopotamia." Rugs made in Iran are still called "Persian" because they sell better than rugs called "Iranian."

My almanac says there are 25 million people in Iraq. One other statistic we know for certain: There are about 135,000 American soldiers there and too many of them have been killed, many since President Bush declared that we had won the war.

Iran is the other country that has only four letters and just one letter is different. It would be as confusing as if there was a state right next to Utah called Utaq.

Iran is bigger than Iraq and has more people (67 million). Iranians speak Farsi, not Arabic, so they are not called Arabs. Out of every 1,000 Iranians, 154 have television sets.

Iraq is about the size of California—not the shape—and only 82 of every 1,000 people have television sets. I suppose those people in Iraq who can't read, watch television. Like here.

Iran is more like the size of Alaska, but Alaska is mostly ice and Iran is mostly sand. It's too hot most of the time and, fortunately for the Iranian people, they don't have to work very hard because under the sand is an ocean of oil they suck up and sell to us.

A lot of Middle Eastern countries are small. Israel, of course, is small. Lebanon, Jordan, Kuwait is even smaller than Israel, but you can see on the map why Saddam Hussein tried to take it over in 1991. Kuwait has a port right on the Persian Gulf, so a lot of oil goes through there. The country pretty much blocks off Iraq from the Gulf.

Iraq just barely touches the gulf near Abadan, Iran. I flew into Abadan once. The end of the world must look something like that. The day I came in, a couple of GIs stationed there were sitting on a bench at the airport watching the planes come and go. I asked one of them what he did on his day off and he just looked at me and said, "This IS my day off."

I hope this encourages all of you to do more research on the Middle East on your own. You might look into such countries as Uzbekistan, Yemen, Oman, Qatar and, of course, Turkmenistan. Perhaps there are real estate opportunities you've been overlooking.

A NOTE TO THE READER: I wrote the following four essays before we attacked Iraq.

A PREEMPTIVE STRIKE

It is possible to imagine a time in five years, after New York and Washington have been destroyed and millions of people killed with biological or nuclear weapons. Won't those Americans left alive ask why we didn't attack and eliminate our enemy years before when we could have done it easily? Like in 2000, 2002 or 2006?

It's easy to imagine our living to regret an all-out attack on Iraq. A great many Americans would object to our attacking another nation for any reason. There are people with strong moral objections to our being the aggressor. Even though we would have saved a lot of time, trouble and American lives if we'd attacked Germany before Hitler conquered all of Europe, opposition to our entry into World War II was strong. It was hard to convince the American people that we had to go to war even after Hitler had moved into France. Stories about concentration camps where Jews were being murdered seemed like propaganda designed to suck us into a war that was none of our business. President Roosevelt was even accused of baiting the Japanese to attack Pearl Harbor as a trick to get the American people to support our entry into the war.

It seems likely that most Americans do not think we should attack Iraq. The Bush administration is ignoring us and proceeding on a course that is going to take us to war. Saddam Hussein is refusing to let UN observers see what he is doing. We have to trust that President Bush and his military advisors know things about Hussein, his weapons and his intentions, that we do not know. We have to believe, as patriotic Americans, that an attack is an urgent necessity or they wouldn't be planning one. We have to put a lot of trust in some people who have not been very trustworthy. As Americans, we have to believe they know what they are doing. The alternative, if we are wrong and substantial parts of the United States are destroyed, is too terrible to contemplate.

Most Americans don't know Iran from Iraq, or either one from Saudi Arabia. Iraq is a little bigger than California in square miles. Iran has the most people, 66 million; Saudi Arabia the most land, if you call sand land. It's three times as big as Texas. Iraq has only 23 million people, slightly more than Saudi Arabia.

These three countries are swimming in oil. The people don't have to lift a finger to prosper. It's as if they have a money tree and only have to shake it to get what they want. They have very little industry and little farming.

Saudi Arabia is on our official list of "friends," but a recent study presented to top-ranking Pentagon officials said that "Saudi Arabia supports our enemies and attacks our allies." The report went on to say that Saudi Arabia "is the most dangerous opponent" in the Middle East.

That briefing included a suggestion that if Saudi Arabia didn't cease its anti-American activities, we should move in and take over its oil fields. This is macho stuff that a segment of our population loves. The idea of gas for 50 cents a gallon is appealing. Saudi Arabians couldn't do much about it if we decided to move in and start taking their oil.

TO WAR OR NOT TO WAR

The majority of Americans support and approve of George W. Bush as their President. It seems strange then that while he is apparently intent on invading Iraq, Americans who voted for him and would vote for him again tomorrow, are not so enthusiastic about it as he is.

President Bush seems almost eager for war. It's as if he knows something about Saddam Hussein that we don't know and for some reason won't tell us. He's asking us to trust him on this and we don't trust him. Bush's critics accuse him of using Iraq to take our minds off the economy which has been so bad during his time in office.

However, it seems unlikely that the Republicans are responsible for the downturn any more than President Clinton and the Democrats should get all the credit for how good things were during Clinton's regime. The economy is something that doesn't ever respond predictably to any effort economists make to influence it.

We're all asking each other now how we feel about attacking Iraq. People ask me what I think, as if I knew more than they do because I'm on television. There is a tendency to invest people in the public eye with an intelligence they don't have—and whether or not we should go after Iraq is beyond my ken.

The idea of using our great power to straighten out the world appeals to most of us. We think that in attacking Iraq, we are the good guys and have the best interests of mankind at heart. The trouble is, war has never done much for mankind.

Americans like the idea of taking action, as if action were always good, but we know that action has often had bad results, too. The administration is calling this current phase "the war on terror" but it is not war. Attacking Iraq would be war.

My own feeling about attacking Iraq is colored by my embarrassing past, which is so much on my mind that I keep writing about it. In college, I had a pacifist professor who convinced me that I was one. I accepted his opinion that it would be wrong for the United States to get involved in the war in Europe against Adolf Hitler. Stories of Nazi persecution of the Jews seemed like hard-to-believe propaganda designed to get America involved in someone else's war. I didn't believe rumors of the persecution of Jews that were oozing out of Germany. They seemed too far-fetched to accept. I did not have the courage of my convictions, however, and after registering for the draft I was inducted into the Army. It was three years later, after I entered Buchenwald, before I realized what a stupid college student I had been. The only way for me to relieve myself of the guilt I feel is to talk about it like this.

And so I am ambivalent about attacking Iraq to eliminate Saddam Hussein. I don't like the thought of so many people being killed—and don't kid yourself, a lot of Americans and a lot of Iraqis are going to be killed if we go in. It's even conceivable that such an attack could provoke a retaliatory biological war by Saddam that would kill millions.

But then I turn over in bed and get thinking that those Americans who oppose an attack on Iraq are making the same mistake I made in college. It occurs to me that it's probably a good thing we have a President who can make up his mind about Iraq . . . because I can't.

OUR UN-UNITED NATION

You can feel it building: the all-American resistance to the idea of the United States attacking Iraq without the blessing of the United Nations. We don't want to do it. It isn't only activists who regularly march in the streets carrying placards for or against something. It's average, everyday Americans who voted for George W. Bush and still approve of him as their President.

There are a lot of things that are hard to understand about Bush's position—or maybe "swallow" would be the better word. The President has chosen to ignore the fact that the UN inspectors haven't found any major weapons in Iraq. We're saying, "We know you have them. We demand you cooperate with the UN inspection team." But why would Saddam "cooperate" by telling inspectors where they are? The word "cooperate" doesn't make sense.

It is apparently so easy to make chemical weapons like deadly anthrax in a small laboratory that it's difficult to catch anyone doing it. They can move their operation by truck or trailer to another location in hours. The inspectors must have known this when they went in. Why did they go looking, then? It makes the inspectors look inept, or Saddam Hussein look innocent.

Hiding the facilities that might produce nuclear weapons is more difficult, and if Iraq was making nuclear weapons, the inspectors would have found them.

Even if Iraq does have major weapons, there's no evidence that Saddam would dream of using them. If Iraq attacked Israel, often mentioned as a target, it would be like inviting the end of Iraq as a nation. The United States would react as though New York had been hit. Politicians and generals wouldn't feel any inhibitions about obliterating Baghdad. They would have the support of the American people—which they don't have now.

The nagging worry now is that President Bush and Donald Rumsfeld have set in motion a military juggernaut that is hell bent for Iraq, no matter what. Before we drop one bomb, the war has cost billions. It would be hard to stop this runaway freight train headed for Baghdad—but not impossible. It might also be cheaper to abandon the weapons and equipment we've shipped to the region than to bring them back.

No one mentions the fact that we have all the nasty weapons we accuse Iraq and North Korea of having. No one suggests we destroy our vast store of biological killers. No one is demanding that a UN inspection team be allowed to take an inventory of the weapons we have in sufficient quantity to wipe out all mankind. We assume everyone knows that, because we're the good guys, we won't ever use them.

This war we're headed for has had a negative effect on our already poor economy. Things are bad and getting worse. The price of oil dominates how much everything else costs. The most ardent haters of George W. Bush are accusing him of planning the attack on Iraq so the United States can take over the country's oil. You have to dislike President Bush more than I do to believe that.

Americans have never been friendly toward the United Nations, but some kind of organization that represents the national interests of the several hundred countries in the world is vital to civilization's survival. We single-handedly destroyed the world's first attempt to organize such a group after World War I when we refused to join the League of Nations. We're in the position now of emasculating the United Nations by attacking Iraq without its support.

There has been life on Earth for more than 3 billion years. Mankind has only been dominant on the planet for something like 100,000 years. Progress has been slow but we've made some. There's no guarantee that life on the planet will not revert to what it was before we organized it the way it is today. Destroying the United Nations by ignoring it would be a step in that direction.

THE PRESIDENT AND HISTORY

No President has ever risked the history books' assessment of his years as the nation's leader as George W. Bush is risking his now. This is it. If we attack Iraq and lose thousands of American soldiers, he will go down in history as a bumbling fool who led us into a war against no one and we lost it. If the economy continues its decline after he insists on tax cuts for the rich, Americans could be in for a worse time than they had during the Depression of the 1930s. This country is not impervious to disaster.

On the other hand, if Saddam Hussein blinks and leaves Baghdad before we attack, or if he is defeated in a quick and bloodless war and the economy bounces back up to where it was when Bill Clinton was President, George W. Bush will be re-elected in a landslide. They'll start carving his visage out of the rock on Mount Rushmore before he's out of the White House.

I'm not so concerned with President Bush's place in history as I am about what we're going to do in Iraq and why. It doesn't seem as though Saddam Hussein is any imminent threat to us, his neighbors, Israel or the world. Why are we doing this?

Many of the soldiers headed for Iraq think they're avenging the Sept. 11 attack. They equate Saddam Hussein with terrorism. The fact that no one in Washington has said that Hussein had anything to do with the attack has not deterred the soldiers from thinking so. It's a curious transfer of blame that helps fire up our soldiers for war and works to the President's advantage.

Americans who are ambivalent about attacking Iraq give the President the benefit of a feeling they have that he must know something they don't. The issues don't enter into their judgment. They either like the President or they don't, and if they don't, they don't like his plans or policies.

I interviewed a class of New York City high school students about the prospects of war with Iraq and was surprised, not only at how articulate they were on the subject, but how profound some of their thinking was. One young man who approved of an attack on Iraq said that he thought the President and his advisors had real knowledge of Saddam's weapons and his plans to use them, but could not sway public opinion in their favor by revealing the information without endangering the lives of our spies in Iraq.

When I asked these sixteen- and seventeen-year-olds how they felt about a draft in view of the fact that they were coming up to the age where they might be called, one boy made a statement worth 10,000 buttonholes filled with American flags.

"Personally," this young man said, "I think the draft is an absolutely legitimate form of service to your country. If you want to live in the most prosperous nation in the world and have all the opportunities that we have as Americans, the least you can do is offer, in some way, service to your country."

MUSLIMS AND DEMOCRACY

It's hard to see the bright side of anything when you look at our whole world these days. There are so many bad spots that if the world were an apple, you'd throw it away.

Too many people on earth aren't civilized by our standards and don't enjoy the comforts of a real home or any kind of cultural life that separates human beings from the lesser animals. Here it is early in the twenty-first century and even civilized nations spend more money on ways to kill people than they spend educating their young.

The military budgets for many countries are a disgrace to mankind. The expenditures are all listed under "defense" even though there's no likelihood whatsoever that most of the countries will ever be attacked and have to defend themselves. If they were attacked, their armies wouldn't be able to do anything about it anyway; they're probably big enough to keep the citizens poor but not big enough to protect them from an enemy.

Take Zambia. I've picked Zambia at random. There are 10 million people in Zambia. They have horrible AIDS and famine problems but spend $65 million annually on what they call "defense." Wouldn't you think Zambia would abandon its military budget and spend that $65 million on trying to correct those problems?

I watched the victory celebrations in Baghdad and have seldom in my life been so pleased to find I was wrong. I did not think we should attack Iraq without the approval of the United Nations. The UN was wrong, I was wrong and George W. Bush was right. Fortunately, he's President and I am not. There's a lot of the world left that needs straightening out, however, and I hope he doesn't set out single-handed to do it with military force.

For some reason I don't understand, we have made our prosperous civilization the envy of many people in the world but, while they like our standard of living, our cars, our music, our food, our technology and Coca-Cola, we have not always made our case for the democratic system that enables us to have those things. Democracy has been so good for us and seems so incontrovertibly the best system of government that we don't understand why the people of every country on earth have not insisted on democracy.

We've had a most notable lack of success exporting democracy to Muslims. About three quarters of the 145 non-Muslim nations in the world are democracies, or call themselves that, but of the 47 Muslim nations, 36 are not democratic. From the President on down, we are religiously correct enough to publicly respect Islam. In private, however, we question what it is about the religion that so often leads its followers to reject the system where the people choose for themselves how they will be governed. One of the unfathomable mysteries of history has been why so many people, given free choice, choose not to be free.

I am optimistic about life in general but specifically pessimistic about the long-term potential for peace on earth.

THE LOOTER MENTALITY

People don't understand looting. It's a crime all its own, different from robbery or theft. We've even made a lighthearted noun of it, referring to "the loot."

Most of the people who loot wouldn't think of stealing. The looters in Baghdad didn't think they were stealing because the stuff they took didn't belong to anyone. It was lying there and if they didn't take it, someone else would. That's the looter mentality.

Whatever else you think of me, you probably wouldn't think of me as a looter but I was one. My first experience came as a reporter in World War II. We came upon a huge cave in a small mountain near Cherbourg that the Germans had used to store thousands of bottles of wine and liquor for their officers.

I went in with a reporter named Al Newman, of *Newsweek*. If Al had found a $100 bill in the street, he would have looked for whoever dropped it so he could give it back. He was absolutely honest, but he filled our jeep with bottles. For reasons having nothing to do with morality, I didn't take any because I didn't drink—a youthful shortcoming that I have since corrected.

It didn't seem wrong. The loot wasn't being taken from its rightful owners. The Germans, dead or imprisoned by this time, had already taken it from whomever the French owners had been.

This was not my only experience with looting during the war. Like every growing boy, I'd always wanted a motorcycle and when I found one abandoned by a captured German soldier, I climbed on and took it. In GI terms, I "requisitioned" it and drove off with "the loot."

On another occasion, I came upon a German command car that had been hit by our artillery. The four occupants were dead but next to their vehicle was a black satchel like the ones doctors used to carry when they made house calls. I opened the leather bag and found it filled with thousands of marks that were to have been used to pay German soldiers. I took the bag with the money. I cannot recall what I did with it, or whether the marks would have been worth anything but, as a looter, the morality of what I was doing didn't enter into my thinking.

When German soldiers were captured, they were relieved of any valuables they were wearing or had in their pockets. Bill Mauldin drew a cartoon showing a group of prisoners lined up in front of an American sergeant.

"Are there any questions?" the sergeant in the cartoon is asking.

A German soldier has his hand raised and asks, "Ven do ve get our vatches back?"

That cartoon probably isn't in any collection of Bill's work because it doesn't project the image of American soldiers that Americans like to see.

The looting in Baghdad may be the worst since Hannibal sacked Rome but not because of the furniture, computers and television sets that were taken. Inexcusable were the actions of ignorant looters who carried off the irreplaceable treasures of the National Museum.

Sad too, is the realization that the Iraqis on whom we visited such destruction were not so different from ourselves. They are civilized people who went to great effort and expense saving the history of their world for 7,000 years back. They had built and maintained the National Museum to preserve their culture. Looting of the collection isn't what we intended to have happen when we set out to destroy Saddam Hussein, and we should have taken steps to prevent it. I am selfishly pleased the looting wasn't done by Americans.

The looting in Baghdad does not mean that human beings are monsters. It only means that war turns us into less admirable people. It takes one to know one.

A VOTE AGAINST DEMOCRACY

I spoke to a class of high school juniors. While I was being introduced by the history teacher, I stared at the boys and girls seated in front of me and idly wished I had the life ahead of me that they have ahead of them. My brain paused and I had a terrible thought: There was a real possibility these good kids wouldn't get to live to be as old as I was.

The phrase "weapons of mass destruction" has been used so often, detached from the details of how death to masses would occur, that the term has become a cliché without meaning.

It would seem to make sense to say we have to find a way to prevent a nuclear, biological or chemical war that could wipe out most of the people in the civilized world—and quite a few in parts of the world that aren't so civilized.

We used to be safe in America, protected by wide oceans on two sides and friendly nations on the other two sides. Those oceans are no longer wide enough and too many awful weapons capable of inflicting death don't have to travel long distances to be delivered. They can be made right here by the enemies among us. Nuclear weapons can be delivered by long-range missiles for which an ocean is no barrier.

The first nuclear or biological strike by one nation isn't going to kill everyone in the country being attacked. That country will retaliate and both nations will go down with their guns smoking.

If that seems too dramatic, too pessimistic, look at the problems we face trying to establish freedom and democracy in Iraq. The Iraqi people don't know us and we don't know them. We assume they want a democracy where the people choose their leaders. It's a shock for us to be learning that the people of Iraq may not want democracy. Since that idea is inconceivable to us, it wasn't part of the plans of retired Gen. Jay Garner, who was put in charge of making Kansas out of Iraq.

We thought our problems were going to be political and economic. We'd talk common sense to the Iraqis and as soon as we got them straightened out, we'd leave. We forgot another important factor: religion. We don't know a Shiite from a Shiksa, and the pictures of bloodied pilgrims who'd whipped themselves with chains in a holy Islamic ritual makes it apparent that talking what we think makes sense isn't going to make sense to them.

The relationship of Christians to Muslims is not like that of Baptists to Catholics, Methodists to Presbyterians, or even Jews to Episcopalians.

General Garner wasn't able to sit down and talk to Iraqis in a quiet, reasonable way about democracy. They pray to a god who's a stranger to Christians, and electing a leader doesn't interest them. They have the only leader they want in Allah.

Religion is more a matter of geography than intellect. Very few young Israelis study the world's religions and choose to be Episcopalian. Most young people in Baghdad didn't grow up and independently think out what they believe. They didn't consider the choices and become Muslim any more than the Irish kid in Boston makes a thoughtful decision to be Catholic. He comes Catholic.

Courtesy and broad-minded good manners in accepting another country's politics is possible. A socialist might listen to a capitalist's argument for free enterprise, but someone else's religion is hard for anyone to accept. Religion is our problem in Iraq—a potential weapon of mass destruction.

WORDS DON'T DO IT

It isn't good for a writer to be introspective. First thing you know, he starts thinking about what he's thinking and he's in trouble. It gets so he can't put words down on paper without considering how wrong, inadequate or idiotic they are and he ends up not being able to write anything at all.

I feel that way about Iraq. I've had so many thoughts about what we did there, what we're doing there and all the complicated issues about whether we should be there at all that I stammer when I try to write about it.

Was I in on any of the meetings President Bush had with Dick Cheney, Donald Rumsfeld, Condoleeza Rice or Gen. Tommy Franks? No, of course I wasn't. Did I read any of the reports the President got from the

State Department, the CIA, the FBI or our spies in Iraq? Sorry, no. Did anyone show me the messages that came to the White House from Tony Blair, King Abdullah of Jordan, or Hans Blix of the UN weapons inspection team? They did not, so what business do I have having an opinion?

My problem is that having opinions is what I do for a living. If I didn't have opinions, many of them uninformed, I wouldn't have anything to write about at all, so I'm reduced to venting my anger about things as insignificant as the words of war. For example, I disliked it when government officials and military analysts used the phrase "coalition forces," as if we had a bunch of countries fighting on our side when we didn't. We had only Great Britain and Australia. It was hardly what you could call a "coalition."

I boiled over when reporters started using the word "troops" as a synonym for "soldiers." "Our troops," they'd say. One reporter said, "Seven American troops were captured." A troop is not a soldier. A troop is a group of soldiers and several groups of soldiers were not captured.

I'm at a loss to know what to think or write now about Iraq. We have found no evidence that Saddam had the weapons we went there to eliminate. It's embarrassing. It seems likely that if we keep looking, we're going to find some barrels of toxic substances somewhere but nothing with which Saddam could have mounted a massive attack—least of all on us.

The United States is standing guard now in Iraq but why, with Saddam Hussein gone, is not clear. I remember a story about a Russian czar who was walking in his palace garden one day and wondered why there was always a soldier standing guard near one little patch of grass. He asked the guard, but the guard didn't know anything except that his captain had ordered him to stand there. The czar went to the captain and asked him, but all the captain knew was that the guard was there because there had always been a guard there.

The czar looked into the story further and found that Catherine the Great, in a previous century, had planted a rosebush where the patch of grass was and ordered a sentry stationed there to make sure no one stepped on the bush. The rosebush had died fifty years before but no one in charge ever thought to say it didn't need to be guarded any longer.

I don't know what I think, but I know I hope we don't stand guard in Iraq after the rosebush dies.

ELECTING A DICTATOR

It seems likely that if there had been a free and open election in Germany in 1940, Adolf Hitler would have been elected dictator. This is the sort of dilemma that democracies do not anticipate or know how to deal with. Right now in Baghdad, which we like to think we've freed of oppressive leadership, it's possible that given a vote, most residents would indicate their preference for a Shiite Muslim leader, who would bring back all the oppressive strictures against women, among other things, that we consider wrong.

A lot of the great things we said we were going to do for Iraq are hard to do because Iraqis are behaving differently from the way we anticipated they would. They don't necessarily want all the things we wanted for them. Many of our boastful predictions of what we were going to do were made for consumption here at home as a way of making our aggression acceptable to Americans.

One of the few good things about boasting is that subsequent to it, the boaster almost always makes a greater effort to fulfill his promises than he otherwise might.

Power is almost never innocuous; someone always gets hurt. We have the power in Iraq now but we're trying to find a way to hand it over to the Iraqis. However, it's difficult to find the right group or person to hand it to. Governments are always formed by relatively small numbers of people who want power.

Because of the faith we have in our democracy, we like to think that an inherent goodness always wells up and leads to the election of the right people—but that's just a dream we have. Most people don't want power, so don't seek it. They'd rather be led than lead. Unfortunately, the people who do want power are not necessarily the best ones to give it to.

The selection of leaders in Baghdad today is like throwing a deck of cards in the air and letting the cards float to the ground at random. There's no order and the people best able to take over probably aren't the best people to do the job. If we decide who is best able to run Iraq, it would no longer be the democracy we promised to give them.

It is apparent that President Bush and his aides are honestly seeking a good solution to the problem. We always try to solve a problem as if there was a good answer, but it's apparent that very often, there is no good answer.

That's all I have to say on this subject now—and it seems like a good thing.

TALK TO US, GEORGE

We've had forty-two Presidents. Of those, twenty-seven ran for re-election. Fifteen made it for a second term. Twelve were defeated. Lyndon Johnson said, "Gee, thanks, but I don't want to do this for four more years."

Re-election is based partly on luck and partly on performance. Right now, President Bush must be worried that he isn't doing well in either category. For example, it must be galling for him to have to go back to the UN with his hat in his hand and ask for help after he so cavalierly proceeded without the UN's approval when he ordered the attack on Iraq.

To rationalize the war, the President always tries to associate Iraq with terrorism, but there is no evidence that, bad as he was, Saddam Hussein had anything to do with 9/11. It is further embarrassing for the President that no weapons of mass destruction have been found.

The President's speech last Sunday night was a speechy speech that didn't sound at all like George W. Bush. When he talks, the President sounds like a regular guy, but that night he wasn't talking to us; he was speaking at us.

If it was the President's intention to set us all at ease about Iraq, newspapers the next morning didn't help him. Just about every paper put the emphasis on how much rebuilding and stabilizing Iraq is going to cost us, not what a great job the troops are doing there.

The *Washington Post*'s headline was typical: "Bush to double Iraq spending."

The *New York Times* said: "Bush seeks $87 billion and UN help."

There simply is no doubt that we're spending more of our money and manpower on Iraq than it deserves as a problem for the American people. There are half a dozen countries with evil or inept governments that the world would be better off without but we can't take on all of them and probably shouldn't have taken on Iraq.

The original budget for the Iraq war was something like $80 billion. The $87 billion Bush is requesting for operations in Iraq and Afghanistan is additional—and we're all familiar enough with our government to know that spending won't stop there. If, as seems likely, we spend $200 billion before we're through, that would amount to more than $800 for each tax-paying American. Not many of us are happy to come up with that.

President Bush also had the unpleasant job of authorizing an extension in the deployment of Reserve and National Guard troops in Iraq—possibly for up to a year. After this announcement, there were stories on television from Iraq and from the hometowns of those soldiers about how surprised and unhappy they were to hear that the Army was extending their stay. Most of these National Guard soldiers had signed up with the expectation that, in exchange for about $400 a month, they would give up one weekend a month and two weeks once a year. It was a bet they lost and one more bit of bad news that no President running for re-election wants to deliver.

APOLOGIZING FOR APOLOGIZING

He didn't mean to do it, but President Bush has made the United States the most detested nation in the world. He displays what is seen by many countries as an arrogance that transfers to all of us.

Bush won no friends at the United Nations in 2002 and we need friends.

We are not all powerful and we ought to get used to it and stop acting as if we were. It's no longer possible for us to impose our idea of how people ought to govern themselves in a Muslim country—or any country, for that matter. There aren't weapons enough on earth for us to make everyone else like us.

There was a time as recently as fifty years ago when we could dominate the world with our military power and money, but those days are lost and gone. The oceans that surround us were moats that once protected us from attack, but with ballistic missiles, supersonic airplanes, chemical and biological weapons, oceans are no more than wet spots on the globe.

Our Army with all its tanks and infantry, our Air Force with all its bombers and fighter planes, our Navy with all its battleships and submarines, are no match for one terrorist with a suitcase full of anthrax or one suicidal religious fanatic with a truckload of nitroglycerine. We are shadowboxing with an enemy we can't see or touch. Our West Point graduates are trained to fight a war there will never be.

It doesn't matter what I think, but I think like millions of Americans, and they matter. I was opposed to going into Iraq without the approval of the United Nations. When we moved so quickly into Baghdad and seemed to get rid of Saddam Hussein, I decided I'd been wrong and apologized.

Now I want to apologize again. I want to apologize for apologizing. The people who thought we should not have attacked Iraq without the sanction of the United Nations were right. It wasn't all President Bush's fault. UN delegates were sitting on their hands. The French and the Germans were against it basically because we were for it and because they had economic interests in Iraq, but now we have to live with our mistake. We're living with it and too many of our guys are dying with it.

The UN has to be a lot smarter than it ever has been to fulfill the promise of the organization. The United Nations has been a namby-pamby group and that's partly because the United States has never supported it with any enthusiasm.

It's foolish of us not to put our wholehearted support behind the UN. There simply has to be some power in the world superior to our own—for our own sake. Iraq is the world's problem, it isn't our problem. There are far too many places in the world that have more problems than we can solve.

I hope we remain the strongest country in the world because we usually do what's right. It isn't a sure thing that we will remain as dominant as we are, however. We can't imagine it any other way, but Great Britain, France and Germany are not the dominant countries they used to be in the world. Japan is fading. It could happen to us—may be happening.

Something I read in college keeps coming to me and I can't remember the source. It was that ancient Greece and Rome didn't go into decline because there was anything wrong with the principles on which their civilizations were based. They went into decline because the people who believed in those principles became a minority and they were overrun by people who didn't understand those principles at all. There must have been some Greek and Roman George Bushes.

HEROES DON'T COME WHOLESALE

The reporting from Iraq has been pretty thin. We don't learn much about what our soldiers in Iraq are thinking or doing. There's no Ernie Pyle to tell us and, if there were, the military would make it difficult or impossible for him to let us know.

It would be interesting to have a reporter ask a group of our soldiers in Iraq to answer five questions and see the results:

1. Do you think your country did the right thing sending you into Iraq?
2. Are you doing what America set out to do to make Iraq a democracy, or have we failed so badly that we should pack up and get out before more of you are killed?
3. Do the orders you get handed down from one headquarters to another, all far removed from the fighting, seem sensible, or do you think our highest command is out of touch with the reality of your situation?
4. If you could have a medal, a raise or a trip home, which would you take?
5. Are you encouraged by all the talk back home about how brave you are and how everyone supports you?

Treating soldiers fighting their war as brave heroes is an old civilian trick designed to keep the soldiers at it. But you can be sure our soldiers in Iraq are not all brave heroes gladly risking their lives for us sitting comfortably back here at home.

Our soldiers in Iraq are people, young men and women, and they behave like people—sometimes good and sometimes bad, sometimes brave, sometimes cowardly. It's disingenuous of the rest of us to encourage them to fight this war by idolizing them. We pin medals on their chests to keep them going. We speak of them as if they volunteered to risk their lives to save ours but there isn't much voluntary about what most of them have done. A relatively small number are professional soldiers. During the last few years, when millions of jobs disappeared, many young people, desperate for some income, enlisted in the Army. About 40 percent of our soldiers in Iraq enlisted in the National Guard or the Army Reserve to pick up some extra money and never thought they'd be called on to fight. They want to come home.

One indication that not all soldiers in Iraq are happy warriors is the report released by the Army showing the large number of them who committed suicide there last year. We must support our soldiers in Iraq because it's our fault they're risking their lives there. However, we should not bestow the mantle of heroism on all of them for simply being where we sent them. Most are victims, not heroes.

America's intentions are honorable. I believe that and we must find a way of making the rest of the world believe it. We want to do the right thing. We care about the rest of the world. President Bush's intentions were honorable when he took us into Iraq. They were not well thought out but not dishonorable, either.

President Bush's determination to make the evidence fit the action he took, which it does not, has made things look worse. We pay lip service to the virtues of openness and honesty, but for some reason we too often act as though there was a better way of handling a bad situation than by being absolutely open and honest.

GOOD DAYS, BAD DAYS

If you were going to make a list of the great times in American history, you'd start with the day in 1492 when Columbus got here.

The Revolution when we won our independence would be on the list.

Beating Hitler. The unconditional German surrender at Reims on May 8, 1945.

The day we put Americans on the moon was a special occasion.

We've had a lot of great days.

Our darkest days up until now have been things like presidential assassinations—four of them. The stock market crash in 1929, Pearl Harbor and 9/11, of course.

The day the world learned that American soldiers had tortured Iraqi prisoners should be put high on the list of our country's worst. It's a black mark on our record that will be in the history books in a hundred languages for a hundred years. It altered the world's perception of us.

The image printed in newspapers of one bad woman with a naked man on a leash did more to damage America's reputation all over the world than all the good things we've done ever helped our reputation. Other guards put hoods over the heads of prisoners, stripped them naked, beat them and left them hanging from the bars of their prison cells by their wrists. The hoods made it difficult for them to breathe. Impossible sometimes, and some died of slow asphyxiation.

What were the secrets they were trying to get from captured Iraqis? What important information did that poor devil on the leash have that he wouldn't have given to anyone in exchange for a crust of bread or a sip of water?

One prisoner reported that a guard told him, "I'm going to make you wish you'd die and you're not going to."

Our general in charge said our guards were "untrained." Untrained at what? Being human beings? Should we excuse the Iraqi who chopped off Nicholas Berg's head because he was untrained?

The guards who tortured prisoners are faced with a year in prison. A year for destroying America's reputation.

I don't want them in prison anyway. Take away their right to call themselves American, that's what I'd do.

In the history of the world, several great civilizations that seemed immortal have deteriorated and died. I don't want to be dramatic, but I've lived a long while and, for the first time in my life, I have this faint, far-away fear that it could happen to us in America as it happened to the Greek and Roman civilizations. Too many Americans don't understand what we have here and how hard it is to keep it. I worry for my grandchildren and great-grandchildren. I want them to have what I've had . . . and I sense it could be slipping away from them.

WE SHOULD LEAVE WHILE
WE'RE BEHIND

Democracy has worked so well and lasted so long for us in the United States of America that we assume popular government is what every country should have. That probably isn't true in a lot of places, and Iraq may be one of them.

The people of Iraq never had what we have. They don't understand democracy and there's no great demand for it from the people. The history of the region is hundreds of years of tribal war. Iraq is a disaster state. The people are largely uneducated, any government they've had has been corrupt and they produce almost nothing of any value but oil. The women weave some nice rugs but it's a cottage industry. Their oil is an accident of nature.

Most Americans are not committed to this war. They are committed to supporting our soldiers, but they don't know a Shiite from a Sunni and couldn't care less about the Kurds.

A democracy like ours, where people decide for themselves what's best for them, depends on the people who vote knowing what's going on. That's why good newspapers and responsible television news are important. Iraq has almost none of that.

I've often thought we should mount a huge advertising campaign in Iraq to convince the people that we're really nice guys just trying to help them, but I'm dreaming. How would we tell them anything? Few Iraqi homes have a television sets. Fewer than one out of every fifty people read a newspaper. It wouldn't help if they had a newspaper delivered to their door every morning because something like 50 percent of the people can't read. And, of course, you couldn't deliver a newspaper to their door anyway because a lot of Iraqis don't have a door to deliver it to.

What kind of a democracy could you have in a country like that? It's a sad state of affairs for the 25 million Iraqis because they are human beings like us, but their lives are beyond our ability to improve.

Before Vietnam, Americans used to enjoy saying we never lost a war. Well, we lost that one and we're losing this one. I don't know what promises we've made to those Iraqis who have worked with us, but I suppose they're one big reason Rumsfeld, Cheney and Bush haven't said we should leave. The friends we have will be slaughtered when we leave, and we ought to devote our energies to finding a way to prevent that. Our incursion into this Middle Eastern morass isn't working. What has it done for us, for the Iraqis, or for the world?

It would be difficult now for President Bush to tell the Iraqis we're leaving after killing thousands of their people and laying waste to half a dozen of their major cities. Here at home, the families of several thousand soldiers who've been killed might never forgive him. It would otherwise be nothing more than politically embarrassing if Bush came out and admitted he was wrong.

Admitting we're wrong has become popular. Everybody is always scoring points by admitting they were wrong. President Bush has got to admit that going to war in Iraq was a serious mistake. He sent our soldiers in there without knowing what they were going to do, or how they were going to get out when they finished doing it.

NEVER MIND WHO WON

I have a friend who spent time in Iraq working for the government as an architect. He says of all the Middle Eastern countries, Iraq is closest to being enlightened. It is not enlightened, he said, but it comes closest. For example, women have more rights in Iraq than in many Muslim countries, and I thought of that when I saw how many women voted in the Iraqi election. Iraqis going to vote looked like average, ordinary people and I felt bad about having distanced myself from them in my mind.

The apparent success of the elections in Iraq is a disappointment to people who dislike President Bush. They're unhappy when the news about anything is good for the President.

I know people who dislike President Bush so much they're disappointed when the market goes up even though they own a lot of stock.

No one in our country knows what the Iraqis were voting for or who won. However, it didn't really matter and most Americans were surprised by the number of Iraqis who risked their lives to vote.

The election was also a pleasant surprise because we had not thought Iraqis cared that much about the democratic process from which they had been so long separated.

Reporters and cameramen don't dare circulate among the people of Iraq because of the danger of being blown up or kidnapped and beheaded, so we haven't been seeing average Iraqi people on television. Most reporters are forced to stay in safe compounds, isolated from the Iraqi people. Some of what they said on camera was even written for them in New York. The joke in network newsrooms was that before going on the air from Iraq the reporter would call the writers in New York and ask, "What's it like over here?"

We're all enthusiastic about democracy in a general way, but there is a limit to what public opinion, as expressed by its vote, can accomplish. People are often so uninformed and dumb that it's a miracle democracy works at all. That must be as true in Iraq as it is here. "The public," someone once said, "is a idiot." It doesn't really know what it thinks and there's no guarantee the people it elects will do what they promise to do anyway.

We aren't talking a lot about it because it's an uncomfortable subject, but religion is as basic to our problem in Iraq, as it is in many countries we deal with where spirituality plays a dominant role. Americans know little or nothing about Islam. They are even uncertain about when to use "Islam," when to use "Muslim," or even whether the word is spelled "Muslim" or "Moslem."

When I was young, Muslims were called "Mohammedans."

TORTURE, AMERICAN STYLE

It's strange for proud Americans who have never doubted the honorable intentions of their leaders to feel tentative with their support right now. That's how the administration's approval of torturing prisoners has made a lot of us feel.

There is no justification for torture. The information elicited can never be trusted. It has been well established by military people who have held enemy prisoners that torture, besides being uncivilized, is not an effective way of eliciting information.

Is there something we don't know? Has the CIA been able to get lists of names of the Iraqis who plan to blow up landmarks like the Statue of Liberty or the Sears Tower by holding prisoners under water until they're close to drowning? This is a torture technique known to the CIA as "water-boarding." Have we been able to get the dates when their operatives plan to attack by water-boarding Iraqis? When an enemy captures American soldiers, which will inevitably happen, will Americans be subjected to water-boarding?

The *Washington Post* published an article saying that the CIA had set up secret detention centers in as many as eight countries. This made a lot of people wonder what was going on in those prisons. The CIA promptly demanded a criminal inquiry into the source of the *Post*'s article. My friend Ben Bradlee, the former *Post* editor, still has a major role there and I worry about him. I don't know how Ben would stand up to torture if the CIA set out to make him reveal where the *Post* got its information.

What has our Central Intelligence Agency learned of vital importance by torturing prisoners? They should tell us about the results they've obtained from torture that make it acceptable to them. Even if they told us, I don't think most Americans would approve of torturing anyone. The prisoners we have done unspeakable things to—including killing some of them during their torture—are mostly Iraqi soldiers. They know as much about the secrets of their leaders as I knew about the day and date of D-Day when I was in the Army in England waiting for the invasion of France in 1944. Nothing. Soldiers don't get in on planning the actions in which they are killed.

In a secret CIA report by its own inspector general, some of the agency's methods of questioning prisoners were said to violate provisions of the international Convention Against Torture. Things like this make it harder for us to continue thinking of ourselves as the good guys.

There's no question we are in danger, as a nation, from terrorists, who are planning, as I write probably, to destroy some landmark buildings in the United States and kill several hundred people in the process. We need the CIA, and our operatives are working, in small, clandestine groups in more than 20 foreign countries, trying to search out potential terrorists. We approve of all that. We do not approve of the kind of torture to which we subjected prisoners at Abu Ghraib.

Many Iraqi prisoners being tortured have been captives for more than a year. Is there an Iraqi so brave, so inured to pain that he would hold back secret information he had after having skin torn from his body? Other techniques designed to illicit information include "impairment of bodily function." I hate to think what that means.

Every once in a while, it occurs to me to wonder where all the women are over there. I don't suppose Iraq has even a token group of women in uniform comparable to ours, but the Iraqis must have wives and girlfriends. Women have all but disappeared in this war. Maybe that's why it isn't nicer. We don't see many American women on the scene, either. Not since the charming Lynndie England dropped her leash.

The Bush administration said that certain restrictions on torture do not apply now because we aren't doing it in the United States. We are torturing prisoners who are not citizens of the United States in foreign countries where those international laws against torture do not apply. Does that make you proud to be an American?

I am nervous about writing so critical a piece as this about the CIA. I could end up on a list—and end up ending up.

NO EASY ANSWERS

For several years now, Americans have been busy asking each other whether we should pull out of Iraq immediately or stay and try to finish what we started. I wish I knew for sure what was right. I even wish I knew for sure what I think. If I knew, I'd state my opinion loud and clear every time the subject of Iraq came up. Unfortunately, I'm ambivalent. Sometimes I'm thinking it's idiotic for us to be there with more of our guys dying every day. The next minute, I'm thinking we're doing the right thing for the people of Iraq. Just as we saved the whole civilized world from domination by Adolf Hitler in WWII, we've saved the Middle East from domination by Saddam Hussein. Was I against WW II? No, so how could I oppose our saving the Middle East from Saddam Hussein now?

In idle moments, I've often thought that if we all had all the facts about something, we'd all come to the same conclusion.

We don't have all the facts, though, and President Bush probably doesn't, either. You'd think that as the people of the world became more civilized, war might have died out as a way of settling international disputes but it hasn't. Instead of using the advances in our technology for the purposes of peace, we've used them to produce more effective weapons capable of killing more people in a shorter time.

I argue with myself about Iraq every day. Last week, just when I thought I'd convinced myself we were doing the right thing there and should finish the job, I read the new federal budget. I saw what our government plans to spend on education in one year compared with what it will spend on what it calls "defense." ("Defense" is the official euphemism our government uses for "war." Years ago, some smart public relations expert arranged to have our years-old "War Department" renamed the "Defense Department.")

The new budget called for spending $439 billion on the military in 2007 and $54 billion on education. If we are the most civilized society on earth, how can we justify spending all those billions of dollars making devices and training armies whose only purpose is to kill people?

War is an industry that makes billions of dollars for a wide variety of businesses. If our Government made all our weapons itself instead of having them made by the so-called arms industry it might eliminate the people who encourage us to fight so they'll profit.

When I was quite young, I thought I might be a pacifist. Pacifists believe that any peace is better than any war. I liked that idea, but I learned that most pacifists were impractical dreamers. It's nice of them to talk about not going to war, but then what do they do when another country attacks theirs to take land or property? Do they sit back and watch because they're pacifists, or do they abandon their ideals and pick up a rifle? The answer is, they fight, and that's why war is inevitable until human nature changes. I should live so long.

It is not clear that Iraq had any plans to take anything away from anyone, and certainly not from us. We get no sense of any civilization in Iraq from reading our daily papers or watching television but there is a great one. We don't see it because of inadequate reporting and lack of interest on our part. We don't want to know that much about Iraq. The fact is, the people of Iraq are not so different from us. They worship a different God than most Americans, or maybe it's that they worship the same God in a different language.

PART SIX

On Politics

It's a mystery why so many men want to be president. What kind of ego would you have to have to think you were smart enough to run the country?

LIBERAL IS A DIRTY WORD

We have never had so conservative a President as the one we have now.

We use the word "conservative" interchangeably with "Republican," as we do "liberal" and "Democrat." In the past fifty years, we've had six Republican Presidents and some of them were more conservative than others. They were Dwight Eisenhower, Richard Nixon, Gerald Ford, Ronald Reagan, George Bush and now George W. Bush. We've had five Democrats: Truman, Kennedy, Johnson, Carter and Clinton.

Even though we almost always associate the word "liberal" with Democrats and "conservative" with Republicans, the words have so many nuances of meaning that this doesn't always work. You'd think that a conservationist would be conservative, but most conservationists are liberal. Under conservationist, the dictionary says: "One who practices or advocates conservation of natural resources." Our ultraconservative President is the last person to fit that definition. Like most conservatives, he believes we should use all the world's natural resources freely now because there's more where they came from. If that proves false, conservatives believe we'll find substitutes or ways to do without certain resources. This is not only a position that can be defended but it's also a more attractive philosophy than the spartan liberal conservationist belief that we have to reduce our consumption of natural resources or we'll ruin the Earth.

President Bush has proposed what he calls a plan for preventing forest fires by letting the lumber companies cut down more trees. He says clearing some of the forests will mean fewer fires. This is comparable to killing every other baby at birth to reduce deaths from starvation.

Most of us have our political opinions and they are seldom formed free from consideration of our own personal or financial interests. For this reason, it's a mystery why so many working people are conservative and enthusiastic supporters of a President who's best friends with their bosses. George W. Bush, the most aggressive pro–big business president we've ever had, got a lot of votes from people who work with their hands for big corporations at an hourly wage. It's hard to understand.

Liberals are having a hard time understanding the popularity of so conservative a president and his conservative Cabinet members.

Many Bush appointees seem to liberals to have contempt for civil liberties. The Bush administration has operated on the theory that the American public would be better off not knowing the details of everything its government is doing. This is why Secretary of Defense Donald Rumsfeld allowed so little information to come out of Afghanistan regarding our troops' activities there.

I have the uneasy feeling that a great many Americans—the majority—agree with the conservative, secretive, pro-business philosophy of this administration. I accept it, but I'm puzzled.

ELECTION DAY

Every election day we decide which politicians we're going to be complaining about for the next couple of years. Congressional representatives only serve for two years. They just get to Congress and they have to start running again, so they don't have a lot of time to pay attention to the important matters.

Running for election is a demeaning thing to do—going around telling everyone how good you are. People would laugh at us if we did that in real life.

No one says so, but I think voters and politicians have a low opinion of each other. When we call someone a politician, we aren't saying something nice. It's an epithet. We treat politicians like dirt.

Politicians don't have a high opinion of voters, either, though they never let on. There are a lot of things politicians can't be honest about. Candidates would never be elected if they didn't deceive us. For instance, politicians don't decide what they believe and vote that way. They find out what voters want and pretend that's what they want.

It's no wonder politicians are contemptuous of voters because most of the voters they meet want something from them. The voters aren't interested in what's happening to their country. They want a law passed that will help their business, or they need help getting their brother-in-law out of trouble.

That's one reason our political system doesn't work very well when it comes to international affairs. Politicians are so busy getting re-elected by sucking up to voters who have petty little problems that they don't have time for a lot of the more serious stuff.

The classic dilemma for everyone in Congress is whether to do what's right or what the voters in their district want. It doesn't seem as though politicians should ever ignore their best judgment to get in good with voters, but they do it all the time.

Paul Wellstone, the Minnesota senator who died in the plane crash, was much admired but little imitated. He was the only senator to vote against giving President Bush the authority to make war on Iraq.

A lot of Americans are put off voting because they don't think their vote counts for much in big elections. There are too many special interest groups that support politicians. Maybe they are union members, veterans, business executives, Catholics, Baptists, women or political party members. The politician has to pay attention to these people because they vote as a block.

Our political system is a mess—no doubt about it—but no other country as big as ours with so many different kinds of people has ever governed itself so successfully for so long as we have.

JUDGING THE JUDGES

The success of President Bush and the Republican Party make it apparent that the people of this country are more conservative in many of their opinions about social issues, the law and the environment than they once were. Those who voted for Republican candidates this year would not have voted for Franklin D. Roosevelt had they been of age in the 1930s.

One of the things that will have the most impact on life in the United States in the future is the conservative judges, at every level, that President Bush is appointing and which a conservative Congress seems almost certain to approve.

There have been six landmark U.S. Supreme Court decisions in recent history. "Landmark" may be a cliché term for them but I can't think of any other. They've had a profound effect on life in this country and it's interesting to consider whether or not any of them will be overturned. I'm proud of myself for having done a little homework and you might like to have your memory refreshed about these decisions. Amaze your friends by knowing these cases:

Brown vs. The Board of Education: The court ruled that separate public schools for black students and white students was fundamentally unequal.

Gideon vs. Wainwright: Defendants charged with serious crimes must have access to a lawyer at government expense if they can't pay.

New York Times vs. Sullivan: The press is protected from being sued for libel for defamatory statements about public officials, even if the charges are in error, unless it can be proved that the paper printed the statements out of malice or deliberate disregard for the truth.

Miranda vs. Arizona: Before they are questioned, suspects in custody must be told they have the right not to say anything and that they can ask for a lawyer.

New York Times vs. The United States: The court upheld the right of the newspaper to publish documents about the Vietnam War that the government wanted to keep secret.

Roe vs. Wade: The court ruled that an unborn baby is not a person with constitutional rights and during the first three months of pregnancy, a woman has a right to an abortion.

Some of those decisions would probably not have been made by a court dominated by conservatives. The one most likely to be overturned by a conservative court is Roe vs. Wade. The U.S. Supreme Court has been a noble institution, though. Over the years, it has usually done the right thing whether dominated by liberals or conservatives.

President Dwight D. Eisenhower, a Republican but a very moderate conservative, appointed Earl Warren as chief justice. Warren was considered a conservative when appointed, but many of the court's most liberal decisions were made during his years in office. While there have always been members of the U.S. Supreme Court whose decisions were 100 percent predictable, over the years many more have been refreshingly independent and surprising.

Looking back, it is apparent that the Court has not always been right but we trust it because its members have been people with great experience, knowledge and wisdom. They have thought about the issues from every angle and made their decisions independent of any outside interests. The members don't have to run for office and they don't get fired. Let's hope that if the President appoints any new members, the U.S. Supreme Court will maintain its even hand and let past decisions stand.

NO UNCONVENTIONAL CONVENTIONS

We complain about our political parties, but it's one of the true things about a democracy that the two-party system works best. As soon as there are three parties or just one, the whole system can break down. It's why so many people were angry with Ralph Nader for starting his Green Party and distorting the delicate Democratic/Republican balance.

The two parties are revving up now for another election and even when the politicians know who their candidate will be, they have to go through the ritual of choosing him at a convention. Every city wants a political convention because it fills the hotels and the Chamber of Commerce thinks it's going to be good for local businesses. (It's never as good for business as they think it will be.)

Chicago has had the most political conventions, twenty-five. Philadelphia is next with nine. There have been five in New York, four in San Francisco and Baltimore, and three in Kansas City, Cincinnati and Miami Beach.

A political convention takes over and dominates most cities, but when a convention is in New York, residents of the city hardly know it's there. The city is so big with so much going on that the convention gets lost.

The parties need approximately 20,000 hotel rooms, so smaller cities don't get the conventions. Philadelphia has just about 20,000 rooms. Chicago has 28,000. New York has 66,000. If you want great food and would like to see a naked lady wrestle an alligator, you go to New Orleans.

When you attend a political convention as a journalist, you are certain to question whether this kind of chaos, some of it not ethical and some even dishonest, is really the best way for a nation to set out to govern itself. The politicians often seem dumber than average citizens as they make long, meaningless speeches just to be on stage in front of a crowd. No one listens to what they say, and it doesn't matter because they don't say anything. The fact is that this process has worked for this country for too long to suggest we replace it. It may not be good, but we have never found anything better.

There are only three ways anyone gets to rule a nation. The person can inherit the job from a father in power, the king usually, or he—almost always "he"—can seize power by force and maintain it with police who suppress opposition. Ours is the third way, and bad as it may be, it's best and it makes political parties necessary.

Considering how important political conventions are, I am embarrassed at how trivial my memories are of the dozens I've been to. Each one stands out in my mind, not for what happened or who was nominated but for some isolated incident. My first convention was in Chicago in 1956. I was writing the *CBS Morning Show* with Will Rogers Jr. The candidates were Adlai Stevenson and running mate Estes Kefauver. The most memorable thing that happened was the morning Bill Rogers, an old cowpoke, rode a horse up the marble steps and into the lobby of the Palmer House Hilton Hotel, the world's largest hotel at the time.

Another memorable scene was the day a police chief stopped Mike Wallace as he tried to enter the hall. Mike laughed and chucked the chief under the chin with his index finger. Mike thought it was funnier than the chief did, and he was instantly arrested, lifted off his feet with a cop at either elbow and carried off.

Political conventions have lost their attraction because the decision about who the candidate will be has usually been made before the delegates vote. It makes a poor television show, and the networks have even considered not covering them in detail. I hope they continue to cover the conventions, dull as they may be, because if they do, I'll be there, hoping to see someone ride a horse up marble steps into a hotel lobby, or Mike Wallace carried off by the elbows.

BEATING AROUND BUSH

When President Bush gave his State of the Union speech (known formally as an "Address"), I sat in my comfortable chair in our living room with my feet up, making random notes.

President Bush was lucky his parents put the initial "W" in his name so that no one calls him "Junior." Eleven presidents have had their father's name and it doesn't seem right. A president should have a name of his own.

President Bush has done a good job of being his own man. None of us thinks of him any longer as being primarily George Bush's son.

Someone must have talked to the President about his persistent mispronunciation of the word "nuclear" because in recent speeches he has often said it properly. He has frequent relapses, though. In one speech in 2006 he pronounced it "nucular" twelve times. It just doesn't make a president sound real smart.

I got two phone calls during one speech of his from friends who said they couldn't stand to watch him or listen to him. It always surprises me that people feel so negative about him. They don't call him "President Bush." They call him "Bush." They spit out his name like an epithet. There were people who loathed Bill Clinton. I'll bet someone in the audience at Gettysburg hated Lincoln's speech there because they didn't like Abe.

They should always announce the name of the person or persons who wrote a president's speech but they never do. Apparently, at least two men, both evangelical Christians, were involved in the writing of this one but they were not mentioned. The writer for any president has to be willing to write anonymously. A man named David Frum wrote the famous "Axis of Evil" line in President Bush's 2002 State of the Union speech. Frum wasn't around anymore after his wife bragged about his having done it in a magazine article.

There were some quotable lines in Bush's speech. Speaking to the troops who will fight if we attack Iraq, he said, "You believe in America and America believes in you."

Speaking about our allies who agree or disagree with him, President Bush said, "The course of this nation does not depend on the decisions of others."

His best line was addressed to the people of Iraq: "Your enemy is not surrounding your country; your enemy is ruling your country." Pretty good, whoever wrote it.

After the Sept. 11 terrorist attack, President Bush made a big thing about capturing Osama bin Laden. He hasn't mentioned him recently.

It's surprising that the President's persistent support of the wealthiest Americans and of Big Business has not hurt his popularity with ordinary Americans who are not rich. He took their side in a big way in the speech both by advocating an end to taxes on stock dividends and by attacking trial lawyers who sue big companies.

The Democratic or Republican response to any president's speech has traditionally been terrible and people don't listen to it. Both parties ought to give up that anti-climactic "response."

WE NEED SMARTER LEADERS

Thinking about government abstractly, Americans are pretty much all in favor of democracy. We speak in grand terms about its virtues. When we talk about it more specifically, though, we aren't so enthusiastic about the democratically elected politicians who run the country for us.

Our leaders should be the smartest Americans, but pursuing politics as a career doesn't usually interest the smartest people. They don't want to have anything to do with government for several reasons. Sometimes it's because they can make more money doing something else, or perhaps they don't want to face the endless unpleasant problems that anyone in public office must. What happens is, we allow ourselves to be led by inferior leaders because no one better wants the job.

A politician's ego is fed by something that doesn't nourish the rest of us. The men and women who do go into politics are attracted by the lure of power. Power is an aphrodisiac to which politicians are addicted. It's not something that appeals to a great many men and women who might make better leaders. Those people are everywhere:

The faculty of any one of our best colleges is, collectively, smarter than Congress.

The doctors at any good hospital are smarter than the politicians in town.

The lawyers who don't go into politics are smarter than the ones who do, and judges at every level are smarter than politicians.

Successful business people are usually brighter than politicians.

Journalists are smarter than the politicians they report on.

To be fair to politicians, you have to admit that they don't do it for the money. There are dishonest grafters among them, but the majority of politicians are honest and their pay is low.

In view of the intellectual mediocrity of too many politicians, it has occurred to me that we're missing something important in our structure of government. We have the legislative, the judicial and the executive branches, and maybe we need one more. I don't know what it should be called but it should comprise a group of fifteen or twenty people with the best brains in the land. Intellect would be the only requisite. It would be like the Supreme Court, but instead of deciding legal issues, this smart group would give its best advice on every important matter that affects the nation.

These days, this Intellectual Council would hand down a decision on whether it was a good idea to attack Iraq without the UN sanction. The council would tell the President, in addition to what to do about Iraq, whether giving the rich a tax cut was a good idea.

We'd pay these super smart people exactly what they were making before they got the job. If they were professors, we'd pay them the salaries their colleges paid them. If they were business executives making a million dollars a year, that's what the government would pay them for this job.

We'd look for people too smart to be always allied with one political party. They'd side with Democrats on some issues and with Republicans on others. They would pledge when they took office to be honest without considering who their decisions would be good or bad for—except the whole country.

Here are some possible candidates for the job: Condoleezza Rice, Walter Cronkite, Tom Friedman, Colin Powell, Arthur Schlesinger, three Bradleys—Bill, Ben and Ed—and me.

CLINTON AND BUSH

Comparisons between Bill Clinton and George W. Bush persist. I don't ever recall the specter of the last president looming so large over the incumbent as Clinton looms over Bush.

If you are going to argue their merits as leaders, you have to exclude their personal shortcomings. George W. had a drinking problem and now his opponents are accusing him of being a liar. Bill Clinton's appetite was not for alcohol but he lied and he may have ruined his reputation for the history books with the shortcomings in his character.

One reason we keep drawing comparisons is they are both the same age, born in 1946. All good Democrats are waiting for a new candidate to emerge about whom they can become enthusiastic. They don't see one yet.

For the first time, President Bush is beginning to look vulnerable. His approval ratings are way down and his critics are louder. It seems likely those ratings will continue to drop if efforts to achieve peace in Iraq don't improve.

Bill Clinton is easier to be enthusiastic about and easier to detest than George W. Bush. Or so it seems to me, anyway. George W. doesn't seem like a Phi Beta Kappa but neither do many of us.

Democrats have always accused the President of lying to us about the reasons for the war in Iraq, about a connection between Saddam and Osama bin Laden, about "leaving no child behind" and about who will benefit from tax cuts. The President's justification for going to war with Iraq was always the threat Saddam Hussein posed to the United States with his weapons of mass destruction. There's been so much talk about those weapons that newspapers are even referring to them as "WMD." I'm not an apologist for the President but his critics see evil that I don't see. I believe he honestly thought Saddam had nuclear or biological weapons that were a threat to us. I believe he believes the tax cuts will help everyone, I believe he believes his plan for schools will help every child. The fact that he may be wrong about all these things doesn't make him a bad person. A little dumb, maybe.

It's probable that we ask too much of politicians. We expect them to be nice, intelligent, honest and of good moral character. That's a lot to ask. We don't demand that of any of our other heroes or public figures. When we look for a doctor, we don't check into his preferences in matters of politics, religion, sex, exercise or food. All we ask is that he be a good doctor. If a politician is experienced in government and expert at leading us, maybe we shouldn't expect him to be of sterling character, too.

YOU DO, I THINK

President Bush got his first seriously bad marks of his presidency in 2002 over the false information he used in his State of the Union speech charging that Iraq was trying to buy fissionable material from Niger for making nuclear weapons. (Niger is not to be confused with Nigeria—with which I confused it.)

I often annoy friends and family members by defending President Bush when they accuse him of perfidy. In the quiet of my own mind on those occasions, I try to think why it is I'm taking sides with a president I didn't vote for and with whose policies I seldom agree.

It may simply be my perverse nature or it may be because I have some sympathy for politicians in general. They're doing a hard job I couldn't do. I keep thinking what terrible work being president is. (In a brief conversation I once had with Bill Clinton, he laughed and said he couldn't tie his shoelaces in the morning without someone complaining that he was doing it wrong.)

The thing you have to give George W. Bush, like him or not, is that he's doing it. There are many important decisions that have to be made and he doesn't sit around worrying something to death before acting on it. The fact that his decisions may have a good or bad effect on millions of people here in the United States and others elsewhere does not seem to keep him awake at night. He couldn't be president if it did.

President Bush is driven by concepts of the economy, world affairs and religion with which I do not agree but it's a good thing he's president and I'm not. I'd be sitting there thinking all day without coming to any conclusions. I'd anguish over how wrong any decision I made would be. I read an article by Nicholas Kristof in the *New York Times* condemning Bush for the "pattern of dishonesty and delusion that helped get us into the Iraq mess." It was a good column—certainly better than Bush could have written—but we're probably better off with Bush as president than Kristof.

The relaxing thing about being a writer is, what you say doesn't really make a damn bit of difference. People may agree with me or disagree, love me or hate me, but what I say has no effect whatsoever on anyone. What I write about the economy doesn't effect the economy. What I write about war, the French, the Yankees, summer vacations or George W. Bush doesn't have the slightest bit of influence on the economy, the French, the Yankees, summer vacations or George W. Bush.

George W. Bush, on the other hand, can't raise a finger without it influencing someone's life—and perhaps the lives of millions of people. That's why thinking is so much easier than doing. George W. Bush is doing more doing than thinking and a lot of us can criticize him for it but we criticize with words which are insignificant compared to his actions.

In a general sense, this is why politicians are taken more seriously than college professors. College professors may be smarter and more profound thinkers but it doesn't matter. What politicians who don't think much actually do makes a big difference to all the rest of us—including college professors.

George W. Bush does not seem to be a profound thinker. The history of his academic life does not suggest he ever was. His political enemies, though, would have to concede that, right or wrong, he does things. He makes up his mind and once made, no well-thought-out argument from an opponent can change his mind.

The deepest thinkers have never been the best leaders. Of course, that doesn't mean we can't wish we had a better thinker in the White House.

THE POWER OF A PRESIDENT

It's difficult to know how important the administration of any one American president is. A president with strong opinions about government, money, justice and the uses of power has a great deal of influence on the country for at least the four years he's in office. Other presidents just seem to come and go, presiding over the status quo without making any changes that rock the boat.

Every once in a while, we have a president who makes a permanent difference in what the United States is like and what it will be like in the future.

Abraham Lincoln changed the course we were on with the Civil War. Whether it was his fault or not, Herbert Hoover will never be forgotten because of the lasting effects of the Great Depression that occurred during his presidency.

In modern times, Franklin D. Roosevelt made permanent changes for the better in the lives of all Americans by pushing the Social Security Act with old age benefits and unemployment insurance into law in 1935.

The backbone of our democracy is the Constitution and you would think it would have a stabilizing effect. However, the Constitution is subject to both alteration and interpretation so there is some room for major change to be made by a president even under it.

President Bush does not seem to have profound theories of government but he has strong opinions that are taking this country in a different direction. It is going to be difficult for any liberal who may be elected in the future to change what has been done or alter the course it has set us on.

The single biggest opportunity a president has to make a difference in our basic process of government is in his appointments of people to positions of power. Franklin Roosevelt appointed half a dozen Supreme Court justices whose decisions consistently pushed the country in what would be considered a liberal direction.

President Bush has led us to the right. That seems to be what most Americans want. It is not clear yet whether President Bush's political philosophy will have a permanent effect on such important matters as the separation we previously maintained between religion and government. He seems to approve of a merger.

President Bush has already had an effect on the direction many of our scientific programs are taking. In April, for example, he urged the Senate to forbid the cloning of human embryos for either research or reproductive purposes. The National Academy of Sciences had said it should be allowed. The people doing the most important work in health, science and technology are often dependent for their enormously expensive research equipment, on government money. If the government controls the money with which scientific equipment is purchased, it can control the people who use it. This takes technology in the direction most favored by a president.

President Bush's refusal to go along with 178 other countries in Kyoto when they agreed on the reduction of the release of gases that produce global warming doesn't have much sex appeal as a news story but it was as important for the world's future as any decision our President has made. And not good.

The U.S.A. PATRIOT Act, the appointment of ultra-conservative judges and Bush's appointment of John Ashcroft as attorney general may have permanently changed the course of this nation. While it does not seem now as though history will consider him one of our great presidents, George W. Bush may have more of a lasting effect on the country than any president since Franklin Roosevelt.

SCHWARZENEGGER FOR PRESIDENT

The words we use for political leaders are in some jobs as unsatisfactory as the leaders themselves. "President" isn't the right word for our most important position. It ought to be reserved for the head of a company. "President" of the United States doesn't really make much sense. The word "mayor" has no roots as a word meaning the chief executive of a city. The word "Congress" confuses us because of the way it includes both senators and representatives. All senators are congressmen or women, but not all congressmen or women are senators. The word "senator" has some historical background that makes it useful, but "representative" is a weak word for an important person in our political hierarchy.

Of all the words we use for our political leaders, "governor" seems most appropriate. It's too late to change, but our president probably ought to have been called governor.

Being governor of a state is the best path to The White House. Nineteen governors have become president of the United States. Before spending a lot of time looking that up, I guessed there were seven. The nineteen were George W. Bush, Texas; Bill Clinton, Arkansas; Ronald Reagan, California; Jimmy Carter, Georgia; Franklin D. Roosevelt, New York; Calvin Coolidge, Massachusetts; Woodrow Wilson, New Jersey; Theodore Roosevelt, New York; William McKinley, Ohio; Grover Cleveland, New York; Rutherford B. Hayes, Ohio; Andrew Johnson, Tennessee; James Polk, Tennessee; John Tyler, Virginia; William Henry Harrison, Indiana; Martin Van Buren, New York; Andrew Jackson, Florida; James Monroe, Virginia; Thomas Jefferson, Virginia.

More governors than senators have become president of the United States. I suspect that's because governors don't have to reveal their political opinions quite so openly on every issue as senators do. A senator has to vote on issues, revealing his or her opinion. We know exactly where he or she stands and it makes it more difficult to run for the next higher office. A governor is not so encumbered.

I brought up the names of governors who later in their careers became president of the United States because there is no chance Governor Arnold Schwarzenegger will ever be president. He's old enough, maybe smart enough, and he's lived here since 1968 but he isn't qualified for our highest office. "No person except a natural born citizen or a citizen of the United States at the time of the adoption of this Constitution, shall be eligible to the office of President," reads Article II. This is all clear to me except the phrase "natural born citizen." Would that exclude someone who was born unnaturally?

THE PERSON YOU ELECTED

One of the few things about our elections that's always made me feel good is that once they're over, Americans pretty much accept the results. We may not like the outcome, but no one throws rocks. Whether our candidate wins or loses, we live with the one who got the most votes—or at least that was true until California decided it made a mistake electing Gray Davis and ousted him from office in 2003.

Gray Davis seemed grossly inadequate from what I saw of him on television but the recall was wrong and contrary to our established practice of taking what we get. Davis was a dull disaster, but Californians should have stuck with what they got when they voted. We simply cannot start overturning an honest election. Arnold Schwarzenegger is certainly a better governor than Davis was, but under our system, voters don't have a second chance to get it right.

I was surprised when Maria Shriver, Schwarzenegger's wife, wore a cross around her neck at his inauguration ceremony. As a Kennedy, Maria would be Catholic, I suppose. I never heard anything about whether Arnold shared her religious convictions, or whether he was religious at all.

I don't believe as many Baptists, Presbyterians or Methodists wear crosses as jewelry as Catholics do. It strikes me as wrong for anyone to press their beliefs on the rest of us in public with symbols of their affiliations affixed to their clothing or body. I even feel that way about men who wear the American flag as jewelry in their buttonholes. President Bush wears an American flag button in his lapel even though he's no more patriotic than I am and his patriotism would not be suspect without it.

WHICH SIDE ARE YOU ON?

What makes one of us liberal and the other conservative is a mystery. It's a mystery why we're both so damn sure we're right, too. It surprises me that Americans are so evenly divided between Republicans and Democrats, conservatives and liberals.

The 2000 presidential election, when George Bush and Al Gore each got about 49 percent of the popular vote, made it clear that there are as many of one group as the other. This is evidence of parity, although I've never seen a poll that indicated whether conservatives or liberals were most apt to vote in an election. If more of one group than the other voted, that would skew the numbers.

The recent surge in the popularity of conservative talk show hosts like Rush Limbaugh and Bill O'Reilly and conservative TV news like you see on Fox, indicates conservatives may be the majority.

I'd like to see a cumulative I.Q. of each group and compare the totals to determine whether liberals or conservatives were smarter. Liberalism probably attracts more intellectuals than conservatism does. Conservatives would be more apt to describe them as dreamers than intellectuals.

Some people—and I think of myself as one of them—are part both. We're liberal about some things, conservative about others. We think of ourselves as sensible and open-minded. Others think of us as indecisive and stupid.

The biggest problem with liberals is that while they're often concerned with social issues that conservatives ignore, they're more apt to make decisions about what should be done based on an overly optimistic opinion of human nature. Considering that there are more working-class people, whose interests you'd think would be best served by liberal officeholders, it's surprising that Democratic candidates don't win every election. The curious fact is, though, there are a great number of working-class conservatives. The coalition between conservative businessmen and -women and right-wing hourly wage-earners is an interesting political phenomenon. Even when their union supports the Democratic candidate in an election, a lot of individual workers with minds of their own vote for the conservative candidate.

The reason may be a bitter anomaly for professional Democrats to face: The successful efforts of previous Democratic administrations on labor's behalf eliminated a lot of reasons working people had to vote Democratic. There was a time when all union members were Democrats because Republican politicians who favored big business were less apt to approve of union demands.

These days, unions have won their point. They are entrenched and union members don't have much to win from Democrats that they can't win as easily from Republicans. They have minimum wage laws, Social Security, unemployment insurance, a range of health benefits and other goodies Democrats got for them.

They may still be striking for more money but their right to exist has been long since established.

THE GOOD LOSERS

Many good men never got to be president. Ben Franklin was brilliant but he never ran for the presidency because he was too busy doing more important things. Franklin was a serious scientist and I don't think anyone who is serious about something serious would want to be president.

Thomas Jefferson lost to John Adams in 1796 and must have thought he was an also-ran but four years later, he won.

Several modern politicians, other than the Democratic candidates, would be good. I think of the bright and principled Republican, John McCain.

I went into a restaurant last week and spotted a friend of mine, the historian Arthur Schlesinger. He motioned me to come over and introduced me to the man he was sitting with, George McGovern. McGovern lost to Richard Nixon. What confidence does that give you in our democratic system?

Herbert Hoover beat Al Smith in 1928. Smith was governor of New York, very capable and a real character. He probably would have been a better president than Hoover but he was Catholic and that mattered more then than it does now. Thirty-plus years later, John F. Kennedy's Catholicism wasn't much of an issue.

When I was in college, a lot of my friends were trying to get Wendell Willkie elected. Willkie may have been the most capable of all the losers in modern history but he never had a prayer running against Franklin Delano Roosevelt in 1940.

FDR, our only four-term president, beat Herbert Hoover, Alf Landon, Willkie and Tom Dewey. Roosevelt is the kind of legend who gets his picture on our dimes. Dewey, governor of New York, was humorless but would have made a good president, too. He never got his picture on a penny.

Adlai Stevenson might have been a great president. He lost to an American hero, Dwight Eisenhower. In one of the great moments in television history, Stevenson appeared on TV to concede and quoted Abraham Lincoln on the occasion of his loss of his seat in Congress: "I'm too old to cry," Stevenson said, "and yet it hurts too much to laugh."

It's fun for me to consider that I can drop the names of five presidents I've actually met. As a reporter for the *Stars and Stripes*, I met FDR in 1945. I wouldn't say we were close friends, but I shook hands with both Richard Nixon and Ronald Reagan. Reagan was more fun to shake hands with than Nixon. I met Ike a dozen times, and several months ago I was eating in a New York restaurant when Bill Clinton came in. He saw me sitting there and slid into the banquette next to me and chatted for twenty-five minutes. He was hard to hate.

The loser I knew best was Barry Goldwater and I didn't vote for him. I did a one-hour documentary called "Barry Goldwater's Arizona" and got to like Barry better than I liked his politics. He was a good guy but not a president. At Barry's retirement party, his unlikely friend, Teddy Kennedy, got a big laugh when he said Barry's motto was, "Ready! Shoot! Aim!"

Strom Thurmund ran for president in 1948 and was, fortunately, a big loser. We've had other potentially bad presidents but no one that bad.

It's surprising, when you think of all the people who want to be president that we've had two sons of presidents who became president themselves. John Quincy Adams, our sixth president, was the son of John Adams, our second president. George W. Bush, of course, is George Bush's son. When it comes to being president, it doesn't hurt if Daddy gives you a head start.

EINSTEIN FOR PRESIDENT

One of the difficult things to determine in life is how much authority to give to someone who is smart about one thing, in an area about which he or she has no experience.

If I had my choice, I'd take the smartest person over the most experienced anytime. Once you've learned something, "experience" isn't anything but repetition. It has amused me over my years, because so many of my friends are in the news business, to note how quickly someone smart can get to know almost everything about someone else's business. A good reporter can do some research and then interview his subject and in a few days get to know 90 percent of everything he needs to know about his subject and his life's work. If a good reporter can do that, there's no reason why a good lawyer, businessman or doctor can't get to know a lot about government in a few weeks. As far as having enough experience to be president, it's a foolish idea. There is no experience a person could have that would familiarize him with being president of the United States.

When Howard Dean ran for governor of Vermont, opponents asked what a doctor knew about running a state government. Dean was elected and then re-elected four times. It obviously didn't take him long to get the hang of switching from medicine and healing to politics and government. (It seems like a step down to me, but that's another matter.)

You often read about some huge corporation appointing a new president. If the corporation makes widgets, the new executive is hardly ever an expert on widgets. He's an expert on running a corporation no matter what it makes.

Albert Einstein had one of the great brains ever born to man, and he used it to the tangible advantage of civilization. It was Einstein who told President Roosevelt in 1939 of the possibility of our making an atomic bomb with the research he had done cracking atoms in the laboratory. He spent his life working on the relativity and quantum theories, which are too complex for any but a handful of us to understand. He also produced a delightful little book of essays about life that are direct and simple enough for anyone who can read to understand. We humans have amazing breadth. We can be stupid and brilliant. We can be good. We can be bad—angels one minute, devils the next.

What often occurs to me about our elections is that we get too many experienced politicians and not enough people like Einstein, who are brilliant in some other form of endeavor. We ought to find some way of embarrassing more of our capable, even brilliant, non-political citizens to get into politics and run for office. We should not exclude our scientists, and they should not exclude themselves.

Einstein, although ineligible because of being born in Germany, would have made a great American president. If he had run, someone surely would have said, "He doesn't have enough political experience." What I want for my president is the smartest person in America. Forget whether that person is experienced in politics.

HOORAY FOR POLITICIANS

It's good fun to criticize our politicians and we all do a lot of that. It's hard not to, but I often feel sorry for them. Most people who are successful in any field have one special talent for doing something well. They aren't successful because of their overall ability. A politician can't specialize like that. He or she (see footnote) has to know a lot about everything.

Believing that you're smart enough to take a public job that involves making decisions that will influence thousands or even millions of lives takes more chutzpah than most of us have. Imagine really thinking that you're smart enough to be President of the United States. Or even a congressman. Such jobs take men and women with self-confidence and I'm glad we have so many of them to lead wimps like us.

Of course, we're always being disappointed by our politicians, even the ones we voted for or plan to vote for. Sooner or later, our favorite says something we hate. The trouble is, politicians have to do and say some terrible things to get elected. They have to say things they don't believe and do things they don't like doing. They even have to pretend they like some things. Shaking hands with 2,000 enthusiastic jerks every day must be a pain. We practically force them to lie to us, or at least force them to be evasive and then accuse them of not being honest.

Plain dealing is impossible for a politician. How do you come out clearly and unequivocally for or against abortion, tax cuts, the war in Iraq or school prayer without alienating about half of the people who were inclined to vote for you? The politician has to find a way to avoid saying what he really thinks as often as possible. John Kerry, for instance, is burdened now with the fact that he voted in favor of the war on Iraq. He has to find a way to squirm out of it every time it comes up. I'd hate to be a politician and have to announce publicly every opinion I've had about Iraq. I'd get run out of the country. Most of us are puzzled and unsure about major issues. We can be persuaded in one direction or the other. A politician doesn't have the luxury of rethinking something, hedging or changing his mind. Voters, on the other hand, can usually avoid taking any firm position. We aren't dead sure what we think.

The philosophy of democracy assumes that the people of a country know what they want and make intelligent decisions about whom they vote for to get it. The trouble is that we're too evenly divided and if one group gets what it wants in the next election, it's certain that almost half of us will be dissatisfied. It won't be "the will of the people," but only the will of about half the people. This makes democracy seem less like a perfect system. It's just that there isn't any other as good.

Footnote: Every time I write I'm faced with the problem of those damn third-person pronouns "he" or "she." We are in desperate need of a gender-neutral word that would include men and women. You used to be able to use the masculine he as if it was universal. That's no longer acceptable, but I'm not willing to write "he" or "she" every time it seems necessary.

CRAB GRASSROOTS CAMPAIGNING

Bragging is not an attractive thing to do so I'm reluctant to tell you this, but I can't resist because I'm bursting with pride. I've just received a personal letter from the Republican Senate majority leader, Bill Frist, telling me that I've been assigned to be "REPRESENTATIVE OF ALL REPUBLICANS" (his caps) living in my voting district.

If you wonder what the Republican Party is doing with $130 million in campaign funds, let me tell you about some of this letter.

On my letter, the "Friend" in "Dear Friend" was crossed out and "Andy" written in by hand over it. This indicates to me that Bill and I are very close. Under that, it says, "Your immediate attention is required." Not requested, desired or wanted but "required."

When this comes out, it's going to be some surprise to my friends and neighbors or anyone else in my voting district. My friend Quinton is going to be especially surprised. He thinks George W. Bush is too liberal and considers me as practically a communist.

I don't think any of the people I know in our little town would have expected that I'd be accorded the honor of being appointed a leader of the Republican Party there. My first duty, the letter says, is to fill out a survey Sen. Frist sent me. "Your answers," he says, "will represent the views and opinions of ALL Republicans living in your voting district."

This survey, the letter says, is an "OFFICIAL REPUBLICAN PARTY DOCUMENT—REGISTERED IN YOUR NAME ONLY and MUST BE ACCOUNTED FOR upon completion of this project." I am unclear about who has to account for it.

The first question on the survey asks, "Should we raise taxes as some liberal Democrats have suggested?" Next, it says, "I MUST find out—as soon as possible—where loyal grassroots Republicans like you stand on the most vital issues facing our nation today. So please take a few minutes NOW to complete your official Republican Majority Leader's Survey . . . And when you do, please include your most generous financial contribution . . . of $500, $250, $100, $50, or even just $25 today."

I have never said publicly whether I'm a Republican or a Democrat because I'm sometimes one, sometimes the other, but I would have to confess that "liberal" is not a dirty word to me.

I hope Bill Frist isn't depending on me for $25 to pay for any part of this letter he sent because, Republican or Democrat, it's one of the dumbest pieces of campaign literature I have ever seen. If I had been going to vote Republican, this letter is enough to have made me change my mind.

Did Sen. Frist write this letter? I don't think so. Did he read it before it was sent out over his signature? He's smarter than that or he never would have completed medical school.

How about these sentences:

"Our Republican leadership are counting on your input." Who is you counting on, Senator"

"That is why I must have your immediate involvement today." Would immediate involvement day after tomorrow be soon enough?

". . . we are counting on each and every one to provide their input." "Their"? With "one"? How about "his or her"?

"Your answers . . . will help me build a strong foundation of grass-roots support."

"Your answers will be used to build grassroots support . . . "

"We must continue to build from the grassroots up . . . "

". . . help build a foundation of grassroots support."

"Our success was fought for—and won—by the heroic efforts of dedicated grassroots Republicans like you."

With grassroots Republicans like me, they wouldn't have to mow the lawn very often.

Whoever in the Republican Party campaign office who put out this semi-literate letter ought to pay for the stamps itself.

A PHONE CALL TO REMEMBER

Everyone else has interviewed Bill Clinton about his book, *My Life*. I haven't cared much for the interviews, so I'd like to interview him myself. Here are some of the questions I'd ask:

Q: I've heard several of your book interviews and everyone asks you the same questions about Monica Lewinsky. Because we all know what your answers are now and because we're all tired of the subject, is it OK if I don't ask you about that?

As I was typing those words, my phone rang. You'll just have to trust me on this. It was 8:23 in the morning on Wednesday, June 23. I picked it up. The voice said, "Andy, this is Bill Clinton." I assumed it was the announcer on the Imus radio show who imitates Clinton putting me on, so I said, skeptically, "Sure."

I had been invited to a book party at the Metropolitan Museum of Art given by Bill Clinton's publisher the night before and I went but he was late, it was a mob scene and I left before Bill showed up.

"That was some party last night, wasn't it?"

"I guess so, but I left before you came," I said.

"Yeah. Sorry I was late. Why don't you do something about my book on *60 Minutes* next Sunday?" I suppose this was the real purpose of his call.

"Bill (I called him Bill, not Mr. President), you're not going to believe this, but I am just writing about you. I'm saying everyone else has interviewed you and I'd like to. Here are some questions I'd ask."

"Go ahead. You got a tape recorder?"

I didn't have a tape recorder handy so I didn't record anything.

"What were you going to ask me?" he said.

"I was going to ask whether you get tired of the same old Monica Lewinsky questions. I've been predicting you're going to stop doing these interviews."

"Well, it does get sort of old," he said.

"I read where the manuscript was in longhand. The book is 957 pages long. How many pages was it as you wrote it out in longhand?"

He laughed. "It was long," he said, "That's why it took so long to edit it."

"It was cut down?" I asked. "You mean it was originally longer?"

"Oh, yeah."

"Do you type?" I asked.

"Well, I type some and some of it was in longhand. But I dictated most of it."

"You dictated?"

"Yeah. I think better when I'm walking around."

I mumbled again.

"Want me to send you a copy?" he asked.

"Can I get one that isn't autographed?" I asked. "It might be a collector's item."

In retrospect, I realize I didn't do very well with the conversation. It took me quite a while to get over the shock and my initial suspicion about whether it really was Bill Clinton slowed me down. I don't very often get a telephone call at eight in the morning from a former president of the United States.

OK. Now then. Where was I going when I started about an imaginary interview with Bill Clinton before he called me and I actually interviewed him on the phone? It was one of the most pleasant and most amazing coincidences of my life.

IN BED WITH BUSINESS

It is commonly accepted as fact that Big Business is at war with Big Government.

I would like to say, in a nice, quiet, polite way that this is horse manure. Big Business is in business with Big Government. They are best friends. Too often they exclude the rest of us from their behind-the-scenes dealings. We don't know what goes on.

About half the people who leave government jobs, including those who served in Congress, go to work for more money as lobbyists. They work for major corporations trying (often successfully) to influence the decisions of the government agencies they left. For some of them, being elected to Congress or getting a government job is just a stepping stone to a job as lobbyist with higher pay. The pay for U.S. representatives and senators is $157,000. The starting salary for a lobbyist with any connections in government is around $300,000 now.

The popular concept is that Democrats favor more government and Republicans want less, but there are more government employees now than there were under President Clinton.

Government spending in Washington increased by a whopping 30 percent between 2000 and 2004 to a record $2.29 trillion.

One of the bad things about the power of lobbyists to influence the laws under which businesses operate is that the biggest corporations with the most money can afford to pay the most influential lobbyists to get things their way. The little guys in small companies who don't have a million to pay an influence peddler are squeezed out. The big get bigger; the rich get richer.

The huge salaries made by lobbyists are a temptation many legislators can't resist. Lobbying companies and trade associations trying to influence government decisions in their favor offer former government officials millions to work for them. Marc Racicot, who made $75,000 as governor of Montana and then became head of the Republican National Committee, is going to get a million dollars a year as president of a lobbying firm euphemistically called "the American Insurance Association." Former Representative Robert Livingston of Louisiana was chairman of the House Appropriations Committee. He knows where the money is buried. Livingston is now president of a thriving lobbying company.

If you think it's only Republicans who are digging in this lobbying gold mine, note that former vice president and one-time head Democrat Al Gore joined the board of directors of Apple Computer for an undisclosed salary that was probably too embarrassingly big to be disclosed. You can bet it was ten times the $175,000 he got as vice president.

Lobbying is a Washington tradition most of us don't like or understand. I, for example, do not like or understand why the American Ambulance Association pays $300,000 a year to a lobbying company. I'm sure, though, that they get their money back and we pay it when we call an ambulance.

Last year, Hewlett-Packard paid lobbyists $734,000 trying to get Republicans to pass legislation that would allow the company to pay a lot less tax on the $14 billion they made in profits from foreign companies they own. I wouldn't want to have to explain it to a class of eighth-graders, but if a company pays Chinese workers 35 cents an hour and sells what they make in the United States as if they had paid the workers $25 an hour, the company makes a lot of money.

If I ever give up writing for a living, I may become a lobbyist. I'll get Congress to pass a law paying old writers $300,000 a year not to write anything in order to give younger writers a better chance.

TIME—BOTH OFF AND ON

Many of President Bush's critics are being critical of him for the five-week summer vacation he's taking at his ranch in Crawford, Texas. I am neither critical nor envious because for half the money in the world you couldn't get me to go to Texas this time of year.

One of the worst things about being president is that someone keeps track of every little thing you do. According to these presidential record-keepers, George W. Bush has made forty-nine trips to his Texas ranch since taking office. He recently passed Ronald Reagan's modern-day record of having spent 335 days away from the White House, and Bush still has a way to go.

James Madison holds the all-time presidential record for one vacation. He left Washington in June 1816 and didn't come back until October. He went to his country estate in Montpelier, Va.

George Washington took his vacations on his farm in Mount Vernon. Mount Vernon is only sixteen miles from where Washington is now. But George's office wasn't in Washington. There was no Washington, no White House yet. Washington didn't become our capital until 1800. George's office when he was president was in Philadelphia.

Vacations are easy for our presidents now. They don't have to go through security at the airport getting out of town because they have their own airplane. They don't have to remove their shoes or empty their pockets. All presidents have to do when they leave Washington is climb the steps to their plane, smile and wave goodbye to us as they get on board.

President Bush's father had a ranch in Texas, too, but didn't go there for his vacations much. He went to Maine, where he fished, played golf and sailed.

They take so much time, a person needs a long vacation. Franklin Delano Roosevelt went to his home in Hyde Park, overlooking the Hudson River but later he went to Warm Springs, Ga., for the therapeutic value of the waters.

President Kennedy took his vacations at the Kennedy family place in Hyannis on Cape Cod. Newspapers always called it "the Kennedy compound." Lyndon Johnson went to his ranch in Texas. Reporters who cover the president, whoever he is, hate it when he leaves Washington because they have to live and work under difficult conditions away from home. Presidents on vacation always arrange to have good pictures taken of themselves doing something that's healthy for them. When photographers went to Texas with Lyndon, they could depend on getting pictures of Johnson riding his horse. There are good pictures and bad pictures and a president on horseback is a good one.

A lot of presidents have gone to Florida for vacation. Warren Harding was the first president to go there but after that Harry Truman went there and Richard Nixon went often and stayed with his friend Bebe Rebozo in Key Biscayne. Nixon also went back to his place in San Clemente, Calif.

Bill Clinton didn't seem to have any roots in a vacation place, so he went with the crowd to Martha's Vineyard. I guess he'd heard that was the place to go. Jimmy Carter went to his peanut farm in Plains, Ga.

Gerald Ford was the best athlete we ever had as president. He had been an All-American football player at Michigan and the thing he liked to do most on vacation as president was ski in Colorado and stay at a Vail resort.

While a great many people who don't like President Bush are objecting to all this vacation time he's taking, the people most critical of him don't object at all. They're in favor of his long vacations. They say things are better in Washington when President Bush is on vacation than when he's at work.

A NOTHING-NOTHING TIE IN D.C.

Congress and the President have been playing a game recently, and so far the score is nothing to nothing.

The executive branch of our government, the President, and the legislative branch, Congress, have been at war. This has happened before in our history but seldom have their differences been so numerous and pronounced as they are today. Even though members of Congress and the President are separately elected and independent, they are dependent on each other for getting something done. Right now, because neither side is winning, the rest of us are losing.

The battle for power that always exists between the President and Congress may be the major shortcoming of a democracy—but it's also its strength. The division of power keeps us from becoming a dictatorship. Over the years, we've had weak presidents and strong presidents. The weak ones caved in to Congress. The strong ones dominated it, but opposing Congress is not, by itself, a test of a president's greatness.

One defect in democracy as a system of government is its ineffectiveness. A dictatorship is efficient and effective. Too often, a democratic government is unable to act quickly on important issues. The governing bodies get tied up in arguments and end up nowhere.

No one is calling George W. Bush a great president but his opponents are calling him stubborn and dumb. Being disrespected by half the American public and much loved by the other half doesn't make George W. Bush special. Plenty of Americans hated the man and disagreed with the politics of Abe Lincoln. As president, Lincoln was so afraid Congress would disapprove of his Emancipation Proclamation that he waited until they'd adjourned before he issued it. Kind of sneaky, Abe.

It seems ridiculous to an outsider, me, that the President and members of Congress aren't sharing what they know and working out our problems together. The President doesn't trust Congress and tells them nothing. Many members of Congress don't trust the President, even some of his own party members, and don't give him the support he needs to get his programs approved.

If you want to be optimistic, you could say that inaction in Washington on the President's proposals is democracy at work. Maybe nowhere is just where we ought to be going.

Democracy is a magic word for us. We never question its virtues, but democracy is not always held in such high regard by other people. We should be making it look good as a way of showing the whole world that it is the best system of government. Having Congress at war with the President is not the way to do that.

GOOD PRESIDENT, BAD PRESIDENT

Considering how much faith we have in the ability of our democratic system for choosing our leaders, it's disappointing to look at how few great presidents we've had over the years. We've had good ones, bad ones and mediocre ones but very few great ones.

If pressed to answer a question about his own standing among the forty-two men we've had for president, I don't think George W. Bush would claim to be one of the great ones. I don't know what he thinks of his performance. He seems satisfied with his work but he also appears modest enough to deny ranking at the top. (As Winston Churchill said of his rival Clement Attlee, "He is a modest man—with a great deal to be modest about.")

Power in the United States is, fortunately for all of us, not so much centralized in the presidency that the occupant of the Oval Office is solely responsible for the course the nation takes. The president, whoever he is, often diffuses his power by delegating a lot of it to others.

President Bush has spread his power thinner than most by turning over so much of his authority to helpers like Vice President Cheney, unelected assistants like Donald Rumsfeld and behind-the-scenes aides we didn't elect and don't even know, like Karl Rove.

It's too bad President Bush is not great because we're in need of greatness right now. We're in competition with Japan, China and the Arab countries for leadership of the world. We're still ahead but they're catching us. Of course, we might be better off if they did, so that the whole weight of the world wouldn't be on our shoulders.

There has often been a shortage of greatness in the White House. To unfairly pick a few examples off the bottom of my head, no one ever accused Calvin Coolidge, Herbert Hoover, Gerald Ford, Jimmy Carter, Richard Nixon or the first George Bush of greatness. Franklin Delano Roosevelt is probably the only president of the twentieth century that future historians will put in the same rank with George Washington and Abraham Lincoln. John F. Kennedy might have been on his way to Mount Rushmore but he was assassinated.

There are supporters who make a case for Lyndon Johnson, Truman and Ronald Reagan, but "great" is not the universal adjective used for any of them. Woodrow Wilson isn't a hero in the history books, although he was the first president to recognize that the United States needed to be part of a world alliance. His League of Nations was a good idea that failed, so he doesn't get any credit.

Our best presidents have found a way to overcome the most serious defect in our democracy—the seesaw balance of power in the relationship between Congress and the president that too often ends in inaction. Politically knowledgeable presidents like Lyndon Johnson knew how to play the House and Senate, but too often our presidents have been stymied by the legislature. President Bush isn't much in charge of either, even with his own Republican majority, and he has a way of alienating them.

There have been times it wasn't necessary for us to have a great president. Dwight Eisenhower wasn't great but he was popular. He was in office for eight years and people liked him. He was easy to take. We were cruising along, so Ike was just what we needed—a hands-off president. He patted us on the head, told us everything would be all right and went out to play golf.

Ronald Reagan polarized the nation. Half of us loved Reagan, half of us hated him. There were not a lot of people in the middle. It's that way with President Bush, and it's half his fault and half ours. It's wrong that so many people enjoy not liking him and wrong that so many like him so much they refuse to admit his shortcomings.

We could use a great president today. George W. Bush's most ardent supporters like him, they like his wife and they support him in general but they don't claim he's great. Too bad.

DIVIDED WE STAND

If we were to have an election tomorrow, President Bush wouldn't win. I have never seen Americans so bitterly divided over their president or the direction their country is taking as they are now. Maybe divided is the wrong word if it suggests we're divided in half, because it appears as if the Americans who dislike the President far outnumber those who support him.

Even many of the people who voted for him are blaming President Bush for not responding sooner to the disaster in New Orleans. They don't blame the weather, bad luck, the government or God for the disaster following the impact of Hurricane Katrina. They blame President Bush. They don't like anything about him:

"Look at that fake smile he has!" "He doesn't walk, he swaggers."

"Where does he get all those inept assistants to do his dirty work for him?"

I don't want to suggest here that I voted for President Bush or that I'm a fan of his. I just think we have to cut him some slack. It's a hard job and he's not an evil guy. I wish he was smarter but he's not evil. It's obvious to everyone, including him probably, that we made a mistake going into Iraq. However, no matter how good it sounds to say, "We ought to get out," the fact is we can't just pick up and leave. There are too many people in Iraq who supported us who'd be slaughtered if we did. President Bush made a mistake going to his ranch for a five-week vacation in July and August. He tried to make it look good by making a few day trips to give cameramen some photo opportunities, but he didn't seriously interrupt his vacation until a couple of days after the flooding of New Orleans.

He made a mistake appointing a political supporter named Michael Brown as head of the Federal Emergency Management Agency. Brown has bungled the operation in New Orleans, and it became apparent when reporters started looking into who Brown was that he had no business having the job. Brown's last job before FEMA was as head of the International Arabian Horse Association—and he got fired from that.

Whether you like George W. Bush or not, he is our president. We're stuck with any president we elect for four years and maybe that's too long, but unless we change it, that's our system. The American people are often dissatisfied with a leader they have elected. Of our forty-three presidents, only sixteen have been re-elected for a second term.

Our senators are elected for six years. Our representatives in Congress only get two-year terms. The interesting thing I don't understand is, our congressmen and women are much more apt to be re-elected than any of their challengers and much more likely to be re-elected than a president. It may be because the work of a congressman or woman is not out in the open as much as is our president's.

I'm no more enthusiastic about President Bush than most of his critics, but even in our democracy, which is supposed to be dominated by the will of the people, an elected official can't answer to all the people on all the issues all the time. The American people elected George W. Bush—although just barely—and now we should let him decide some issues without first asking us what we think. For one thing, we may be smart collectively as a democracy, but individually we're pretty dumb about a lot of things. After all, we did elect him.

NO MORE GAS GUZZLING

The President's suggestion that we all cut down on driving to use less gas seemed sensible to me, and I want to cooperate. I'm trying to accommodate the President's wishes by making plans to use my car less. I have the good of the country at heart, but $3.29 per gallon enters into my consideration, too.

Like millions of Americans, I drive to work. My apartment in New York is only eighteen blocks from the office. It's 1.3 miles and there is not a shorter way, so there's no way to economize there. About twice a week, I take another street two blocks away because there's a store where I buy coffee, oranges and sometimes milk and a box of Grape

Nuts. I have gauged this on my odometer. It is two-tenths of a mile longer so, by walking to the store the night before to buy what I want, I could save one mile's worth of gas every two and a half weeks. How's that for cooperation, Mr. President?

My car gets about twenty-three miles to the gallon, so I'd be saving about 30 cents a month, too.

The President has recently made seven trips in Air Force One to the area where the hurricanes hit. Air Force One holds 47,200 gallons of fuel. It costs $86,000 to fill a 747. It burns $6,000 worth of fuel an hour. The trip from Washington to the Gulf Coast is a little more than two hours, so it costs $15,000 to fly the President there from D.C. Then, of course, he has to get back. If President Bush drove to the Gulf Coast or bicycled, it would save all of us a bundle.

Just a few weeks ago, President Bush visited the UN and I was excited to be on East 62nd Street when his motorcade came through. I stood, entranced by the drama of it, as eleven limousines, lights flashing and windows darkened, passed by. Try as I might, I could not determine which car the President was sitting in. That was on purpose, of course. The use of eleven cars would make it difficult for a potential terrorist to know which one to blow up.

My suggestion here is for the President to save gas by cutting the dummy limousines by two. It would not greatly increase the risk of travel for him and gas consumption for the cavalcade would be cut by two-elevenths. If the train of cars used 100 gallons of gas that day, two less would mean a reduction of 19 gallons. We have to think of our President's safety, but we have to think of our gas, too.

The best way for all of us to save gas would be by planning our shopping trips carefully. We should not go to the hardware store for some small item early in the morning and a few hours later, go to the bank, the grocery store or the drugstore. Leaving the car in the driveway instead of putting it in the garage every night might save gas, too.

I am determined to help the President save gas before he flies his gas-guzzling 747 to Louisiana again.

NOT AN INTERVIEW WITH BUSH

I try not to be one of those people who hates everything President Bush says or does, no matter what it is.

I'd like to ask the President some questions but he's too busy to grant me an interview. I've been thinking of some of the questions I'd ask if I got the chance.

Q: What's the best part of being president?

Q: What's the worst part of being president?

Q: What is your greatest weakness?

Q: What's your greatest strength, or would you rather not boast?

Q: Your approval ratings aren't very good this week. What do you think the history books will say about you in the future? Be honest, now.

Q: Whom do you really hate? Pick someone we all know.

Q: There are about fifty White House correspondents. Who's your favorite? Whom do you dislike the most?

Q: Why?

Q: When you meet a foreign dignitary and have to do all that hugging, would you be embarrassed to have your real thoughts about the guy appear in a little comic strip bubble over your head?

Q: How's the White House to live in . . . you know, as home?

Q: If you owned it, what would you change?

Q: Who is your best speechwriter? Shouldn't a president give more credit to the person who wrote it when he reads a speech written by someone else?

Q: Could you write a speech yourself if you had to?

Q: Do you type?

Q: Do you cut your own fingernails? Toenails?

Q: Who's the brightest person you know?

Q: Who's the dumbest person you know in public life? We won't tell him you said so.

Q: You used to drink quite a bit. What did you drink—scotch, bourbon, vodka, gin . . . all four? Do you miss it?

Q: Ever sneak one upstairs at night in the White House?

Q: When you and Laura are home alone, going to bed, do you talk about what you did right and what you did wrong that day?

Q: Does Laura ever tell you what you did wrong before you ask her?

Q: In your opinion, who is the best president we ever had?

Q: All right, in the past 50 years, who was the best? Let's leave your father out of this.

Q: It often seems as if your father is a little critical of you. Does his attitude bug you sometimes?

Q: You've said you don't get much advice from your father—that advice comes to you from a higher power. Are you suggesting God took us into Iraq?

Q: After your term is up, would it be any fun to get together at dinner to talk about your experiences as president with Bill Clinton, Jimmy Carter, Gerald Ford and your father?

Q: No marriage is perfect. You and Laura seem to get along but what do you do that bugs her? What does she do that bugs you?

If President Bush agrees to being interviewed, I'll let you know.

EX-PRESIDENTIAL PERKS

We now have four living ex-presidents. They are Gerald Ford, Jimmy Carter, George Bush and Bill Clinton.

Being an ex-president of the United States is a good life and I'll bet President George W. Bush wishes he was one of them right now. Everywhere you go you are honored. People don't remember the mistakes you made in office. Your opinions are taken seriously. You get a yearly salary of $182,000 and that's just a small part of your income.

An ex-president has Secret Service bodyguards, if he wants them. In 1997, Congress voted to limit that protection for presidents to ten years after leaving office. I guess they figured if anyone hated a president enough to try to harm him, they'd get over it in ten years.

A former president gets $96,000 to pay an office staff. He gets government paid travel, house rental, telephone, postage, supplies and equipment. And then, in addition to all that, they build a library with his name on it so he has a place to put all the junk he saved over the years.

Of our four living ex-presidents, Bill Clinton is the youngest. He's only sixty and he can expect another twenty-five years of life so he doesn't have to worry about doctors' bills because all his medical expenses are paid for. Last year, Bill made $850,000 in speaking fees. That was less than he made speaking in previous years but he made up for it by writing the book *My Life*, which made him a couple of million.

Gerald Ford is ninety-three and he has never taken being a former president seriously. He was an excellent athlete and he still plays golf almost every day. Jimmy Carter and George W. Bush's father, George, are both eighty-two. Former presidents don't always get along but George Bush and Bill Clinton formed an alliance when they got together this year to help in the Southeast Asia tsunami relief effort and then in the aftermath of Hurricane Katrina.

Even though former President Bush got along well with Bill Clinton, he often seems remote and even a little amused by his son's presidency. We know less about the activities of George H.W. Bush than we know about most former presidents. I don't know what he's doing. If you know what he's doing, write me.

Jimmy Carter seems to work hardest at being an ex-president and some historians say he's the best one we ever had. He's always bustling around doing good works but that's his idea of a good time. He won a Nobel Peace Prize in 2002. He has an easy way of seeming to be a good guy and he has never cashed in on his status by taking $100,000 fees for speeches. No one hates Jimmy Carter. You could call him "beloved."

Bill Clinton had a $460,000 house rental bill paid for him and a $54,000 telephone bill that he got free as an ex-president. He must spend a lot of time gassing on the phone. Bill is by far our most expansive and expensive ex-president. The Congressional Research Service lists his other expenses. One item is listed simply as "Other services: $146,000."

Jimmy Carter spent $15,000 in government money on stamps. George Bush had the most travel expenses. The government paid $54,000 for his airfare. I suppose he doesn't fly coach.

I'll bet George W. Bush can't wait until the day he gets to be an ex-president with all the perquisites that go with the non-job and none of the headaches he's had in office.

TALKING HEADS

TOM: How do you feel about immigration?

ED: Who, me?

TOM: Who else am I talking to? Yes, you. How do you feel about immigration?

ED: Well . . . promise not to tell anyone what I say?

TOM: No.

ED: OK. I'll tell you anyway. I don't want 'em here. We already got plenty of people, especially foreigners. Let 'em stay where they are.

ED: They really want to come here, though. Some of them will make good Americans.

TOM: Yeah, and some of them will make lousy Americans. Our country is full, anyway. Every vacant lot in our town is built on now. We can't take in the whole world.

TOM: A lot of good people would like to come here. Some of them already have family here.

ED: I don't like foreigners except when they're in their own country, anyway. They're OK if they stay home. We don't need 'em, don't want 'em. We got a great place here and I don't want a lot of strangers coming in from other places and lousing it up. Half of them get jobs and send money home instead of spending it here.

TOM: But overall, they'll help our economy, and anyway, taking them in is the American thing to do.

ED: Baloney! They'll just make things more crowded and more expensive for us. They'll drive cars on our roads and make more traffic. We'll have to build new roads.

TOM: Didn't your grandparents or great-grandparents come from a foreign country?

ED: Naw, not really. They came from Ireland. That's not foreign like say, Poland, Yugoslavia, Guatemala, Mozambique, Nigeria, Nicaragua, Syria, Thailand, Turkey, Yemen. Places like that. People from there are foreigners. That's what I'm talking about. The Irish talk funny but they talk English. I mean, you know.

TOM: But we're proud of America being the great melting pot.

ED: Forget about it. Half the people who come here these days don't melt. After ten years here, they still don't speak English. I say, "You don't like our language? Leave then. Go back where you come from. Speak whatever language that is if that's what you like but speak it there, not here."

TOM: But our country is made up of foreigners. Everyone here except a few thousand Indians came here from someplace else.

ED: Well, yeah, but that was a long while ago. We got enough now. Close the damn door, I say.

TOM: Who's going to do the dirty work if we don't have immigrants? You know, run the garbage trucks, do the heavy lifting on construction jobs. Who's gonna mow the lawns of rich people like you?

ED: If I can't get anyone to mow it, I'll mow it myself, or just let it grow. Lots of Americans are unemployed.

TOM: No, you got that wrong. Technically, they aren't all what you call unemployed or out of work. Some of them don't want to work. If they aren't looking for work or don't want to work because they don't have to, they aren't unemployed. You can't count them. They're retired.

ED: Yeah, or lazy. They just like getting unemployment insurance.

TOM: You don't approve of unemployment insurance?

ED: Yeah, but if someone's on it for a long time, they ought to lose it. They should get out there and look for a job.

TOM: Boy, you're tougher than President Bush.

WORKING FOR BUSH

A President of the United States has more work than he can handle so he needs plenty of help. President Bush has surrounded himself with assistants he trusts and, according to the people who watch him closely, he takes a lot of advice from aides. Some White House experts don't even think it was the President's idea to attack Iraq.

President Bush's most important assistant for several years was Andrew H. Card Jr. but he quit the job in 2006. I guess he wanted to spend more time with his family. That's what they always say even if they don't have one. Card was called "Assistant to the President and Chief of Staff." Most of us will never know the real reason why someone like Card decides to call it quits—or did President Bush decide for him? The President has regularly denied that there were going to be any major changes on his staff. However, he must have been looking for someone to point at after the precipitous decline in his popularity. Maybe Andy Card was his choice.

I have in front of me, as I write, an interesting document that lists everyone on the White House staff, what their jobs are and how much each is paid. The top pay is $161,000. That's what Card and ten other top assistants got. In the business world, $161,000 is peanuts. The heads of most big corporations wouldn't put on a tie and come to work for less than a million dollars a year.

This list is for 2005 but I don't think it's changed much. Melissa S. Bennett is on here. She has a hard job. Melissa is "Deputy Assistant to the President for Appointments and Scheduling." She gets to tell the President where to go.

Liza Wright Renner is "Special Assistant to the President for Presidential Personnel." In other words, the President has so many assistants working for him that he has to have an assistant in charge of the other assistants.

Anita McBride is "Deputy Assistant to the President and Chief of Staff to the First Lady." I don't see why "Deputy Assistant to the President" is part of her title. Does she have to check with George before she does something for Laura?

Dennis Grace is called "Special Assistant to the President and Deputy Director, Office of Faith-Based and Community Initiatives." I guess he's in charge of religion.

Janey Roell Naughton and Elizabeth Ann Horton are both called "Ethics Advisor." I don't know about that, either. It seems to me President Bush ought to know what is ethical and what isn't without having two women tell him.

Janet Lea Berman is "White House Social Secretary." That could be a hard job. She makes $92,100. After they have a party at The White House, maybe she gets to take home some of the leftover sandwiches.

Marguerite Murer is "Director of Presidential Correspondence." She reads the mail, I guess. That would be a hard, important job if she also has to answer it. Nuts are always writing to the President and I suppose she has to be polite to them. Marguerite makes $92,100. There's also a "Director of Mail Analysis." She must get to tell the President when people really hate something he did.

Misty Marshall is the "Director of Correspondence" for the First Lady.

There are thirteen speechwriters listed. Someone named "Joan R. Doty is called "Senior Writer" but she only makes $36,900. I wouldn't write "Nice to be here" for the President for that kind of money. Robert Thomas Pratt Jr. is a "Senior Writer" and he gets paid $42,800. They don't list any "junior" writers. The writers must have to wait on the table the President is speaking at to pay the rent.

Lee F. Bockhorn was also listed as a speechwriter. He was making $40,900. Lee's name is just below Sarah Penny's name, and Sarah makes $41,000 as the West Wing Receptionist. You can see how important they think writing is in the White House.

Clare Ross Taplett is "Deputy Director of the Gift Office." She must help decide where to throw all the presents people send the President.

Julia Phillips is a "Gift Analyst." She must decide how much a present is worth.

After reading this list, I can see why Andy Card decided to quit his job in the White House and look for work.

THE KYOTO DECISION

My daughter, Ellen, lives in London working as a photographer. Recently, she got an assignment in Cuba. She emailed me her hotel phone number there because I wanted to call and see how she was doing in Havana. I picked up the phone on my desk and started to dial the number. Suddenly, I had a terrible thought. I slammed down the receiver.

"Wait a minute," I said to myself. "If I call Cuba on my telephone, someone in the FBI is going to put me on a list of Americans who call Cuba." I had never been ashamed to be American before.

We Americans think of the United States as the greatest nation on earth. In the view of most of the rest of the world, we're objectionable about it because they think our pride exceeds our greatness.

I'm one of the objectionable Americans who probably has a higher opinion of our country than it deserves. What worries me is not the high opinion I have of it but my diminishing sense of pride because of things like not daring to call Cuba because it would get me on a list of people suspected of being un-American.

Our country no longer seems as great as it once did. We are no longer the good guys always doing the right thing as the leaders of the free world.

We have always been best friends with the English and they're still doing fairly well. China, Japan and even Russia are doing better, and I don't want to see my country fall behind any of them in any category. Every country on the planet has its strengths and weaknesses but some have more strengths and fewer weaknesses.

It isn't popular to say, but it still seems incontrovertibly true that the people born and raised in some countries are less capable at living than the people of other countries. I think the accomplishments of the civilizations of Europe and North America have exceeded those of the South American and African countries by any standard you can name. There is no explanation for why this is true and I know that it's politically incorrect of me to mention it.

It would be interesting to have the people of every country in the world take an I.Q. test so we could match the collective intelligence of a nation with its standing in the world. If we lived by our professed belief that "all men are created equal," the scores for all nations would be equal. However, we don't really believe that. Something has gone wrong in some nations along the way. Climate may make a difference.

The character of the population of the United States is changing for a variety of reasons, and our image around the world is changing because of that. About one million people are entering the United States as legal and illegal immigrants every year. They are no longer primarily European, as they once were.

This country was made great by the people whose initiative made them pick up, leave home and come to America for a better life. It is not certain that the people coming here now are motivated by the same things as the immigrants who made their way here 100 or more years ago.

There's no question that the United States has a lower standing among nations today than it had a 150, 50 or even 15 years ago. It was hardly noted by most Americans, but the single most damaging blow to our international reputation came in 2001 when the Bush administration refused to comply with the Kyoto Treaty designed to reduce global warming.

The treaty, which sought to reduce the kind of pollution that has trapped heat around the earth and produced a warm band was signed by 141 nations. Under the influence of the major manufacturing corporations who didn't want to spend the money to clean up their act, their friend President Bush opposed the treaty. This has had a lasting and negative effect on our standing in the world community.

PART SEVEN

My Life

People trying to be nice say, "What's wrong with being old?"
It's a dumb question to which I have a ready answer: "I'm
going to die before you do—that's what's wrong with it."

HOPELESSLY COPELESS

The comedian Roger Price, long gone now, invented and used the word "copeless" in describing himself. He was unable to cope, he said and I often think of the word—which is not in any dictionary—in relation to myself.

I was stopped by the flashing lights of a New York City police car last week. Unaware of having done anything wrong, I assumed the cops were after someone in front of me and wanted me to move over so they could get by and apprehend the culprit. It turned out, I was the culprit. One officer came to a position slightly behind the window of my car and said, without inflection "Registration and license, please." It was a bloodless "please" and did not suggest I had a choice.

"What did I do?" I asked.

"License and registration," he repeated, without the "please" this time. My license was in a small leather case I carry instead of a wallet. I opened the door to get out.

"Where you going?" he said not in a friendly voice at all.

"It's in my pants pocket," I said. "It's easier to get if I'm standing."

I had forgotten, in a moment of angst, that when a cop stops someone in a car, he stays well behind the driver and, as a precaution against the possibility the driver has a weapon, does not permit the driver to get out.

I showed him my license but could not find my registration. Like my clothes closet, my desk drawer, my garage and my basement, my car looks like an unemptied wastebasket. Everything is right there somewhere but I don't know where.

"You have an outdated sticker on your license plate," he said. "I'm going to let you go this time but get that sticker and put it on." I thanked the cop more effusively than he deserved and drove off.

If I were arrested for every sticker I hadn't stuck, every form I've failed to fill out, every item to be returned that I had not returned, I'd be in prison for life. I don't fill things out and return them. I don't know my social security number. I don't know when I pay the doctor and when some plan pays him. Neither do I know one medical plan from another. My bank writes to say I should change over from one plan to another and I don't understand whether it's something I should do for my own good or whether it's another bank sales gimmick, better for them than for me.

I hesitate to say so in print, but I do not keep track of what I have in my bank account and if the bank stole from me, I'd never catch them.

My company informs me that they are going to have a new system for the company retirement plan and will I please fill out the form and indicate that I want it, don't want it and how much of it do I want—or not want. The fact that I don't plan to retire is not an option they offer.

The details of the difference in the plans grew unfathomable to me and I do what I always do. Nothing.

Yesterday I read a story about the rivalry between the personal computer business and television interests. A new device called a Moxi is a digital box that goes on top of your television set "designed to serve as an integrated digital video recorder, CD player, DVD player, MP3 music player with an Internet connection and a high-speed wireless home network."

I am still struggling with channels higher than 13 on the television set. Is the whole world more able to cope with the new technology than I am?

It's a good thing I can type and put down one word after another on a sheet of paper because, if I couldn't, I don't know what would happen to me. I'm copeless.

ON BEING A COLLEGE PRESIDENT

To save them embarrassment, I'm not going to name the college I attended. Their president resigned and they've sent me a letter saying I'm a candidate for the job.

If this is a joke, I am mildly amused but should tell them that I prob-ably take myself more seriously than they do. If this is some kind of a fund-raising gimmick—nothing is too outrageous for a college fund-raiser—I object and may stop giving them "funds," which I call money.

If the college is serious, I can only say that if nominated, I will not run. If elected, I will not serve. Are they crazy or something? Do they really believe I'm capable of being a college president? Do they think I'd give up my day job to do that even if I was capable of doing it?

Along with the letter informing me that I'm under consideration by the search committee, there's a ten-page outline of the job. On page 8 is a section titled DESIRED QUALITIES and I don't have any of them. According to the outline:

"A viable candidate must:

"Be a good listener."

Count me out there. I'm not a good listener. If anyone else is talking, I'm impatient until I get a chance to say something.

"Be able to make timely and difficult decisions."

Not me. Half the time, I can't even make the easy decisions.

"Maintain a strong commitment to openness and consensus building."

No, I'm not committed to being open-minded. You can carry being broad-minded too far. By this time in my life, I know what I know and I know what I think and it's very damned unlikely that I'm going to change to build what you call a consensus.

The fact is, I'm no more capable of being a college president than I am of being president of this country. Maybe less. The president of the United States gets help from hundreds of capable assistants. A college president is out there all by himself fighting off the wolves.

Being a college president is one of the worst jobs known to man or womankind. Everyone is out to get the president. He has to quarrel with the Board of Trustees. This group is made up largely of business people who know nothing about education but have been appointed on the strength of the size of their contributions to the college.

There's always a faculty contingent that opposes the president on philosophical grounds.

Parents want the president's attention and he doesn't have time to give it. He's not leading an educational institution along a path to greater learning. He's out there raising money more than half the time at an unending series of alumni functions.

Let me ask a couple of questions of the search committee that thinks I might be college president material:

When I'm in office, will it be OK with you if I cut the number of football scholarships to zero?

Will I be able to go over the list of faculty members and see if I can put my finger on the ones who aren't really teaching?

Will I be able to rewrite the schedule for the academic year so that instead of having classes on just 126 days out of the 365, the university would hold classes something like 240 days a year? I'd give students one month off in the summer. Classes would start the day after Labor Day and continue until a Christmas vacation of one week.

There would be a spring break of one week in March or April. There would be classes every weekday and Saturday mornings. Class attendance records would be routinely mailed to parents so they'd know they were getting what they paid for.

If I were president of the college, students would not be treated like young adults. They would be treated like old children—which they are.

Do you still want me?

CARS I HAVE KNOWN

I call the odometer on my car a speedometer. It rolled past 60,000 this morning. That's when I start thinking about buying a new car. I don't do it right away; I just start thinking about it. I usually get close to 100,000 miles before I actually turn a car in.

Not many of us buy a new car because we need one. A new car is irresistible once you get thinking about it, even though there's nothing wrong with your old one. The tires do it for me. I don't like to spend the money for a new set on a car I know I'm not going to drive another 50,000 miles.

To pass the time on long drives, I've often tried—and failed—to remember and count all the cars I've owned. I'd list them, but no one under 50 would know the names. Is Borgward familiar to you?

We own four cars now. That sounds silly for two people but I leave two of them in the garage in the country from early October until mid-May. One is my 1987 Jeep Cherokee. It's a good car with about 90,000 miles on it, but the dealer would give me only $5,000 on a trade so I've kept it.

The other part-time car is my great 1966 Sunbeam Tiger with the Ford V–8 engine shoehorned into its little body. I paid $3,600 for the car and wouldn't sell it for $100,000. It was rebuilt in 1988 and is in pristine condition. I drive it with the top down through the rolling hills around our country house in upstate New York. It makes me feel young again, but I think I can hear people by the side of the road whispering, "Look at that old fool."

My parents owned a memorable Packard when I was growing up. It was one of the best cars ever built in the United States—one of the best of anything ever built anywhere—and this fact makes me suspicious of the free enterprise system. A company manufacturing such a superior product should not be forced out of business for lack of business. When we used to make the 75-mile trip from home to our summer cottage in 1936, my mother drove the Packard at 70 mph, the same speed I would drive my 2006 model car today.

The first car I bought and paid for with my own money was a 1942 Chrysler New Yorker. I bought it secondhand in Albany, right after being discharged from the Army in 1945. I had sold a book to MGM for $55,000 and was hired to write the screenplay. We bought the car for $2,500 and set out with all our possessions for California. The New Yorker, one of the last cars built before all carmakers suspended production during the war, had been owned by a funeral home and never driven more than 12 mph. The dark blue velvet upholstery was unruffled. It was a beauty.

I am foolishly sentimental about a car. I don't treat it like an inanimate object. I feel disloyal and sad when I turn one in. It's as if I was leaving an old dog with the vet for the last time. I still feel a twinge of regret when I think of my 1980 Ford station wagon, which I pushed past 120,000 miles before abandoning it for the jeep.

I was influenced to get rid of the station wagon by a remark made by a stranger when I was stopped for a light in New York. The car bore the evidence of its age in the scrapes and dents that pockmarked the body.

The pedestrian looked up, recognized me and said, "Aw, come on, Andy. You can do better than that." I traded the car within the month.

It'll be about a year before I actually buy a new car but that gives me time to anticipate the pleasure and think of ways to get a better price from the dealer.

ANOTHER LOST WEEKEND

I had a good feeling on my way home from work last Friday. There were a lot of satisfying little jobs to do around the house and we didn't have any plans for the weekend that would keep me from doing them. Even if you have the money and don't mind spending it, you can't find anyone to do little jobs around the house. I'm not really handy, but I have a lot of tools and I'll take on anything except plumbing or electricity.

Saturday morning, we sat in the kitchen reading the newspaper over a third cup of coffee. If you're looking for a way to delay getting at doing odd jobs Saturday morning, one good way is to make a list. Making a list is a job of its own and it delays actually going to work.

"Don't forget to put the air conditioner in the window in our bedroom," Margie said. "I wish you'd turn the rug in the living room, too."

"I'm making my own list of things to do," I said. Actually I didn't "say"; I "snapped."

"Well, just don't forget to get rid of that awful-looking mat by the front door. You said it was just for the winter and it's May. I asked you to take that hook off the door, too. The one we hang the Christmas wreath from. It looks terrible."

"I'll do it when I have the ladder out to get the leaves out of the gutter," I said.

The first item on my Things-To-Do-Today list was "Plates."

The new Connecticut license plates for my car came last week. The plates are a different color than the old ones and I don't like the new color. I never like the new color of license plates as much as I liked the old color.

With nine items on my TTDT list, I got up from the table and announced that mounting the new plates was my first priority.

"Don't waste your time on that," Margie said. "You've got enough things to do without that. I'll take your car to the gas station Monday. They have a mechanic who'll do it."

"A mechanic?" I asked, incredulously. "To change my license plates? You're kidding. It's a ten-minute job."

I backed the car out of the garage so I'd have more room. Some stuff I needed on a shelf on the passenger side is hard to get at when the car is in there. Cars must have been narrower when they built our garage. Or maybe it was a mistake putting those shelves along the wall.

The plates are attached to my car with inch-long metal screws with hex nut heads. Three of the screws came out with a few twists of a pair of pliers. The fourth was jammed. I sprayed the reluctant screw with WD40. Still no luck. Obviously I needed a set wrench. Or maybe WD41.

I judged the nut to be three eighths of an inch and went to the basement for a wrench. I had a half-inch, a five-eighths, a three-quarters and several larger ones but no three-eighths.

Frustrated, I climbed in the car and drove to the gas station. The mechanic loosened the screw with his three-eighths-inch wrench. While he was at it, he secured the front and back license plates to the car. I said, "Buy ya a beer," gave him $10 for three minutes' work, and drove off.

There was no reason to bother anyone with the information that I'd had to go to the gas station to get the license plate off. It was past noon by now, so I went out to the kitchen and made myself a tuna fish sandwich.

I poured a Coke and took the sandwich into the living room and got watching Serena Williams and Jennifer Capriati. My eyelids started to droop so I turned off the sound on the TV set and took a little nap.

I can do those odd jobs some other weekend.

REUNION: TO GO OR NOT TO GO?

Because I had never seen any of my college classmates' wives in their nightgowns before, last weekend's reunion was outstanding.

The get-together was with about with thirty classmates in the picture-perfect little college town.

Reunions are bittersweet and sometimes more bitter than sweet. This one was good. It is usually the most successful graduates who return and they are also the most interesting.

I went to college for three years before being drafted into the Army. I was one year short of memories that most of the others shared. However, our son and grandson are both graduates of the same college and this gives me an added affinity with the school.

Some of the people I enjoyed seeing are better friends because of past reunions than they were because of any association we had in college. Some of my friends in college were, for one reason or another—mostly one—sadly missing.

The college, and particularly the part of it known as "the development office," is alert to the potential of graduates as gift-givers and they are friendly and helpful. Because our class was one of the older of the returning groups, we were given priority consideration for accommodations at the Inn, which is owned by the university. The Inn is a three-story wooden hostelry with forty-six rooms that backstops one end of the town mall.

On Saturday night, we had our class dinner at the Inn. The dinner was an improvement over the food the college had provided at an all-class lunch. (It occurred to me when I sat looking at the lunch that if you wanted to make a television show on bad cooking, our meal would have been a good example.)

At about 10:30 P.M., we decided we'd had enough and went to our third-floor room. Shortly after we got to bed, we were abruptly awakened by the sound of an urgent alarm. I opened the hall door to determine the source and got back in bed with the raucous noise precluding sleep. Two minutes later, there was a loud banging on our door accompanied by a voice yelling, "Fire! Everyone out! Fire! Clear the building!"

I pulled my pants on over my pajama bottoms, wishing I had brought pajamas the top of which wasn't frayed where it buttoned down the front. I looked to see Margie starting out the door barefoot. I yelled over the alarm for her to put on shoes. She grabbed her shoes but continued down the hall barefoot. The three-story stairway looked formidable so, ignoring the small sign with red letters reading, "IN CASE OF FIRE DO NOT TAKE ELEVATOR!", I pressed the button and we took the elevator. Long experience has taught me that the overwhelming number of alarms, relating to anything, are false.

Outside the lobby door, there were several glass-topped tables and wrought iron chairs. Half a dozen people who had not yet gone to bed were still drinking and greeted the refugees from inside as if they were hosts.

The fire engines arrived and the firemen, in boots and helmets, axes at the ready, stormed inside ready to extinguish the inferno.

We sat down and watched as other guests poured out. Many of the women who'd arrived at the reunion determined to look their best, no longer did, although I was much impressed by the high-fashion silk, flowered dressing gown worn by the wife of one classmate. I couldn't help noticing that she looked better in her bedclothes than she had at dinner. Had there been no fire alarm, none of us would ever have seen the grandness of her nocturnal habiliment. Such a waste, I thought . . .

and thank goodness for the false alarm that added so much to our re-union weekend.

THE KASHMIR EXPERT

Courses on how to write seldom produce any good writing because the students are so young they have no background or experience on which to base anything.

When I read about the potential for nuclear war between India and Pakistan, I dismissed it as a subject to write about because I know so little about the issues. Then my eyes fell on the word "Kashmir." I thought to myself, "Although I am uncertain about the difference between Cashmere and Kashmir, I can write about Kashmir. I've been to Kashmir."

When World War II ended in Europe in 1945, my editor sent me to China and India. It was assumed, after the Germans surrendered, that several million American soldiers in Europe would be shipped to India and China to invade Japan. My assignment was to write stories about what it would be like for American soldiers when they got to China and India.

On the flight from France to New Delhi, the C-54 cargo plane stopped for fuel in Cairo. The pilot misjudged our distance from a telephone pole on the side of the runway and clipped off a few feet of our left wing. I was pleased with the accident because it made necessary a three-day stopover for repairs and provided me with a tourist-eye view of Cairo. I stayed at the Shepheard's Hotel, with which I was familiar as the locale of some movie I saw as a child.

When I arrived in New Delhi, it was 110 degrees. I was still wearing my wool uniform and all I wanted to do was lie down on the relatively cool, mosaic floor of the airport and die. I had no interest in India or my assignment. After I pulled myself together I jotted down some story ideas.

American soldiers on leave in India often wangled their way on board one of the cargo flights to Kashmir, so I decided to write a story about where American soldiers in India went on leave. I was surprised but delighted to find The Vale (Valley) of Kashmir one of the garden spots of the universe. It is in a verdant bowl eighty miles long and twenty-five miles wide surrounded by majestic, snow-capped mountains. There is not a more spectacularly beautiful place on earth. The snow on the mountains releases some of its water as it melts under the hot sun during the day, and a thousand streams of water make their way down the rocky crevices to the town. Many of the streets are waterways, much like Venice, and people use small boats to get around.

I found a barge-like boat with rooms for rent to visitors. The only other occupants were three British sergeants from New Delhi. We quickly became friends and on the second day I joined them on a horse-back expedition into the mountains.

I had never ridden a horse. Mine was a broad-backed, sure-footed animal thoroughly familiar with making his way up the icy slopes. We followed one of the streams, often crunching along on the frozen layer of ice covering the running water beneath it. The day was pleasantly warm and we took off our shirts. I soon realized it was going to be a long day. Eight hours later, we returned our horses to their owner and went to our boat. I could barely walk, crotch bound from eight hours in the saddle and so sunburned that I could neither walk nor lie down comfortably.

Several years after I left, Kashmir was divided between India and Pakistan and they've been fighting over the region ever since.

This is all I know. It isn't much, but at least I've actually been to Kashmir and, to that extent at least, if you haven't been there, I know more about it than you do.

MAN IS DOGS' BEST FRIEND

We had a guest at our summer home for the month of July. Spencer summers with us every year. Spencer is our daughter Emily's great white English bulldog. Dogs are nicer than people. Why are so many dogs so good when so many people are so bad?

It's strange that there are so many distinctively different breeds of dogs too, each with its own personality. The ethnic differences between people of the various races do not begin to be as great as the differences, physically and mentally, between a bulldog and a chihuahua, or between a St. Bernard and a Shih Tzu.

The American Kennel Club lists 150 different breeds among its membership. The ten most popular breeds are listed in order in 2004 as: the Labrador Retriever, Golden Retriever, German Shepherd, Beagle, Yorkshire Terrier, Dachshund, Boxer, Poodle, Shih Tzu, and No. 10, the Chihuahua.

Labradors and Golden Retrievers certainly belong at the top of the list. Friendly and smart are the two most important attributes for a dog and you can't stop a Lab or a Golden Retriever from being friendly.

The surprises to me on that list are the Dachshund at No. 6, the Shih Tzu at No. 9, and the Chihuahua No. 10. I've never known any of those breeds but I suspect that one reason for their popularity is the convenience of their size. Chihuahuas don't appeal to me at all and Shih Tzus are cute, but I like more in a dog than cute. I am offended that the English bulldog, the best of all possible dogs, doesn't appear on the list until No. 14.

Spencer is old now for a bulldog. He's twelve. Emily never took him to an obedience school and, if she had, Spencer would have failed and probably been kicked out. He's not deliberately disobedient. He just doesn't care what you want him to do if he feels like doing something else. He'll listen attentively when you tell him to do something and then do what he pleases.

When I was growing up, my mother did a favor for a woman who raised Pekingese. As a token of her thanks, the woman gave my mother the prize of a litter of Pekingese puppies. My mother was pleased with the gift but aghast at the breed. She couldn't conceal her dislike for this two-pound Pekingese. The woman, who attended a lot of dog shows, asked Mother what she'd like instead. Mother chose an English bulldog. He came already named "Spike" at three months old, and Spike and I grew up together. In my mind, Spike is related to every bulldog I've ever seen. There are traces of him in Spencer.

When our children were young, we bought a bulldog pup and named him "Gifford" after the football player. He became "Giffy" and part of our family—and part Spike, part Spencer.

My relationship to dogs now is mostly to those I meet being walked by their owners in New York City. You can tell if a dog and its owner want to be spoken to and I respond to every wagging tail. The dogs are glad to see me even if they've never seen me before. Dogs are happy to be out for a walk; they love the whole world. What makes dogs so happy? Most get to eat only once a day, they're cooped up and alone much of the time and have little or no sex life. It doesn't matter. When they get to go for a walk they're happy all over.

I never pass a bulldog without stopping to talk. Owners are sometimes leery as I approach their dogs because they know a lot of people are afraid of so fierce looking an animal. It becomes instantly apparent that I know bulldogs and both the dog and the owner greet me warmly. When I'm driving along a street anywhere and see a bulldog, I pull to the curb and jump out of the car to talk to the dog. We're always instant best friends. It's like seeing Spike, Giffy and Spencer again.

It would be a better world if people were as nice, uncomplaining and easy to get along with as dogs.

YOU'VE PROBABLY HAD IT

I'm on sick leave, but I'm not leaving.

Until you've had some physical problem yourself, you're usually unaware that almost everyone you know has had the same thing before you did. If they haven't actually had it, their brother or their father or their best friend had it. Until I was diagnosed with carpal tunnel syndrome, I had heard of it but thought it was a rare disease. Alas, it turns out to be as common as the common cold. Everyone I tell has had it or knows someone who has.

The tunnel is formed by eight bones at the base of the wrist and it carries the tendons that let the fingers move (I think). If the sheath that covers the tendon becomes irritated and swells, nothing works and everything hurts. Anyway, don't get it if you can help it.

This summer, during my so called "vacation," I spent ten hours a day, seven days a week, finishing a book called *Common Nonsense*. I forget who came up with the title but that's it whether I like it or not. If it sells a lot of copies, I'll get to like the title.

Carpal tunnel syndrome is brought on my some repetitive action with your fingers and it was all that typing that brought on my problem. I'm about to have surgery on my right hand to correct it. If I could cross my fingers and hope everything comes out all right—which I can't—I would.

My doctor sent me to an orthopedist, who sent me to a hand specialist. Hand specialists don't have a name for themselves like dermatologists, cardiologists, urologists or gynecologists. They're special, though, because they don't do anything else. I have some foot problems and you'd think this hand surgeon could look into that, but they don't do feet.

Once my right hand heals after the surgery, I'm going to have to have my left hand done. I don't know how specialized these hand surgeons are. For all I know, I'll have to find someone else who just does left hands.

In anticipation of not being able to type for a few weeks, I bought something called ViaVoice, made by IBM. Theoretically, you speak into a microphone and your voice comes out as words on the screen of your computer and you can print out the page.

"You talk, it types" reads the slogan on the box. Simple enough, right?

To test my new toy, I first read a fifteen-minute selection from *Treasure Island* that the manufacturer recommended as a way for the device to get familiar with the sound and inflections of my voice.

It appears as if my voice is not the one IBM had in mind when it made this device. Here's a sample. I was fooling around, ad-libbing, but this is what I said: "Each of us has more anniversaries than he or she has time to celebrate. Tonight marks my 24th year on *60 Minutes,* or I may be wrong about that. It may be my 23rd year, or perhaps even my 26th year, but frankly I don't give a damn."

This is what came on the screen of my computer: "As more anniversaries and he\she has time to celebrate. Tonight marks I 24th year 16 at I may be wrong about that it maybe Irene 23rd year perhaps even my 26 year frankly I got now or dividend."

You can see that IBM is not sympathetic to carpal tunnel sufferers and I'm going to have to find some other way to get my words down on paper. I'd demand my money back from IBM except what happened was probably partly my fault and anyway, I charged the new ViaVoice to CBS.

If I qualify as handicapped because of my carpal tunnel problem, I won't need wheelchair access, but they're going to have to make handicapped bottle tops that I can take off, handicapped doorknobs that I can twist, handicapped shoelaces that I can tie, handicapped shirts that I can button and handicapped newspapers whose pages I can turn.

A LESS THAN MERRY CHRISTMAS

Merry Christmas? Well, interesting but not all merry.

We were fifteen and assembled at our country house in the Helderberg Mountains of New York State, which look toward the Catskills. Two came from London, four from Los Angeles, four from Washington, two from Boston, two from Connecticut and one from Saratoga.

Everyone came bearing gifts and food. We had eleven loaves of rye, raisin, pumpernickel, sourdough and French bread. Emily and her daughter, Alexis, brought the twenty-five-pound turkey. We brought the ham for Christmas Eve. Martha had fixed beef stroganoff, which she brought from Washington. Les and Ellen got through airport security with an odoriferous wheel of Stilton.

Ben, Justin, Leo, Martha and I went to a local farm to buy an eight-foot balsam Christmas tree. That's all the living room ceiling will take. After it was trimmed. Ellen, the severest critic in our critical family, unendeared herself to us by saying it was "the worst tree we ever had." She always says that. It's a Christmas tradition.

Snow started falling early Christmas morning. We opened our presents, merry enough, and by noon faced the snow piling up outside. Before it stopped, we were to get thirty-four inches, a lifetime experience for two young grandchildren who live in California.

I was determined to get the newspaper at a store 12 miles away. Les, our British son-in-law, volunteered to go with me so we took off in blizzard conditions in my old jeep. It was a bad decision. Halfway there, the snow was blinding and the windshield wipers were icing up so we stopped. I opened my door and stepped out. Under eight inches of snow, there was a sheet of ice. My left foot slipped out from under me and my right foot went under the car. The car door, still open, hit my head as it went over me. Briefly stunned, lying in the snow, I did not notice the car moving until it rolled over my right leg just two inches below the knee. I had inadvertently put it in reverse.

It seemed certain my leg was broken. The jeep was still backing down a slight incline and Les ran to it and stopped it 100 feet from where I'd been run over. My leg hurt, but Les helped me up. I could hobble and concluded the bone might not have been crushed because of the cushion of snow. We continued to the store, bought the newspaper and made it home.

As I lay in the downstairs bedroom with my grossly distended right leg, which Cecile had covered with an ice bag, someone called the local rescue crew and, on Christmas Day they arrived in minutes. It was small-town America at its best, ready to help a neighbor who needed it. The trained medic looked at my turgid leg, now twice its normal size and turning black, and announced he was calling the ambulance to take me to the Albany Medical Center thirty-five miles away. Brian and Martha followed in Emily's Subaru down the treacherous mountain road to the hospital.

If every visit to a hospital was as good as this one, I'd go more often. Three doctors X-rayed me, poked and prodded my leg and determined nothing was broken. They warned that I'd have severe pain in the night, but by 7:30 I was released. Without the guiding ambulance taillights, we started the thirty-five-mile trip back up the mountain in nearly impossible driving conditions.

If Brian wasn't an ABC News correspondent, he could get work as a truck driver. Feeling his way along the road, sometimes at 5 mph an hour with his nose just inches from the windshield, he got us home by 10 P.M. It's a humbling experience to have a son do something you could not have done.

By cell phone, we had insisted the rest of the family go ahead with Christmas dinner. When we arrived, we were served ours in style at a small table set up in the living room in front of the fireplace, surrounded by family members alternately telling me to keep my leg up and making rude remarks about the wisdom of going for the newspaper.

At midnight, we all said "Merry Christmas" one last time and I took my aching but unbroken leg to bed.

I never did read the newspaper.

TALKING THE TALK

We were invited by the producers of a Broadway show to a party in a New York City restaurant that was not really big enough to hold all the people they had asked to come. It was hard to talk to anyone and my mind slipped into its writing mode. I got thinking about party conversations.

The first person I met was a big, friendly guy who seemed to know me, although I didn't seem to know him. We shook hands and he started talking about the show. I quickly realized he was one of those people who stand too close to whoever they're talking to. He kept leaning forward to emphasize a word until his nose was inches from mine.

I tried to edge away, but every time I took half a step back, he took a full step forward. As a defense, I extended my left leg in front of me and leaned way back on my right leg. He leaned forward. The next person I met had a familiar conversational style. He repeated himself. He didn't think he'd made himself clear the first time, so he rephrased his statement and said it again: "This is a mess in Iraq. We got ourselves in a real mess over there. We never shoulda got in this mess."

There are other people who end almost everything they say with a question and insist on an answer. "Don't you think that's true?" "Do you agree with me on that?" "You know what I mean?" Yes, I know what you mean. Now can I go and talk to someone who doesn't ask a lot of dumb questions?

Several times a year, we go to some event in a hotel ballroom where they're giving awards and they have an orchestra on stage. There may be people at your table you'd like to talk to, but conversation is impossible. I don't know why orchestras don't understand that no one wants to hear them play loud music incessantly. We not only don't want it loud, we want them to stop playing altogether once in a while and give us some silence so we can chat.

There was no orchestra at the New York party, but I still had trouble talking to several people. One man I know only because he's so rich that his name appears in the newspaper regularly, greeted me in a friendly way. We shook hands and he said something. It may have been a question but I couldn't hear it. He always mumbles. If you're rich, you don't have to talk loud to get people to listen to you. I always think that what someone says quietly is more important than what someone else shouts.

When I noticed that this quiet-talker had stopped because I didn't see his lips moving, I leaned forward and said, "I'm sorry, I didn't hear what you said."

He repeated it but I couldn't hear him the second time, either. There are just so many times you can rephrase, "What?" so I just smiled and nodded. I hope I shouldn't have shook my head in the "no" gesture. I had briefly considered several responses to what I couldn't hear. "Very much," I could have said if I thought he was asking if I enjoyed the show. Or I could have said, "*60 Minutes*" if I thought he was asking where I worked. "Andrew, but people call me Andy," if it was my name he might have been asking for.

If I had to write down everything I heard in the two hours we spent at the party, I wouldn't be able to come up with two sentences.

MISSING FIVE HOURS

Often about 5:30 in the afternoon, I sit at my desk and try to remember where the day went.

I usually go to bed by 10:30 P.M. because I get up early. I don't know how anyone with a job watches Letterman or Jay Leno. My alarm is set for 5:27 A.M., but I wake up before that and turn it off. That's about seven hours. Spending a third of the day sleeping seems like too much.

I'm in the bathroom for maybe fifteen minutes. I shave with an electric razor. I used to shower before I shaved, but I read where a beard cuts better if it isn't soft, so now I shave first.

My dermatologist said you shouldn't use real hot water and you shouldn't stay under it for long so I don't linger. I dress in five minutes.

It takes me an hour getting to and from work every day. I think or listen to the radio. You can't do both. Driving home, I listen to two men who do a terrible sports show. They are so annoying that hating them makes the time pass faster.

I estimate that I spend about an hour and fifteen minutes eating on an average day.

I make coffee in the office in the morning and have a grapefruit at my desk but it takes only ten minutes. The same with lunch. I hardly ever go out. In the evening after I get home at six, we spend a pleasant hour having a drink and watching television news.

We have a dining room but don't eat in it more than ten times a year. We eat in the kitchen or the living room. When I get dinner, doing the dishes takes longer. I figure an hour for dinner and cleanup. Dinner in a good restaurant takes longer, but we don't eat out often.

After dinner, I read the parts of the paper missed in the morning. Someone should publish a digest of the morning newspaper. There's too much in it.

I watch some television at night. I'll assign an hour for that. You can do two things at once if one of them is television, so I go through a pile of mail while I'm watching, separating the wheat from the chaff. It's mostly chaff.

Everyone complains about television but there's often more I'd like to see than there's time to watch.

The telephone both saves time and wastes time. There are people who enjoy talking on the phone but I'm not one of them. I'm not lonesome. Even so, I suppose I spend half an hour a day on twenty calls. I talk to one or more of our four kids every day.

Most of the day, I sit at my keyboard, writing. I write quickly but hardly ever get it right the first time and usually have to do it over, so it's a slow process. I start to write a lot of things that don't work out too, so I'm at it at least five hours a day. People ask me how long it takes me to write my newspaper column and my *60 Minutes* comments. I always tell them if it's any good, it doesn't take long but if it isn't good, it takes all day.

I waste time. I must waste at least an hour a day pretending I'm doing something necessary that isn't. Instead of working, I'll clean out a desk drawer, rearrange the bookshelves or wash the car. It's the little time that's hard to count. The elevators in the building where I work are slow. I wait ten minutes a day. Friends drop in and we talk. I wait in line at the store. I decide to cut my fingernails. I sit and stare.

Now, all that comes to a little over nineteen hours. What I want to know is, what did I do with those five missing hours?

THINGS I LOVE TO HATE

Rummaging through a box of odd bits and pieces of paper I've saved, I came across a column by Dick Burdette in a yellowing old clipping from a newspaper. The column is headlined, "These are a few of my favorite things." I don't want to steal his column or lose my image as a complainer so I'll go in the other direction. Here are a few of my least favorite things:

The customer in front of me in the "under 10 items" line at the checkout counter in the supermarket who pays with a check and takes five minutes to do it.

The trash or garbage collector who leaves more than he takes.

The waiter who keeps filling your glass with water you don't need but disappears when you want something.

When you're browsing in a clothing store, the sales clerk who hangs over you asking if he can help, as though you were too bashful to ask about buying something.

Clever messages on telephone answering machines.

Junk mail that regularly exceeds mail of any value or interest.

The newspaper story "continued on page 27" just when it gets interesting. If it's continued in the second section, Margie has that.

The driver who takes up two spaces when he parks.

Hitting the "caps lock" key on the computer by mistake when I'm typing and not looking at the screen until I've typed two lines in capital letters.

Fitting two cars in a two-car garage that's only big enough for one by the time you put your junk in there.

Car doors that lock automatically.

Packages I can't get into without a jackhammer or tops I can't remove without a crowbar.

Margarine, skim milk and Diet Coke. I'd rather do without butter, milk or Coke than eat or drink a substitute.

Semicolons.

Melting snow.

My birthday. The last one I enjoyed was when I was eight.

Sticky windows that are hard to open.

Yellow cars.

A melon that was expensive but nowhere near ripe.

Subscription forms and advertising fliers folded into newspapers and magazines.

Books that won't stay folded open when you lay them flat. (I also dislike the confusion among lay, laid, lain, lie and lied.)

The Super Bowl halftime show.

Almost all television, with the exception of news, sports, documentaries and a few comedy shows. I don't have a preference between Jay Leno and David Letterman.

Impossible books with dedication pages by the author that say, "To my wife, Charlotte, without whose help this book would not have been possible."

Astrology.

The American flag worn as an ornament in a man's buttonhole.

PURSUIT OF TRUTH, NOT FICTION

My life is one of unread books. I don't have the time or space to name all the books I have not read. In recent years, I have overcome the shame I once felt when asked if I'd read something and had to answer "No," by converting my shame into pride. When asked now if I've read *The Da Vinci Code* for example, I say, "No, I never read novels. I like my own real life too much to want to be transported into someone else's fictitious world."

This is not really an intellectual answer to the question but it sounds thoughtful if you don't think about it and people nod. It is true, too, that I never read fiction. I started not reading fiction in about the ninth grade when an English teacher assigned our class the novel *Lorna Doone* I got away with not reading "Lorna Doone" by reading a brief resume of it and have never felt uneducated for having skipped it. I have plans to read *Silas Marner* when I get on in years.

Over the years, I have broken my rule about fiction ten times. I read *Slaughterhouse Five* because Kurt Vonnegut, who wrote it, is a friend of mine and I didn't want to have it come out inadvertently, when we were talking, that I was ignorant of his masterpiece. I have not read

A Farewell to Arms or *The Sun Also Rises* by Ernest Hemingway, because I knew Hemingway, too, and thought he was a boob.

Putting my mind to fiction I have read, I come up with ten great books: *Lord of the Flies*, *Heart of Darkness*, *Death Comes for the Archbishop*, *The Bridge of San Luis Rey*, *Winesburg, Ohio*, *Darkness at Noon*, *Brave New World*, *The Catcher in the Rye*, *From Here to Eternity* and *Lolita*. I should really leave out *Lolita* because I read that years ago as a dirty book, not as literature, although it's both. Half of those titles were assigned by a teacher when I was in high school or college.

Reading fiction is a form of entertainment. You read nonfiction for information. Someone famous said that those who read nonfiction read to remember, and those who read novels, read to forget. I read the newspaper or a magazine for about an hour a day. That seems like as much time as I should spend on someone else's words.

Not reading novels doesn't make me special. There are something like 290 million Americans, and a popular book like Tom Wolfe's *I Am Charlotte Simmons* may sell 400,000 copies. That means about one of every 725 Americans bought a copy. I'm one of the ones who don't read bestselling novels, so I'm not alone. I'm being generous, too, suggesting that everyone who buys a book reads the book. I suspect that a lot more books are bought than read.

The most omnivorous reader I ever knew was Harry Reasoner. When he anchored the *CBS Evening News*, substituting for Walter Cronkite, he would sit in the chair before the broadcast, and while everyone else around him was frantically tending to last-minute details, Harry would sit quietly reading a novel. When the producer yelled, "Thirty seconds!", Harry would finish the paragraph, put down the book and look into the camera ready to read the news from the TelePrompTer in front of him.

I don't mean to sound proud of not reading novels, nor do I advocate not reading them. I have respect and admiration for people who read fiction. I think of them as culturally and intellectually superior to myself.

A SHIP AT SEA

Last Saturday, I looked out my office window, where normally I see nothing but a dull stretch of New Jersey across the North River, and there was the magnificent new *Queen Mary* practically in my back yard. It looks like a fifty-story hotel laid on its side in the water. One thing that struck me was that there were no portholes, just rectangular windows in every stateroom.

I couldn't remember when Mary was queen of England. I lived in London for a year. I like London and the British people, but the idea of a grownup country having a king or a queen is ridiculous. Even in a college history course, I never mastered all their names.

My almanac lists two Marys who were queens of England. The first was known as "Bloody Mary" for good reason. She must not have been the queen the majestic *Queen Mary* sitting outside my window was named after. There was another Mary, undistinguished, who co-ruled with her husband, William, who came to the throne in 1689. It seemed unlikely the ship was named for a co-queen, either.

The naming of the original *Queen Mary* may have been a fluke. The story is that in 1934 Cunard officials wanted to name their new ship *Queen Victoria* after Britain's longest reigning monarch. They went to King George V and said, "Can we name our ship for Britain's greatest queen?"

George, whose wife's name was Mary, said, "Certainly. My wife would be delighted." So they named the ship *Queen Mary* after a woman who was only a queen by marriage.

To me, the name written as *Queen Mary 2* has no class anyway. At the very least, they should have used Roman numerals and called it the *Queen Mary II*. One of the biggest liners before the Marys and Elizabeths was called The Leviathan after the legendary water giant from Greek mythology. A better name.

When I was five, my aunt and uncle lived across the river from where the big ships dock and they always took me to the cliff overlooking the harbor when one of them came in. The ships always had three smoke-stacks. *The Queen Mary 2* doesn't seem to have any smokestacks.

In about 1965, I sailed on the original *Queen Mary* with the great, though almost forgotten, Garry Moore. Cruising on a big ship is a luxurious way to cross the ocean, but dull. You just look out at the water, sleep and wait for the next meal. Fortunately, we ran into a monster storm. The propellers were coming up out of the water as we rolled over waves the size of mountains and that made things exciting. The captain said it was "the worst storm he had encountered in thirty-seven years at sea," but afterward, when I told someone about it, he said captains always say a storm is the worst they've encountered in thirty-seven years.

I had an unusual experience with the *Queen Mary* several years later after it had been retired and parked in Long Beach, Calif., as a tourist attraction. We were filming the United States from a helicopter for a documentary and thought the docked *Queen* would make a good picture. It was warm and the sun was hitting me sitting in the bubble next to the pilot.

As we banked over the *Queen* for the cameraman, I dozed. I had a still camera, binoculars and a tape recorder in my lap. As I slumped over, my arm hit the latch and the door flew open. I didn't go out, but my camera, binoculars and recorder dropped like rocks into the water next to the old ship. I had removed a jacket with my wallet carrying my credit cards, licenses and cash. That went out but it was light enough so it floated over land. As the pilot landed the helicopter, a truck roared up next to the *Queen*. The driver was laughing and waving my jacket.

"I got it," he yelled. "It drifted out over the road!"

Looking out at the new *Queen Mary* from my office window, I had a lot of memories.

A STAR-SPANGLED TRIP

France is one of the best names to drop when you want to impress people with where you've been. I have just been to France. The reason for my trip was the sixtieth anniversary celebration of the D-Day landings in Normandy. My special interest in the event stemmed from my own arrival on the beach June 10, 1944.

I entered Paris for the first time in the early morning of Aug. 25, 1944, as U.S. and French armored and infantry divisions took back the city from the Germans who had occupied it for four years. It was one of the great moments of my life and going to Paris is still exciting for me. I know just enough French to make a fool of myself.

Like most Americans, I'm ambivalent about the French. They can be maddening one minute and lovable the next, but one thing is certain: they are more French all day long than Americans are American. They live better than we do because they work to live. They don't live to work. They direct their lives toward simple pleasures. It accounts for why their food is incomparably better than ours.

I was surprised and pleased by the French attitude toward American veterans. Walking down the street in Bayeux, less spryly than I used to, and obviously old enough to have been there sixty years ago, two young Frenchmen came up to me, held out their hands and said, "Thank you." I was moved and I don't move easily.

There were a few scattered demonstrations. One small group held signs saying, "WE LIKE AMERICANS BUT WE DON'T LIKE GEORGE BUSH."

Tom Brokaw, the NBC News anchor, was staying in Bayeux and graciously invited this lower level CBS employee to a small dinner at the famous Lion D'Or restaurant. At the table were two Medal of Honor winners, Tom's attractive wife, Meredith, Jimmy Buffett the singer, Tom Hanks, the actor, and Steven Spielberg, the producer. This is not a circle I travel in and I was greatly impressed with myself for being there. I was further impressed by how easy Tom Hanks and Steven Spielberg were to talk to. Jimmy Buffett's wife was on my right, but I talked more to Tom Hanks because I was afraid of revealing that I was not very familiar with Jimmy's work.

We ate late and at about 10:30 there was a flurry of activity as two NBC producers came in and whispered to Brokaw. Tom immediately stood, raised his wineglass and said, "President Reagan has died. To the President!"

We drank a toast and Tom left to go on the air.

The next day was the actual anniversary of D-Day and there were ceremonies and speeches everywhere, including one by President Bush. I did not attend. Instead, I went away from the crowds and visited places in my memory from the days when I had been a reporter for the *Stars and Stripes*. There could have been no speech so eloquent as to match the emotion I felt driving alone into the town of St Lo. I had done the same thing under fire with elements of the First Infantry Division sixty years before.

During my six days in France, I ate in a dozen small restaurants. Each time, as I savored the food, I thought that, just by luck, I had found the best restaurant in town. That's the thing about little French restaurants in little French towns. They are all the best restaurant in town.

At one point, I could hear the far-away strains of "The Star Spangled Banner" floating my way. I hear it played at the beginning of New York Giants football games and am immune to any sensation but listening to it in a foreign country, I always tingle.

When "The Star Spangled Banner" ended, another band in the distance struck up "La Marseillaise." I listened intently and had an un-American thought. Not only is French food better than ours, but so is their national anthem. But that's as far as I want to go being nice to the French.

THINGS TO DO TODAY

There are some things I've been meaning to do. For one thing, I've been meaning to make a list of the things I mean to do:

Try to be nicer to people I don't like.

Try not to dislike so many people.

Sharpen all my pencils.

Do a better job reading the newspaper.

Clean out the trunk of the car.

Make bread in the bread maker I bought three years ago and never used.

Lose eighteen pounds by not eating ice cream.

Either wear them or take some of the old shoes and old clothes in my closet to Goodwill.

Go to see my doctor about that problem I've been having which goes away when I go to my doctor.

Organize the stuff in our two-car garage so I can get one car in it.

Fix the leg on the dining room table.

See the movie that's going to win all the Oscars before it wins them and is too hard to get into.

Put a new washer in the nozzle of the shower so that one errant spray doesn't get me where I don't want to be got.

Pay more attention to things that matter.

Organize my life.

Thank Blanche for the oranges she sent at Christmas.

Get a haircut.

Have the oil changed and the tires rotated on my car.

Read a book. Finish the book I started two years ago.

Look at some of the television shows I've saved on tape to look at later.

Buy new undershirts and socks to replace the ones with holes in them.

Learn how to touch-type. (This has been on my list for fifty years now, during which time I've written fourteen books with three fingers.)

Find out how to get on the Internet and use Lexis-Nexis so I don't feel like the dumbest guy on the block.

Get to bed earlier.

Find out how to program the VCR so I can tape a program I want to see that's going to be on a week from next Tuesday at 10:30 because I'm going to be out that night.

Redo my tattered old personal telephone and address book, eliminating all the names of people I don't talk to anymore because I don't like them, because they moved away, or because they died.

Try to be the kind of person who really knows what he's talking about more often.

Oil the hinges on the closet door in the bedroom that squeaks.

Stop drinking so much coffee.

Call several old friends I haven't called.

Buy a supply of stamps to put on the penny postcards I've bought over the years that need more postage than when I bought them.

Keep everything I'll need for my income tax in one place this year so I'll have it when I want it.

Get more exercise.

HOW TO SLEEP

Considering how much time we spend doing it, little has been written about lying in bed. If you're not sleeping, it changes your whole attitude toward being there. Lying in bed asleep is bliss; lying in bed trying to get to sleep is agony.

It seems like a waste of time to spend seven or eight of every twenty-four of our hours in bed, but that's what we need. I usually get six or less, but then I get sleepy after lunch and ruin my night's sleep with a nap. A five-minute nap seems to mean as much as an hour's sleep at night. I realize I'm luckier than most because I've been on the job for so long at CBS that I have a couch in my office. I'd rather have the couch than a raise or another week off in the summer. Naps are one of the best things in life. They have all the good feeling of a night's sleep without taking so much time.

It seems wrong that most of us cannot lie in bed in the position that should be most restful—flat on our back. If I lie on my back, my mouth drops open and I snore or gurgle. Even worse, I have bad dreams. I only have bad dreams on my back.

I am puzzled over how God thought we'd lie down to sleep when he designed our bodies. It's apparent to me that He didn't mean us to lie on our backs or He wouldn't have me snore or have nightmares when I do it.

He didn't intend us to lie on our side either because He put our shoulders and our arms right where we would be lying. They fall asleep before we do because we put them in such a position under the body that blood can't circulate very well.

There are people who can sleep on their stomach but I don't know any of them intimately enough to have them show me how, so I have no firsthand knowledge of how they do it without suffocating.

There are people who are proud of themselves for preferring a hard bed. They call it "firm." It isn't firm; it's hard, and I dislike hard mattresses. One bed I use in our house in the country is mushy soft. Perfect. It's like sleeping in a hammock.

In the Army, I had to make my bed, and that's what turned me off bed making. You were supposed to have the top blanket pulled so tight that if you dropped a quarter on it from three feet above, it would bounce. I could never do it. Margie sent me an air mattress when I was at Fort Bragg and that worked for a while. Sgt. Fishuk couldn't figure out why, all of a sudden, I was able to make my bed so that a quarter bounced when he flipped it. On the third day, he became suspicious. He found that I was using an air mattress and made me throw it away. Is it any wonder I am psychologically incapable of making a bed?

The only sense in which anyone could call me sexist is, I don't make my bed. I'll often get dinner or wash the dishes, but I don't make beds. If I were alone in the house, I wouldn't make my bed from one year to the next.

A bed I sleep in really needs making, too. I tend to bring the sheet and blanket with me when I turn over. During the night, I suppose I turn both ways an equal number of times, but by morning, my bed is a rumpled mass of tangled sheets and blankets. Whoever makes the bed always seems to tuck it in at the foot. I'm in no position to complain about how the bed is made inasmuch as I won't make it myself, but I don't want the blanket tucked in at the bottom. Tucked-in blankets give me claustrophobia. At home, my sheets are changed once a week, and I hate the first night in them. After that, the sheets are rumpled and comfortable. I know what I'd like to have, but it would be unconscionably expensive to pay some clean person to sleep in my clean sheets the first night to break them in for me.

While I like clean sheets once in a while, pillows are another matter. Perhaps I'll write about pillows some other time. Perhaps not, too.

A FULL HOUSE

Our house is full. There's no longer an empty place to put anything. Whoever designed the house put closets where they thought anyone living there would need one. But no one can decide for anyone else where they need a closet. A house should be built with places to store things that no architect could imagine anyone needing. Some of the closets need closets.

My clothes closets are hanger to hanger with no room in between to squeeze in so much as a necktie. All my hangers have something hanging on them. If I bought new hangers, I'd buy new clothes.

My dresser drawers are full of clean shirts from the laundry and frayed shirts to wear Saturdays. I have more frayed shirts than Saturdays on which to wear them. I used to wear clean, un-frayed shirts just once to the office, then they went to the laundry. It costs $1.50 to have a shirt washed now so recently I've taken to wearing a shirt twice.

My sock drawer overflows with eight balled pairs and seven single socks for which I can find no mate. Some of them have been single for years. I don't throw them out because I still hold out hope that a mate will show up some day.

I went up to the attic yesterday and it's filled with clothes too good to throw away but too old to wear. There are suitcases I don't dare open up here and boxes of Christmas tree ornaments that haven't been used since I started storing ornaments in the garage eight years ago.

In the front part of the basement, which I use for an office, three of the drawers in the five-drawer filing cabinet are filled with old tax returns. I know I could throw out 1981 without any danger of being hauled in by the IRS for a review. However, I write for a living and there are valuable tidbits in there about my life that year that might be useful in my biography—which I'll be writing any minute now. As soon as I clean out my closets.

The drawers in the dresser in Brian's room are full, although Brian left home twenty years ago when he got a job in Rochester, and there isn't much of his stuff left. I noticed a new pair of pajamas in the bottom drawer, which I think are mine. I forget when I bought them, but I don't need new pajamas. I like old pajamas. I wear my pajamas long after most people would have thrown them out. A missing button in front bothers me but a ragged edge on the sleeve does not.

In casting about for someone to blame for my storage problem, I've settled on architects. Our house was built in 1888, so the architect is long gone. It is apparent that he tried to outguess future occupants about how much stuff they'd have and where they'd put it. Architects think they can plan a place for everything and they think we'll put everything in its place. That's not the way things work in anyone's house.

In my office, there are boxes of scripts I've written over the past fifty years. For five years, I wrote a ten-minute radio show five days a week and the scripts take up five feet of shelf space.

My advice to young people is, when you buy a house, don't ask how many bedrooms there are. Find out how many closets it has.

THE V-E DAY I KNOW

We all like knowing something other people don't. I take smug satisfaction every year when May 8 is called "V-E Day" from knowing that Victory in Europe came May 7, not May 8. It isn't much but it's mine. Victory in Europe was achieved the minute German Gen. Alfred Jodl signed the surrender papers in a room on the second floor of an undistinguished school building, the Ecole Professionale, in Reims, France.

May 8 got its official status as V-E Day because Dwight Eisenhower, then a four-star General Eisenhower, promised the Russians he wouldn't release information of the German surrender to the Allies until after they had also surrendered to the Russians. That was scheduled for the following day and that's how May 8, not May 7, got to be called V-E Day. If Eisenhower had been in charge, Christmas might be Dec. 26.

After years of war, the whole world was waiting anxiously for the word that it was over. After the D-Day landings on June 6, 1944, American soldiers, with help from the British and Canadians, had fought their way across Normandy and into Paris on Aug. 25. The U.S. 9th Division crossed the Rhine on March 7 and headed across Germany for a meeting with the Russian army that was squeezing the Germans from the other direction. The two forces met at the town of Torgau on the Elbe River on April 25, 1945, and it was apparent to everyone that the war was winding down and the Germans would have to give up.

On the night of May 6, 1945, seventeen reporters were flown by Supreme Headquarters Allied Expeditionary Force from Paris to Reims, France. They realized their mission was to report the surrender they knew was imminent. Before being taken to Reims, the reporters were sworn to secrecy. They promised not to write the story until they were given permission by Allied headquarters.

Seventeen reporters came to a large classroom in the school at 2:10 on the morning of May 7. At 2:40 the Germans and Americans came in for the signing. The meeting lasted about five minutes, just time enough for several generals to sign the surrender papers. There were four cameramen. One had brought a ladder and was perched on top of that to get a better view of the participants at the table. Others were precariously perched on chairs. The seventeen reporters were standing taking notes.

After the brief signing ceremony, the reporters were ushered out of the room, put on a bus for the airport and flown back to Paris with a great story in their pockets they were forbidden to tell.

It was my first exposure to a dilemma that every reporter is faced with at some time in his life. Here they were with great and important information that the whole world was waiting for but they were inhibited from writing it for what was, basically, a political reason—good relations with the Russians.

One reporter, Ed Kennedy of the Associated Press, couldn't wait. He made the decision to break his promise. He wrote the story and dispatched it to AP headquarters in New York from which it was sent around the world. Kennedy later said he thought the story was too important to keep to himself one minute longer. The world read about the surrender in their newspapers in fifty different languages the next morning, May 8.

The sixteen reporters who had lived by their promise were furious. Ed Kennedy was banished from the company of other reporters. His credentials were revoked by the Army, and he was shipped back to New

York in disgrace. But his story was printed around the world while the rest of the reporters sat with theirs in their pockets.

I was as angry as anyone but, wrong as I thought Kennedy was that day when he released the story, I am not so certain today. The world had been waiting five years for the end of that war. There was no element of military security and keeping that information from the worried world for one more day was probably wrong. It is almost always wrong for a reporter to withhold information for any public relations reason. Ed Kennedy may have been right. V-E Day was May 7.

FUGEDDABOUTIT

Some days, it seems as though I have so much to do I can't get anything done. It happens a lot around Christmas.

When I left for the office this morning, a red light appeared on the dashboard of my car that said, "Service soon." I've been meaning to read the manual, but whenever I get in the car I'm going someplace and don't have time. I'm driving to the country this weekend, though, and ought to take the car in before I go but I have some other things to do first.

When I left the house today, I dumped a suit, a pair of slacks and a sweater in the back of the car to take to the cleaners, but I had so much to do I decided not to stop.

My hair is too long and has been for about two weeks. My barber is over near several department stores, so maybe I'll get my hair cut and do some Christmas shopping at lunchtime—tomorrow, though.

I don't even want to think about Christmas. I have to get presents for Martha, Emily, Ellen, Brian, Cecile, Alexis, Ben, Justin, Emma, Katherine, Beryl, Leo, Les and Nancy. Just getting to a store is hard and they probably won't have anything I think is right, anyway. As usual, I'll probably wait until it's too late to have anything sent, so I'll have to take it with me.

I should put the Christmas wreath on the door this weekend and string the Christmas lights on the hedge. I hope I can find the lights. I may have put them in the attic. If I get the chance, I'll go up and look for them. Come to think of it, though, the lights may be on top of that shelf in the garage. I keep the Christmas tree in the garage so it doesn't get snowed on before we put it up in the living room Christmas Eve. I'm worried about the garage because it isn't heated. The automatic garage door caught on some of the insulated ceiling panels last summer and tore off one of them. There are pipes up there that bring heat to the back bedroom and they're exposed now and could freeze. I ought to get that insulation panel replaced and get a plumber to put some radiator pipes in the garage. I'm not sure who does that or how much it would cost. I don't even want to think about that now.

As if I didn't have enough things to do around the house, I've got more than usual to do in the office.

60 Minutes is going to need two extra pieces next week because they want to get the Christmas and New Year's day shows put together early. I'll have to think of something to do and then shoot the pieces. I should get my hair cut before I do them.

Next to my computer I keep an in/out file tray. There must be twenty-five letters. They're either things like phone bills or messages from old friends I feel guilty about not answering. I've set those things aside for two weeks, though, so I guess another day or two won't hurt.

If I can get my Christmas cards out, that will satisfy some of those letters I should have written. I'm not sure where our Christmas card list is. Last year, I added the names of people who sent me a card even though I didn't send them one.

Some of the things I put off because I've had a cold. My nasal passages have been stuffed up for weeks, so I called my doctor and he gave me a prescription, which I took to the drugstore last Tuesday. They couldn't fill it right away, so I paid for it but I haven't had time to go back and get it.

I love Christmas but I can't wait for it to be over.

FOOD FOR HOLIDAY THOUGHTS

We all look for that perfect day when we have enough to do but not too much. There's a fine line and we usually cross it. At this time of year, most of us have so much to do that there isn't time to sit back and enjoy our holiday.

We had a cocktail party for sixty friends and family on the Friday before Christmas, but we think seventy-five showed up. It was good except two of our closest friends were left off the invitation list by mistake. No amount of apologizing helps in a case like that.

I made eggnog with eggs, cream and plenty of nog (I use rum and bourbon). Some people make the mistake of thinking it's a toy drink and it is not. I put nutmeg and a grater next to the punch bowl. I don't know what nutmeg is but I like what it tastes like in eggnog.

We had fifteen family members for most of nine meals and grandson Justin brought his girlfriend, Gayle, which made us sixteen. It was our second Christmas without Margie and we don't get over missing her. I jerry-rigged a board with legs and fastened it to the end of the dining room table so it would accommodate everyone.

Food for sixteen people, three meals a day for three days is a lot of food and a lot of work. Martha, the most organized of the four children, drew up a chart listing who was on duty for what job and stuck it on the refrigerator door but no one paid much attention to it. After the guests left the party Friday, we had two huge dishes of lasagna left. Martha had made them in advance. They were good with a salad and easy.

Emily's daughter, my granddaughter Alexis, had to get back to Washington to be at work for Fox at 6 A.M. the day after Christmas, so we decided to have our Christmas turkey dinner Saturday night so she'd be in on it. Emily brought the turkey from a farm near Boston. Less than half of the stuffing went into the bird and the rest was baked separately in an open pan. It was better than that cooked inside the turkey.

For the first time, Brian carved. I relinquished my role reluctantly because being the carver puts you in a special position of authority, but I conceded that he did a better job than I would have. I've done it about fifty times over the years but still have a hard time finding where to cut the joint of the drumstick and thigh so that they break off and leave the breast easy to slice.

Ellen made the cranberry sauce and argued with Emily about whether to put slivered almonds in it. Ellen was adamant about not doing that, but I noticed that when it came to the table in the cut glass dish, there were almonds in the sauce.

There were several desserts, principal among them a dense, lemon pound cake called a "62nd Street Cake," named after the great baker Maida Heatter, who first produced it in her shop on 62nd Street in New York. My sister, Nancy, has always made our 62nd Street Cake.

There were a lot of arguments. One ensued Christmas Eve when I insisted on grinding coffee beans instead of using the coffee in cans people had brought. Ellen's British husband, Les, was not interested in the argument. He quietly made himself "a nice cup of tea."

For Christmas dinner, we cooked a huge roast beef. I made Yorkshire pudding, which cooked in the fat after the beef had been in the pan for several hours. (Yorkshire pudding is the same recipe as popovers.) Emily peeled, then braised several pounds of pearl onions until they were brown. For dessert, we had my specialty, peppermint stick ice cream. I crush and melt in milk and cream one pound of peppermint candy canes, which produces a lovely pink mixture. I put that in my six-quart ice cream freezer for about forty minutes and serve it in chilled dishes with slightly bitter homemade chocolate sauce.

Breakfast was hard because not everyone showed up at the same time. I made waffles one morning in a waffle iron we've had for fifty years. The kids always used to fill the holes with maple syrup.

There are still leftovers in the refrigerator, which Les refers to with a British term as "lurkies"—food that lurks in the 'fridge.

PART EIGHT

On Money

My family and friends think of me as cheap. I think of myself as careful with money.

OUR POOR ARE RICH

We should help the poor because we're rich and they aren't but then after we've helped them, it seems to me we have the right to ask a lot of people of the world, who resent the success of our civilization, why they haven't done more to help themselves.

Men and women from the poorest, most underdeveloped countries make their way to the United States and prosper in our society. Professional and business people from economically retarded countries come here and frequently distinguish themselves. Individuals are not responsible for national failures. So who is?

Almost all of Europe, South America, Russia, China and Japan have working economies, stable governments, police forces, a judicial system, roads and public services like water and electricity. At the same time, dozens of countries in other parts of the world do not have the amenities of civilization. The United Nations has estimated that half the people on earth live in poverty.

If it weren't for television, which occasionally shows it to us, we wouldn't understand poverty at all. Poverty to us means a handful of dysfunctional homeless people in our town. Few are in danger of starving or freezing to death. Real poverty means whole countries whose people not only don't have jobs they don't have an organized society, houses, food, clean water, places to go to the bathroom. Forget bedrooms, two-car garages, swimming pools, refrigerators, central heating and air conditioning. They don't have houses.

Poverty anywhere in the world is a concern to us because we're nice guys and we're pained to see hungry and unhappy humans anywhere. We are also concerned because it's only human of the world's poor to resent our prosperity, and we don't like being hated.

You look for reasons why so many countries are what we euphemistically call "backward." Many of the most depressed countries are under the heel of some oppressive potentate who keeps himself rich and the people poor. However, it isn't easy to determine whether a dictator in a poor country is a cause or a result of the nation's problems.

It's a mystery why the people living in the warmest parts of the earth are often the worst off. You'd think that not having to expend money, energy or resources staying warm would be an advantage but that doesn't seem to be so. Africa is the warmest continent but it has many of the least successful societies.

Warm weather should give the people of Africa and the Arab countries a head start on prosperity. Even in the United States, for no discernible reason, the South was for years the poorest and most backward part of the country. In the past 50 years, the South has developed into one of the most prosperous parts of our country. Maybe it's coincidence, but the change seems to have been concomitant with the development of air conditioning. Maybe we ought to raise the money to air condition the earth. It would be cheaper than war.

While I'm not comfortable using the term "Arab" because the definition of the word is vague, many Arab countries are not among the world's most successful. If it were not for oil, they'd probably be destitute because they haven't created any kind of economy for themselves independent of that natural resource.

There was a time in history when the Arab world led all others in the knowledge of geometry, astronomy, chemistry and medicine. Europeans in the Middle Ages learned a lot of what they knew of science from the Arabs. The world has not learned much from Arab countries in recent centuries.

I don't know how it can be done, but it's important that we find out why the people of some parts of the world prosper while others live lives desperately devoid of pleasure or the basic necessities of the good life. You wonder why the poor cling to life as tenaciously as do those of us who have a life so clearly worth clinging to.

IT CALLS FOR A REVOLUTION

The oddball poet and professional character, Gertrude Stein, said, "Money is always there but the pockets change. It is not in the same pockets after a change, and that is all there is to say about money." I always remember but probably ought to forget this statement because there's a lot more than that to say about money.

On a dozen occasions, I've addressed the graduating class at a high school or college. All the kids want is their diplomas so they don't listen to what you have to say, but you're supposed to say something important anyway. One of the things I usually say, trying to sound important, is that I hope, when they finish school, they'll set out to make something other than money.

Enron, the seventh-largest company in the United States, just went bankrupt, basically because it didn't make anything but money. Enron stock fell from $90 to 26 cents per share. Top executives who knew what was about to happen sold their stock while the price was still high. The other 20,000 employees lost most of their savings because they were not allowed to sell their stock and abandon the sinking ship.

Despite the hundreds of news stories about Enron, if you asked most Americans today what the company made, they still wouldn't know. I can tell you. Enron made money for a small handful of dishonest executives. There was no product. The company was a collection of natural gas salesmen and a small collection of sleight-of-hand money managers who stole millions from the public, quite possibly without breaking the law.

Except for the superlatives involved in its demise—Biggest Bankruptcy in U.S. History—the story of Enron Corp. isn't very interesting. The details of what happened are vague, buried under layers of obfuscated deals, reports, accounting and mergers that no one but someone in the money business could understand.

What is interesting is the absolutely disgraceful connection, made with huge sums of money, between Enron and elected officials. You begin with President George W. Bush and next drop all the way down to Vice President Dick Cheney. The details of the connection are unknown but certainly exist. In 2000, Enron gave half a million dollars to Bush's presidential campaign.

While three quarters of all the money the company gave went to Republicans, one quarter went to Democrats—and it wasn't peanuts. Because they got less, does this make Democrats more honest? The chairman at the first Senate hearing was Senator Joseph Lieberman, who must be relatively honest because he hasn't taken any money from Enron since the $2,000 he got in 1994.

After George W. Bush and Cheney, the next highest public official to have benefited from Enron's generosity is former Attorney General John Ashcroft, who received about $58,000 from the company for his failed Senate re-election bid in Missouri.

If we all weren't so dumb and happy and relatively prosperous, we'd start a revolution in this country.

FREE ENTERPRISE ANARCHY

Enron did as much to make capitalism look bad in the year 2002 as Joseph Stalin's Soviet dictatorship did in the 1930s to destroy any favorable opinion idealists in the world had about communism.

Socialism still has the communist stigma attached to it because of the disastrous Soviet experiment. It will be interesting to see if Enron and other corporate giants do any lasting damage to our confidence in free enterprise. It is unlikely Enron was the only major corporation that hid its devious financial dealings behind the capitalist curtain.

There are too many ways for a big company to avoid paying its fair share of taxes. However, any company that doesn't engage in what most of us would call cheating—even if it isn't strictly speaking illegal—is at a competitive disadvantage. By employing such practices, corporate giants shift the tax burden to individuals who don't have offshore (off tax) bank accounts.

There must be thousands of corporations shaving their taxes with bookkeeping tricks of which the average citizen knows nothing. They give free enterprise a bad name and make ordinary Americans yearn for more, not less, government oversight of Big Business.

It's really strange that while the religions so many people profess to believe in are generous in their philosophies about the distribution of money, the majority of religious Americans approve of the dog-eat-dog economic premises of capitalism. We are all becoming more aware that too many people are not getting a fair share.

A relatively small number of people are smarter, more energetic and more capable than others, and they end up getting 90 percent of all the good stuff. Without discouraging this able minority, we have to find a way to keep the Enrons of our capitalist society from stealing so much that they turn all of us off the free enterprise system.

There are still lots of great corporations making big profits from producing good products, but in recent years, too many American companies have been making nothing but money. Their only product is on paper; they don't make anything but stock market statistics. They shuffle their books, buy out small competitors, borrow and loan money so fast that bookkeepers can't keep up.

It seems inevitable that more people will begin thinking we have to devise a better system than either communism or capitalism for distributing the good things on earth. The great power of big business is out of control.

ALL HAIL THE RICH!

We Americans wave the flag and admire our own greatness but fortunately we have a mitigating tendency to be critical of ourselves. We agree with the articles we read about ourselves saying we're decadent. We know we have too many luxuries and spend most of our effort trying to acquire more of them.

We nod, agree with the criticism and keep working to get all we can. There's no question that we have an unlimited appetite for the limited supply of good things on earth. Neither should there be any argument that, with a lot of exceptions, the most capable people get most of the good things. These are the people we call "the rich." We call anyone rich who makes a lot more than we do. We have a natural aversion to the rich. We hate them but we want to be one of them.

The rich are the bad guys. If anybody needs a PR agent, it's rich, successful Americans. We take great satisfaction in complaining about the kind of people we're working so hard to be like.

You never hear anyone say anything nice about the wealthy. When politicians talk about taxes, they want to raise them on the rich. Politicians never say they want to reduce taxes on the rich. Something like 6 percent of Americans pay more than 50 percent of all personal income taxes the government takes in. The top 1 percent of people pay 36 percent of all income tax. You'd think it would dampen their interest in being rich but it only whets their appetite for more.

The number of luxuries we enjoy can seem ridiculous in a world where so many people are starving to death. Expensive clothing, jewelry, pampered pets, five-bedroom homes for two people—do we need all this in a world where so many people don't have enough to eat? Should we feel guilty because 20 million American families own three cars while there are whole countries still using donkey carts?

There are good things to be said about the rich that no one ever says. So help me for saying so, but I don't think the poor work as hard as the rich. Is this blasphemous? Will I go to hell for thinking so? Is this just an arrogant American attitude? You don't see a lot of lazy rich people.

I cannot stop thinking that people seeking to acquire the luxuries of life work harder to get them than people working for the bare necessities. Many people work an eight-hour day, knock off and go home.

They sleep and watch television until they get up and go to work to-morrow again the next day. They have enough to buy what they need to eat and pay for a roof over their head.

The appetite successful people have for more has created more, and that's not all bad. There's no limit to what they want and try to get. They are never satisfied because as soon as they get one thing, they want something else. They want to go out on the lake, so they buy a rowboat. First thing we know they want one with an outboard motor. What they really want is a yacht.

Desire is a great motivating force. The fact that our desires are so often for things that provide physical pleasure doesn't diminish their importance as the principle driving force behind American business. We probably ought to have some motivating force superior to greed but we can't seem to find one. Schools haven't taught one. Religion hasn't come up with anything. The businessman who goes to church on Sunday is no less acquisitive at work Monday morning than one who never goes.

We ought to start being nicer to rich people.

THE BILLION-DOLLAR POOH

One of history's great injustices is how often the great artists of any age—painters, musicians and writers—fail to make a comfortable living from their work. Long after Gauguin, Beethoven and Shakespeare were gone, their work still produces billions of dollars. In their lifetime they got small change.

Listening to the radio last weekend I was fascinated by a report involving literary rights and the Walt Disney Company. It's always fun when you know some things about the story that the reporter telling it does not.

Amy Wallace, a very good writer for *Los Angeles* magazine, was giving details of the problem Disney is having with a lawsuit brought by

Shirley Slesinger Lasswell. Her husband, Steve Slesinger, who died in 1953, owned the rights to A. A. Milne's characters, including Winnie-the-Pooh.

Apparently, Pooh is making more money, billions a year, for Disney than Mickey Mouse and, while Disney has been paying about $12 million a year to Steve's widow, she claims that's peanuts compared with what they ought to be paying her. She is known in Hollywood now as "The Pooh Lady."

I knew Steve Slesinger well. At the end of World War II, I had written a book about my experiences with the Army newspaper, the *Stars and Stripes*, with my friend Bud Hutton. Steve was operating as a sort of literary entrepreneur and we took the book to him to see if he thought there was any chance of selling it for a movie.

Over our first lunch together, Steve told us how he got started. When he finished college, his parents gave him $2,000 as a graduation gift. He decided to go to London. While he was there, he sought out A. A. Milne. He had always loved Winnie-the-Pooh. This was about 1930, the beginning of the Depression, and prices on everything were down. Steve offered to buy Winnie-the-Pooh rights in the United States for $1,500. A. A. Milne was not rolling in money at the time and he accepted the offer. It was Steve's $1,500 that has, since about 1960, been producing $12 million a year for his dissatisfied widow.

Steve was easily likeable and disarming. In his back offices, an artist, Fred Harman, worked on a cartoon strip called *Red Ryder*, which appeared in 400 newspapers. Amy Wallace said the strip was Steve's idea, but I believe Fred Harman took it to Steve, who then bought the rights from him. That's the way Steve worked. Fred always said Steve paid him "about $60 a week."

Steve was a merchandizing genius. He went to the Daisy Air Rifle Company and sold them a deal to make a Red Ryder BB gun. In Hollywood, Republic Pictures agreed to pay Steve for the rights to make ten B movies based on *Red Ryder*. Fred Harman, meanwhile, was cranking out the strip in Steve's back room for $60 a week.

Steve called one day to say that MGM was buying our book for $55,000 and we were going to work at MGM as screen writers for $1,500 a week. We were two young men just out of the Army where we'd been making $135 a month as staff sergeants and MGM was going to pay us what seemed like half the money in the world.

We were so naive as business people that Bud and I hardly noticed that Steve was taking 50 percent of the $55,000 and half of our salary. It never occurred to us to resent him.

It's hard to side with a greedy corporation like Disney in this lawsuit. But when the creator of all this, A. A. Milne, was paid a mere $1,500 for his genius and sixty years later the widow of a smart operator who had nothing whatsoever to do with the literary invention of Winnie-the-Pooh is unhappy with $12 million a year, something seems wrong.

NAME LOTTERY LOSERS

There is nothing more stimulating to the brain than getting mad. I am easily angered (grade school English teachers correct me when I use "mad" for "angry") and there are so many things in the world to get mad about that my brain is seldom at ease.

Nothing so regularly angers me as much as stories about lottery winners. There were big headlines recently about the man in West Virginia, Andrew Whittaker, who won $315 million.

There ought to be a law forbidding newspapers, radio or television stations from reporting the name of a lottery winner unless, at the same time, they listed the name of every single loser. The names of everyone who bought a losing ticket for the same lottery won by Mr. Whittaker would not fit in all the pages of any newspaper. Governments are empowered to do for people what people are not able to do for themselves. They should protect idiots from their natural inclination to take chances with astronomically high odds.

If you wonder who buys lottery tickets, look at the people who line up to buy them. They are invariably the poorest, least-educated, most unemployed among us. Some people on welfare wait for their checks, not to buy groceries but to buy lottery tickets. I feel sorry for them but I also think we should help them by making it impossible for them to waste their money—and ours—on lottery tickets.

This all came to me this morning, driving to work, when I heard a radio commercial imploring people to buy tickets for the New York State lottery. When I got to the office, I set out to find how much the state spends on commercials like the one I heard. Last year, the state spent $24 million on lottery advertising. Am I the only one outraged to find that the state is spending that kind of money inducing its citizens to participate in so stupid a thing as buying lottery tickets? Originally, proponents of a state-operated lottery said that people were going to gamble whether it was legal or not. The mob bosses were already making a fortune on the illegal numbers racket. They argued that as long as people were going to gamble anyway, the state, not the mob bosses, should profit from it.

If people were going to gamble anyway, how come the state has to spend $24 million a year talking them into it with advertising? State officials promised to do all sorts of good things for education with lottery money. Have you noticed a big improvement in our schools because of all the lottery money pouring in?

Gambling is a national sickness that has become epidemic in the last twenty-five years. Thirty-seven states now have lotteries and twenty-nine allow gambling casinos. It wasn't long ago that gambling was restricted to a few places like Las Vegas. Atlantic City, a once prosperous seashore resort, somehow lost its luster, went broke and talked New Jersey into letting it open an East Coast gambling operation to compete with Las Vegas. Then some smart operators, preying on the guilt feeling we have as a nation about the desperate condition of Indians in our country, opened "Indian" casinos, most of which are about as Indian as I am.

Lotteries are immoral and stupid. They produce nothing. It is the transfer of money from the dumb poor to the smart rich. It undermines the American work ethic of which we're so proud. It suggests that anyone can be successful and live handsomely without working for it. All he or she has to do is guess the right number and retire for life.

THE HORSE RACE ECONOMY

Predicting whether the economy is going to get better or worse is about as much a science as picking the winner of a horse race. The race may actually be an easier call because at least you know the horses are honest.

Just when things look as if they're getting better, they get worse, and just when things look as though they're getting worse, they get better. The decline in employment is more under President Bush than it's been in twenty years. This is the first time since the 1930s in which the actual number of people working is less than in the previous administration.

The last time there were actual job losses for four years in a row, Herbert Hoover was President. The total reached 7.7 percent. Under Franklin D. Roosevelt, the number of jobs increased by 18 percent. The job loss statistics today are amazing—and don't think you're not going to hear about them at election time. The number of jobs increased by 22 percent under Bill Clinton's presidency, the biggest jump in history. Under George W. Bush, overall employment is down 2.37 percent. It may not be his fault and Bill Clinton may have been lucky, but Democratic candidates won't be telling you that.

A headline this week read: "Jobless rate at 9-year high."

Of all the things about the economy I don't understand, I understand unemployment the least. There isn't any work that needs to be done? Is that what unemployment means? I look at the business I'm in and see nothing but work that needs to be done. I look at my own personal and home life and see nothing but jobs that need doing that I can't get anyone to do.

Too many of those things that need to be done at home are things I either don't know how to do or they're things that would take me longer than is worth my time. We all draw the line somewhere. My hourly wage is more than I'd be willing to pay myself to do the work. I'm looking for someone down the wage scale to do it for me. It's a cold, cruel world.

The reason the unemployment rate is so high is that a lot of people looking for work have a higher opinion of their value than the people who have work that needs to be done have of it. It's also true that many people draw a line between blue- and white-collar jobs, and those who think of themselves as white-collar, college-educated, never consider doing physical work, no matter how badly they need a job.

It's clear that we need more people who know how to do things with their hands. We should forget this collar color division. We have enough administrators, computer technicians, sales engineers and board-of-directors directors. What we're short of are people who actually know how to make something, do something, or fix something. We long ago passed the point where the hourly wage for a skilled craftsman exceeds that of the average office worker.

I took my 1966 Sunbeam Tiger to a mechanic last week because the brakes weren't working. He told me it would be a while before he could get at it because he lost the two men who'd been helping him. He was working alone. He'd hire a capable mechanic in a minute, he said, but he can't find one because almost everyone goes to college now and they don't teach what he needs done in college.

I don't know how we ever got thinking that physical labor was demeaning. I wish more colleges would set out to convince students that reading good literature, knowing something about history and philosophy and having a good education is not inimical to working with your hands.

IT'S THE ECONOMY, STUPID

The politicians running for President don't really give us much to go on. They make it hard to decide who we want to vote for. Most of us feel more strongly about who we're against than who we're for. It's easier to get someone to say they hate one politician than that they like another.

Polls show that Americans are more worried about the economy now than about Iraq, but most of us are economic ignoramuses. We know, in a general sort of way, whether things are going well or badly because we see the headlines about stock prices being up or down. Economic theory eludes us, so we don't really know what we're worried about.

When I was quite young—before I went to college—I had a temporary love affair with the ideas of an American journalist writing from Moscow named John Reed. He was Harvard educated, a brilliant writer—and a communist. He was the only American apologist for the kind of government that ruled Russia after the revolution. I wasn't smart enough to be a communist—or a capitalist.

I got over my infatuation with John Reed, but I've never given up my suspicion that there's something wrong with the capitalist, free enterprise system. Selfishness is the God of Capitalism. It doesn't seem right and it's a disappointment to me that it works. Success is the only thing in capitalism's favor. There is no intellectual defense for it.

In the real world, businesses cheat to get ahead and the quality of the product always gets worse when a big company takes over a smaller one. Unfortunately, however, we can't devise a system that works any better.

As early as the late 1800s, a handful of businessmen like the Vanderbilts, the Rockefellers, DuPonts and Morgans had accumulated so much money, while millions had none, that it became apparent to lawmakers something was wrong with pure, unregulated, winner-take-all capitalism. The business tycoons were known affectionately as "The Robber Barons." To curb their excesses, Congress passed the Sherman Antitrust Act in 1890.

The Antitrust Act provided government regulation designed to prevent a big, rich company that could afford to do it, from selling its product below cost until the smaller companies selling the same product were forced out of business. At that point, with no competition, the corporate giant could charge anything it wanted.

Most people in business are personally honest, but it's sad and true that most of our laws pertaining to business assume that business would cheat the consumer if it were not inhibited by law. What's sad is the assumption is true. The ethical standards of too many businesses fall short of the personal standards of the people running them. I don't know why that is. Kenneth Lay, the chairman of Enron, stole millions but wouldn't pick your pocket or cheat in a poker game.

The biggest problem anyone like me has in supporting government regulation of anything is not economic theory or Republican inclinations. What's wrong is the assumption that elected officials are smart enough to run business any better than businessmen. (I call women in business "businessmen.")

The fact is neither pure socialism nor pure capitalism works. So we lean one way or the other and draw the line between being conservative and liberal on business issues. If the administration is dominated by Democrats, we draw the line one place. If it's dominated by Republicans, we draw the line another place. President Bush has tried, successfully, to draw the line closer to where the business community likes it. As an elected Republican President, he gets to do that.

What we all have to conclude when we vote is that the success of our country depends, not on any system, but on having honest, smart people running it. They may be there but they're hard to find among campaigning politicians.

RICH MAN, POOR MAN, BEGGAR MAN

Bill Gates is the richest man in the world. I wonder if he thinks about that in the middle of the night when he can't sleep because of worrying about something other than money?

Forbes magazine, once owned by one of the richest men in the world, Malcolm Forbes, publishes as annual list of the richest people. About two years before he died, Malcolm Forbes invited me to have lunch with him in the small dining room in the magazine's offices in New York. That's about as close as I've ever come to hanging out with someone really rich.

I have met seven of the 587 people on the Forbes list, including No. 1, Bill Gates, and I liked all of them. It's probably easier to like them if you don't have to do business with them. But considering that rich men are usually the bad guys in any movie they're in, they all seemed nice and normal to me. I don't know whether they're proud and pleased to be on the list or would prefer prosperous anonymity.

There are fifty-three women on the richest list, although some of those inherited their money from fathers or husbands. One of the great exceptions is J. K. Rowling, author of the Harry Potter books. (Her name is Joanne Kathleen Rowling. I never heard why she uses just her initials.) Her books have sold 250 million copies and, at about $18 each, that begins to add up even without what she makes on the movies.

Eight of the ten richest people are American, including an incredible five Waltons of Arkansas and one from Texas, owners of the Wal-Mart stores. Forbes doesn't publish a list of the 587 poorest people in the world, although some of them probably live in Arkansas, too.

Next to us, Germany has the most people on the richest list. There are a surprising number of Russians and a lot of potentate types. (It is important to know that 1 billion is 1,000 million, not merely 100 million.)

There are a lot of interesting things about rich people. For one thing, if a man is really rich, he doesn't carry much cash around in his pocket. You'd think he would but he doesn't. I guess if you know how much money you have, you don't have a whole lot. My rich friend Steve Slesinger would go into a restaurant he'd never been in before, order meals for four people and when the waiter came with the check he'd say, "I don't have any money. Send me a bill, will you please?" I was reaching for my wallet to see if I could help out, but the restaurants always accepted his request to bill him.

I grew up during the depth of the Depression and it has influenced my attitude toward money all my life—when I didn't have much and now that I have quite a bit. It was good for me. I'll drive several miles out of my way to buy gas for a few cents less a gallon. I'm annoyed with grandchildren who go to the refrigerator, take out a soft drink, take a few gulps from the can or bottle and then leave the rest of it on the kitchen counter to die un-drunk.

The funny thing about my attitude toward money (when I step back and look at myself) is that I'm more careful with small amounts of money than with large amounts. It irritates me that women spend so much on shoes. I don't get used to how much my own grown children spend on things I'd do without. Emily stayed with us last weekend and did some shopping. Last night, I opened the refrigerator and found a pint of raspberries for which she paid $4.30.

I'll bet Bill Gates doesn't spend that kind of money on raspberries.

THE SAVING GRACE

I save things. It comes from a time when we didn't have as much money as we needed. The Great Depression had its effect on me even though my father made $8,000 a year during the 1930s, which was a lot in those days. That made me the rich kid on our block, but I was aware of my friends who were not so lucky. My bad years, during which I had my own personal depressions, were 1949 and 1956.

My car takes 89 octane gas. When 87 octane gas costs $3.25 a gallon, 89 octane costs $3.39 and 93 octane costs $3.51, I sometimes buy five gallons of 87 octane and five gallons of 93 octane which gives me ten gallons of 90 octane gas at about $3.38 a gallon.

Money is not the only thing I save. I save things. I save any piece of paper I've written on. It's the writing, not the paper that I'm saving. I dream of immortality for anything I write, even if it's drivel. I save elastic bands, paper clips, coffee cans and big envelopes that came with something in them which I threw out.

Why do we throw out perfectly good manila envelopes that have been used once? There are convenient labels with glue that easily conceal any previous address and a once-mailed envelope is almost as good as new.

I refold and save big, brown paper bags, cardboard boxes, empty Altoid cans and old jelly jars with screw tops. I keep the boxes new shoes come in—sometimes for longer than I keep the shoes.

Our refrigerator is loaded with things I've kept—commonly known as leftovers. I spend generously on airtight plastic bags and the freezer contains a treasure trove of half-eaten meals. More than a year ago, my stingy little heart almost broke when a storm caused a power shortage that warmed the contents of our refrigerator and turned all the good things stored inside into a compost heap fit for nothing but the garbage pail. Never mind the leftovers I even lost an unopened pound of butter.

It is inconsistent, even paradoxical, that while I save pennies to the point of being cheap, I almost always buy the most expensive brand, style or kind of anything. I equate high price with quality, even though this isn't always the case. Poor people pay the most for the worst. If there are two items that appear to be similar but one costs several dollars more, I buy that one. A high price is to me is a guarantee that it's best. I carry this belief to ridiculous lengths. If a store had identical pairs of socks, one priced at $6 and the other at $8, I'd pay the $8 because of my unfounded conviction that expensive is better.

Even though I buy expensive things, I save so much, I think I'm gaining on them.

ALL PLAY AND NO WORK

One of the things I wish we'd get over is the idea that someone who works with his hands and does what is known as manual labor cannot possibly have a good education. There has always been a vague stigma attached to those who work with their hands.

Because the time seems to be coming, or may already have arrived, when plumbers, house painters, carpenters, mechanics, electricians and bricklayers make more than teachers, sales clerks, poets, editors or in-surance salesmen. Then the social distinctions will probably disappear.

We have a great need for more people who know how to do some-thing more important than selling something. We have to encourage more bright young people with an education to get into the hands-on jobs. Putting a new bedroom over the garage takes as much brains as managing an office payroll.

Anyone who owns a home has to laugh when someone talks about not being able to find work. The hard job for a homeowner is finding anyone to pay who knows how to do anything. If someone can't get a job, the chances are he or she is looking for the wrong job. If more people knew how to do what we all need to have done, there wouldn't be any unemployment. More English majors ought to buy themselves a tall ladder in addition to a computer when they graduate from college and learn how to fix a leaky roof. They can read Shakespeare or browse the Internet when they get home at night.

There are 10,000 little jobs that are short of people who know how to do them. The gutters on the roof by our kitchen door leak and it's hard to find anyone to fix them. I have a suit sitting in my closet because I caught the pocket on a doorknob and tore it. It's easier to buy a new suit than to find a tailor. The gas cap on my new car won't stay closed. When I took it to the dealer, there was an attendant outside showing me where to get in a line of fifteen cars waiting to be checked in before they were serviced.

The people who know how to do anything are all so busy they can't take a small job. Real estate agents ready to sell you a house are more numerous than people who fix gutters. No one wants to repair anything. Throw it away and buy a new one. There's no shortage of jobs. There's a shortage of people willing and able to do them.

I don't even know what happened to kids who used to make pocket money after school cutting grass in the summer, raking leaves in the fall and shoveling snow in the winter. They don't come to our front door looking for work. I guess they're all home now on the Internet accom-plishing nothing.

Our inventors, in collaboration with our manufacturers, have produced a great number of labor-saving machines, tools and other devices. But no machine is ever going to replace the guy who has a capable pair of hands and knows how to use them. Machines produce new things but they aren't good at fixing old ones because every fix-it job is different. A machine doesn't know how to handle a problem it has never seen before. That's why there's never going to be a time when we don't need people who know how and are willing to work with their hands.

There is no meter, no mechanical gauge by which we can judge satisfaction, but it seems certain that it is as satisfying to complete a physical job as a mental one.

We need different qualities in different people. We need more plumbers, carpenters, mechanics and electricians than we need poets, but we need poets, too. From the poetry you see in periodicals, it appears to me as if there are more bad poets than there are bad electricians or bad carpenters. I wish we could encourage the bad poets to turn their attention to fixing leaky toilets or cutting broken limbs off high up places in big trees on our front lawns.

FREE ENTERPRISE IS EXPENSIVE

The free enterprise system may be best but it sure is heartless.

Like most Americans, I enjoy spending some of my easy-earned money going to the store to buy something I don't need. It's one of life's simple pleasures and a form of entertainment.

When I was a small boy, my mother often sent me to Evans grocery store around the corner from our house. Customers didn't wander through the store and pick what items they wanted off the shelves themselves. You told Frank Evans what you wanted and he got it for you. If it was on a high shelf, he used the long stick with pincers on the end to reach up and bring it down.

Once a month, we got a bill and my mother sent me to the store with a check. I liked doing it because when I got there, Mr. Evans always gave me a Baby Ruth or a Mars Bar.

Evans' store is long gone, but more than twenty years ago, all the grocery stores I shopped in began to change. Year after year, the big ones were taken over by something bigger. And then the bigger ones were taken over by something bigger still.

There are still a few high-priced little food stores where you can pay extra in exchange for not having to stand in the long line at the checkout counter in the supermarket.

After the grocery stores were gobbled up, locally owned drugstores started to go. Growing up, I walked the two blocks to Graves drugstore, although I more often bought ice cream than drugs. Drugstores all sold ice cream. They had counters with stools where you could sit and sip soda. They had a few small, round, white tables with three-legged wire chairs, which were triangular so that four of them fit together, like pieces of a cut pie, under the table.

If my mother sent me to buy something like cough syrup, I went to the back of the store where Mr. Graves worked in the white smock that distinguished him as the druggist. He must have made more on ice cream than on drugs.

One by one, drugstores like Graves were eaten alive by Duane Reade, Rite Aid, CVS and Walgreens.

Like most communities, we no longer have our own hometown drugstore. For ice cream, now we have to go to an ice cream store.

The owners of bookstores were special. Invariably, Mr. Clapp had read the book we came to buy and was explicit about its virtues. Bookstore owners were not only sellers of books, they were lovers of them. Borders and Barnes & Noble have driven them out. Clerks now are most familiar with the price of a book.

And what of giants like Home Depot? They have to mind their backs because COSTCO has come. COSTCO has most of what ShopRite, Rite Aid, Borders and Home Depot has—and for less.

What do I do as a loyal customer of the local grocery store, the hometown druggist, the bookstore and the handy hardware store? Why, I go to COSTCO, which is bigger and cheaper than any of them. If I want a diamond ring, a lawn mower or a bag of potato chips, I can get it there.

I just have to keep in mind that it's wholesale and whatever I get I have to buy twelve of.

WRITE TAX LAWS IN ENGLISH

Our government is collecting something like 2 trillion dollars from us in taxes this year. There are a thousand billion in a trillion, and a thousand million in a billion. Two trillion has 12 zeroes. It looks like this: $2,000,000,000,000.

I don't object to that figure except I know darn well Congress ends up spilling about a quarter of the money. They sneak in riders to bills.

The riders are designed to bring money into the district that elected the member proposing them. One member of Congress will initiate a perfectly sensible bill, then another congressman will attach some ridiculous paragraph that brings boondoggle money into his or her district. Congress passes the bill, rider and all, because no one wants to vote against the good parts of it.

For several years now, Congress has said it was trying to simplify our tax laws, but it has not. I wanted to look at some of those laws, so I borrowed the two-volume "Internal Revenue Code" from an accountant I pay to make out my tax form. There are 7,283 pages of tax laws, and I don't think the person who wrote them could explain what most of them mean.

I'm not a happy and contented American at this time of year because, while I don't object to paying taxes, I do object to the inscrutable language used in our tax laws that make them impossible for the average person to understand.

Our tax laws read as if the people who wrote them have a sweetheart deal going with H&R Block. If the tax laws were written in plain English, as they should be, H&R Block would be out of business. As it is, their business is booming.

In New York City, where I am, they open storefront offices all over town at this time of year, and desperate taxpayers flock in for help.

Here's one paragraph from the Alternative Minimum Tax form that I defy anyone to explain: "Step 6. If you did not complete Part III of Form 6251, enter the amount from line 28 of Form 6251 on line 17 of the AMT Form 1116 and go to Step 7 on page 8. If you completed Part III of Form 6251, you must complete, for the AMT, the Worksheet for Line 17 in the Form 1116 instructions to determine the amount to enter on line 17 of the AMT Form 1116 if: Line 53 of Form 6251 is smaller than line 54, and Line 41 of Form 6251 is greater than zero."

I was careful in retyping that to include the punctuation, spelling and capitalizations just as they appeared. I was alternately amused, confused and infuriated by its stupidity. Who at the Internal Revenue Service decided to use the small letter "l" twice in "line 28" and "line 17" and then in the fourth line suddenly capitalize the "L" in "Line 17"?

Who was the genius at the IRS who decided that, in the phrase "Step 7 on page 8," the word "Step" would be capitalized, but "page" would be lowercase?

Why is the word "Worksheet" capitalized?

A fourth-grade teacher would give a paper like this a failing mark.

We haven't always had income taxes in this country. For many years, the government supported itself mostly with taxes on liquor and tobacco. I suppose our Founding Fathers thought of smoking and drinking as evil and decided taxing them was the best way to raise money without making people mad.

The first real income tax came in 1862 to pay for the Civil War. War always eats more of our taxes than anything good for us, like health or education. Even back then, the tax was progressive. The rich paid a bigger percentage of their income than the less well off. Even the rich have always had a hard time arguing against that inequity. In recent years, however, there has been a movement that would have everyone, rich and poor pay the same percentage of their income in taxes. I can't figure out whether I'd do better or worse.

What we should do is take a few million of that 2 trillion dollars next year and send the people who write the tax laws to a school that would teach them how to use the English language in a way that doesn't read like Greek to us.

RAISING MY BLOOD PRESSURE

Several times in the past five years, I've had some medical attention from doctors like ophthalmologists, orthopedists and cardiologists, or semi-doctors like podiatrists, optometrists and chiropractors. In each case, I've showed my card from United Healthcare, with whom I am insured as a CBS News employee. As I've left these various offices, the person at the desk says something like, "The co-pay is $25." I pay and leave.

Several months ago, I had a bad toenail and chose a "podiatrist" from the yellow pages. The man seemed competent and after he worked on my foot, I put on my shoes and stopped at the front desk. The woman there said, "Your part, the co-pay, is $35." That seemed about right for what the podiatrist did, so I wrote a check.

The woman's "Your part" rang in my ears, though, and I said, "How much was the other part?" She shuffled through her papers and said, "Your insurance provider pays $475."

Something is seriously wrong with our health care system. A General Motors official said this week that health-care benefits for employees were adding $1,500 to the cost of every car. It's wrong because the money has little to do with our health, and it isn't the doctors or the nurses who are benefiting.

Last month, I came to the office one day and didn't feel good. By noon, I felt worse, so I called my doctor and went to the hospital where he has an office. He checked me over, poking in all the old familiar places, and couldn't find anything wrong. He was apprehensive about a possible heart problem and said it would be a good idea if he admitted me to the hospital overnight.

I had a room with just one bed and was impressed by the attention I got. You can't tell who's a nurse in a hospital anymore. Nurses used to wear cute little hats but they don't anymore so you don't know who's a nurse and who isn't. And everyone wears a stethoscope. They used to be doctors, but now even the people who empty the wastebaskets wear stethoscopes.

From early on to all night long people kept coming in to take things. They took my temperature, my blood pressure, blood samples, urine samples, and they kept hitting me on the knee with that little rubber hammer to see if I jerked.

At one point, when one of them started to take my blood pressure by wrapping my arm in the elastic bandage, I said, "Someone just did that five minutes ago."

She ignored me and proceeded to take it again. I liked all the unnecessary attention, oblivious to the fact that each test was being entered on a chart at the desk for cost-accounting later.

My doctor came in with a cardiologist he had asked to look at me. They were impressive professionals, although neither wore a stethoscope. I spent the night with bells ringing in the hallway and the stethoscope women coming in every half hour to wake me and ask if I was sleeping OK.

I was released from the hospital the next day. In the following weeks, I got a bill from each doctor. I paid them.

Yesterday, I received a statement from United Healthcare notifying me of my one-night hospital charges.

The breakdown from Mount Sinai Hospital reads:

Room and board, $2,875. Not covered, $525.
State of NY Surcharge, $207.98

Mount Sinai Hospital Misc. Services, $4,856.95. Amount allowed,
$2,725.93.

State of NY Surcharge, $241.24

TOTAL: $8,181.17

WHAT GOES UP NEVER COMES DOWN

News of the economy is not the story I read first in my newspaper. My
eyes glaze over with money talk because I don't understand it.

There have been a lot of stories recently indicating that there is very
little inflation in our economy. Officials in Washington concede that
the price of gas is higher, but they claim other things aren't costing
much more than they did a year ago. They put the increase at less than 1
percent. If the inflation rate is only 1 percent, how come when I go to
the store the stuff that used to cost me $20 now costs $35?

Does anything you buy cost the same as it used to? I'm talking about
ordinary things like a cake of soap, a loaf of bread, or a pair of shoes. I
saw a pair of sneakers in a store for $83. Sneakers? Whatever happened
to Keds for $7?

Last weekend, I made a 250-mile drive. The small country road I
took met the Thruway, and I was ready for coffee. There's a small place
there where I often stop. "Small, black to go, please," I said. A pleasant,
courteous young woman went about drawing the coffee.

"How much is that?" I asked as she put the top on, foolishly fishing a
dollar bill out of my pocket.

"A dollar eighty-two," she said.

Everywhere you go you're faced with price increases no matter what
economists say about there being no inflation. Motion picture attendance is down sharply this summer. The producers are puzzled and have
offered a half-dozen reasons why people aren't going to the movies as

much as they did a few years ago. Have they given any thought to their prices? Obviously, one reason people are staying home is that it costs them nothing to watch a movie on television in their living room but they have to shell out $9.50 a person to get into a theater. A bag of popcorn is $3.50 and a soft drink $2.50. I'm waiting for theaters to start charging people for using the bathroom.

The price of a hotel room has soared. In big cities, it's usual for a room to cost more than $200 and, if you order breakfast, it costs more than the room would have cost a few years ago.

Our telephone bill came the other day and I was shocked to see that a call I made to information for a local number cost $1.99. Didn't information used to be free?

A pint of Poland Spring's water costs $1.35 in the cafeteria in my building. The price of gas may be high, but if gas cost as much as water in those little bottles, you'd be paying $162 to fill your car with fifteen gallons.

In Florida, farmers say they're growing more oranges than they're selling. Has it occurred to them to reduce the price so all of us up here can afford to make a glass of juice for less than $5?

I'd like to have dinner some night at a good restaurant in Washington with a government economist and have him pay the check, just to give him a more realistic view of inflation.

THE GAS BILL

I haven't heard yet today, but I suppose gas prices hit a new high. They always do. The last time I filled my tank, I hit a new personal high. It cost me an even $50. I've never known exactly, but I think my tank holds seventeen gallons and it must have been almost empty. My personal low cost for a tank of gas came when I was in high school. I remember getting five gallons for $1 at the Shell station. I was loyal to Shell for several years and then loyal to Texaco. Now, I buy gas where it's cheapest. I think it all comes from the same place. It's the same gas.

Oil was $73 a barrel the last time I bought any, according to news on the radio. I don't know why they always tell us how much oil is a barrel. No one ever buys a barrel of oil. How would I get it home if I did? They'd probably charge me extra for the barrel itself.

The price they give for what a gallon of gas will cost at the pump on any given day never bears any resemblance to what I pay.

New York borders both New Jersey and Connecticut, and gas is cheaper in New Jersey because the gas tax is less. The tax is 32 cents in New York, 25 cents in Connecticut and 14.5 cents in New Jersey. Georgia has the lowest tax, 7.5 cents per gallon but I'd have to drive about 700 miles to get it.

I often drive to upstate New York, and I make a point of driving a route that takes me through New Jersey. After driving about 30 miles, I come to the New York State Thruway. I always try to get to New Jersey when I'm low on gas, then I drive to a gas station that's just before the New York border and fill up there.

I drive 130 miles north and two days later, after the weekend, I return and can usually get back to New Jersey before I have to fill up again. I continue on into New York and can usually get home with more than three quarters of a tank left. I don't save much but it makes me feel wonderful.

If radio announcers want to tell us something we don't know about gas, tell us how much the guy who owns the pump pays per gallon. Tell us how much the wholesaler pays the big oil companies. That's what we'd like to know.

There are seventy gallons in a barrel of oil, but the oil in the barrel is the crude stuff, straight out of the ground. From that, refineries can produce only about thirty-five gallons of gas that we can burn in our cars. Let's say a barrel of crude costs $70, I figure a gallon of gas would cost an oil company something like $1.40 a gallon to produce. With gas selling for more than $3 a gallon at the pump, even after all the costs they must factor into their prices—things like trucking, rent and salaries—gas station owners and wholesalers must still be making a big profit. For the most part, I don't think it's the gas station owners who are ripping us off. The wholesalers make more than the retailers.

Oil company profits are sky high with the new prices and this gives capitalism a black eye. Oil companies shouldn't make a single penny more on a gallon of gas when the price goes up. They should make the same profit on gas selling for $3 a gallon that they made when it was selling for $2 or $1.50 a gallon.

I have some ideas for saving gas myself. I'm going to put a note pad in my car and every time I get in I'm going to write down where I'm going. I'll start the car, go where I said I was going and no place else. I'll go directly there and directly back home. No wandering around. I'll cut my gas bill in half without ever having to go to New Jersey.

DON'T BE GREEDY

About four years ago, I was a guest on Martha Stewart's television show. I was impressed with her charm, competence and attractive appearance. I liked her a lot, although I was amused by her aggressive personality, which was apparent in everything she did. More recently, I was impressed with the classy way she behaved during her five-month stay in prison. She just took it. When she came out, she was so open and public that she came off more as a victim than a criminal.

The only thing wrong with all that is, my semi-friend Martha did something wrong and deserved what she got. She contributed to the lack of confidence a lot of Americans have in our economic system. A jury concluded she lied when she said she didn't have inside information before she sold 4,000 shares of a stock that plunged the next day.

There is plenty of reason for all of us to worry about this sort of thing. Our economy is based, to some extent, on trust. We have to trust that the people who run the institutions primary to our economy, in business and government, are honest. It's bad for all of us when we have good reason to lose confidence in such important people.

It was bad public relations for our free enterprise system this week when the chief executive of Boeing, Harry Stonecipher, was forced out for having an affair with another Boeing employee. It wasn't the affair that did Harry in; it was being a hypocrite.

Events like these make the rest of us think the stock market deck is stacked against us and we're right; it is. Something like 70 percent of Americans are invested in the stock market. Dishonesty in high places makes us aware that we don't have the same chance of profiting that business executives do. In spite of laws prohibiting their taking advantage of information about their companies, they know where the cards are in the deck and we don't. Martha knew and took advantage of this. If an average American makes money in the stock market, it's more apt to be based on luck than financial perspicacity; by happy accident, they picked the same stocks that people picked who had inside information.

Specific incidents like Martha Stewart's stock sales and Harry Stonecipher's foolish behavior undermine our confidence in the system that needs our confidence to prosper. Two great systems, democracy and capitalism, are sort of tangled together in our minds. They are in mine, I know. We think of them as equal, and they are not equal. Democracy is a great, high-minded idea. As a theory of government, it is unassailable. The prosperity and freedom of the lucky people of the world who have lived, as we do, under a democratic system of government, are proof enough of that.

Capitalism's credentials are not so unassailable. The defenders of capitalism speak of it as though it was an economic religion but it is anything but that. It depends for its effectiveness on one of the least admirable of our traits: greed. The free enterprise theory is that if everyone takes as much as he can get for himself, things will work out best for everyone. Well, they don't. If the theory is right that everything works for the best for everyone when selfishness is God, it's a sad day for all of us.

But uncontrolled capitalism doesn't work and we've known it since Congress passed the Sherman Antitrust Act in 1890. Unfortunately, we've been undermining the strength of that law recently.

One flaw in capitalism is that it's at the mercy of dishonest business people, and I hope we scared a lot of them by making an example of the exemplary Martha Stewart.

THE BUSINESS OF WAR

When the Pentagon announced its intention of saving $48 billion by closing 62 major military bases and 775 smaller ones, there was an outcry from local people near the bases. Their complaint was that the communities would lose jobs.

There's no doubt that when we close a base, lots of people lose their golden-egg-laying goose, but the purpose of a military base is not to provide jobs. The purpose of a military base is to contribute to our national security.

The people who contend that military spending makes jobs claim that a billion dollars spent by the Pentagon on weapons, soldiers and supplies creates 25,000 jobs. It's been pointed out by people who are not so enthusiastic about the arms industry that the same billion dollars would create 37,000 jobs if it was spent on mass transit, 36,000 jobs if it was spent on housing, 41,000 jobs if we spent the same amount on education and 47,000 jobs if it was spent on health care.

We were kidding ourselves, or our military establishment was kidding the rest of us, when they renamed our "War Department" the "Defense Department." It sounds better, even though we obviously don't have to defend ourselves against being attacked by Russia, France, Zambia or Zimbabwe.

We spend almost half of all the money the whole world spends on weapons. Our military establishment costs every single American, man, woman and baby girl and boy $1,533 a year. We are paying for weapons for wars there is no chance we'll ever fight. We have not dozens but hundreds of military bases for which we have no need. Our military establishment is bloated and overweight.

In the last ten years, our so-called "defense industry" has sold $142 billion worth of weapons to foreign countries. If we ever got into a war with a country like Turkey, Uzbekistan or Colombia, we'd be battling ourselves.

The respected Stockholm International Peace Research Institute keeps figures on military spending. Last year, we spent $455 billion on our military. Japan spent $42 billion, Russia spent $19 billion, South Korea, $15 billion. Italy spent $28 billion.

The United States has about 1,393,000 men and women in uniform. We have a total of 1,155,187 enlisted men and women and 225,373 officers. There are about 55,000 first and second lieutenants, 70,000 captains, 44,000 majors, 28,000 lieutenant colonels, 11,559 colonels, 435 brigadier generals, 271 major generals, 128 lieutenant generals and 36 full generals. A general's base pay is $144,932. We're paying 3,011 retired Army generals and 1,300 retired admirals.

One of my life's heroes is Dwight Eisenhower. He was a great general and good, if not great, president. No one ever said anything truer about our arms industry than what Ike said as he was leaving office:

"The country must guard against the unwarranted influence of the military industrial complex. The potential for the disastrous rise of misplaced power exists and will persist."

PART NINE

The English Language

One of the main reasons I'm pleased to be an American is that I'd hate to be a foreigner and have to learn the English language. It's too complex.

ENGLISH FOREIGN TO TOO MANY

Right after deciding to walk on two legs instead of on all fours, the greatest thing humans did for themselves was develop language, a system of words with which they could exchange information. It was a big improvement over grunting.

It is certain that the world would be a better place to live if everyone spoke the same language. The languages spoken by the most people are, in order, Chinese, Spanish, English, Bengali, Hindi, Portuguese, Russian, Japanese, German, Javanese (not "Japanese") and Korean. French isn't even in the top ten, and it makes me wonder why I studied it for five years in school. One strange linguistic aberration is that more people speak Portuguese in Brazil than in Portugal.

There's still plenty of room for misunderstanding even when we're all speaking the same language. But when more than one language is being used—or a proliferation of them—this can lead to a total lack of any kind of understanding. This is already happening in the United States. Twenty percent of the people living in America today speak a language other than English at home.

Where you stand on any of approximately ten popular issues identifies you as either a liberal or a conservative. If you're anti-abortion, hate the United Nations and oppose gun control, you're a conservative. I'm a moderate liberal with a couple of strong conservative opinions. One of those is that English should be the official language of the land.

In twenty-six of our fifty states, there are laws of varying strength that make English the official language. I have no patience with anyone who chooses to come to this country to live, to work, to raise a family, but who refuses to learn and use English.

Last year, liberals were angry with five conservative members of the Supreme Court who turned down a challenge to an Alabama law that makes English the state's official language. The case came to the court through a suit brought by a Spanish-speaking woman named Maria

Sandoval, who argued that her civil rights were violated because she was unable to take the test for a driver's license in Spanish.

Until our traffic lights read both STOP! and PARADA! driver's license tests should be in English. We drive in English. What language did Ms. Sandoval expect to hear when she came to the United States?

Language is an important, unifying force in a country. It is divisive to have large segments of our population speaking languages other than English. It's not only bad for the country, it's bad for the people who insist on using a foreign language. It's a quick way to end up on the public payroll for lack of a job.

In New York City, I frequently ride in taxis, and many of the drivers can barely communicate in English. They often have their radios tuned to a foreign-language station. I always ask what language the drivers speak at home and, without exception, they tell me they speak their native tongue. Many of them learn what little English they speak from their children who are in public school. The ability to speak English fluently ought to be a requisite for getting a license to drive a cab in New York.

English has become the whole world's second language. That is partly because of our cultural and economic dominance. It's also because English, screwed up though it may be, in many ways is still the best language. It has the most words and, while there are prettier languages, English communicates the most effectively.

You can usually make out in any foreign country with English because invariably, someone you're dealing with speaks it. I do not defend boorish Americans in foreign countries whose solution to not speaking the native language is to shout louder in English.

The United States should have a policy making it clear to those who plan to emigrate to this country that, as part of the deal, we expect them to learn our language.

ENGLISH AS SHE IS SPOKE

It has been said by someone other than me that no language that pronounces the word colonel "kernel" is perfect. In spite of some flaws, English is a great language. It isn't easy, though. I write a lot of English and never stop running into problems.

A recent newspaper story said, "The teachers asked the students to read the papers they had written." It isn't clear who wrote the papers—the students or the teachers.

It's easy to slip into redundancies. "Purchase price"? What other kind of price would it be? People speak of "the end result," as if some results were not the end.

How come someone who writes a play is a playwright and not a playwriter?

We use a lot of ungrammatical short cuts, which seem OK to me. We say, "I'll be home tomorrow." No one bothers to say, "I'll be at home tomorrow."

When I write a sentence with a quotation in it, I put the period or the question mark that ends it after the last quotation mark but editors often change this. They put the period or question mark inside the final quotation mark. My question is, "Why?"

In Don Marquis' delightful stories about archie and mehitabel, archie the cockroach typed everything lowercase, without any capital letters. He couldn't use capitals because, as a small cockroach, he had to dive headfirst at the keys to make them hit the paper. He couldn't simultaneously hit the key he wanted and the "caps" key, so everything archie typed, including the united states of america, looked like this.

Archie had an excuse, but there's no excuse for e-mail being spelled without a capital E. (For years I have objected to the policy of many newspapers not capitalizing the word "president" when it refers to the President of the United States. Maybe the policy was established for newspapers written by archie the cockroach.)

Written English is at its best when it's plain and simple. Henry David Thoreau said, "If one has anything to say, it drops from him simply and directly like a stone to the ground . . . he may stick in the points and the stops wherever he can get a chance."

I always liked that but Thoreau used "one" the first time, then a few words later in the sentence he drops "one" and goes to "him." Once you start with "one," you have to finish with it and I wouldn't ever start with it. It must have sounded less pretentious in Thoreau's time. Writing was more formal.

It's wrong, but I routinely use the word "like" as a conjunction in place of "as" both in writing and speaking: "I write like I speak," not "I write as I speak."

There are 10,000 phrases that may not be good grammar but which are too useful to ignore, such as, "He wants out."

I don't like to use "whom." "Who" suits me just fine for any occasion. I seldom use the subjunctive, either. I write, "If I was home . . . ," not, "If I were home."

There are English words that can be used to mean a dozen different things, even though the spelling never changes. The word pretty is an example. We all know what it means when someone says, "She's pretty." The meaning of that word becomes complex, though, when you say, "She's pretty pretty." It means she isn't beautiful, just fairly pretty. And it would be hard to explain to anyone who spoke another language what we mean when we say, "He's sitting pretty." (I seldom start a sentence with an "and" like that.)

It would be hard (difficult) to come to the United States from someplace like Korea without any knowledge of English and have to start learning it. How long would it be before you understood all the nuances of "pretty"?

DOWN WITH THE SEMICOLON

Writers try to make concessions to what interests readers but inevitably they end up writing about what interests them. I spend so much time writing that punctuation looms large in my life. However, I recognize that a lot of people couldn't care less about it—or "could care less," as the expression has become even though it doesn't make sense.

There are ten punctuation marks in that first paragraph of mine and they all serve a purpose. The period or dot used as an unequivocal stop to a flow of words is one of the great inventions of all time. It's simple and there's no doubt about what it means. It's interesting that it has recently acquired a whole new use in computer language as ".com" When you speak it, you say, "dot com" not "period com."

I especially like dashes in a sentence, like the one in my first paragraph, although I don't think they were even an acceptable punctuation mark when I started taking English classes in the fourth or fifth grade. A dash is somewhat similar to but different from three dots in a sentence . . . if you know what I mean.

Commas are useful in making the meaning of a written sentence clearer to a reader but newspaper copy editors have turned against them and I don't understand why. There are many fewer commas in newspaper stories than there were twenty years ago. (I'm not sure, of course, whether it's the editors or the writers who are using fewer of them, but I often have to reread a sentence to understand it because of a missing comma.) I like using parentheses like that occasionally, too. It indicates the thought is sort of a side remark being made to the reader. If you use brackets, they convey a different meaning. Parentheses are rounded marks to set off a group of words. Brackets are a different shape, usually with right angles at top and bottom. I think of them as strong parentheses and hardly ever use them even though there are keys for them on every keyboard. No one writes as he speaks and no one speaks as he writes, but when you put words down on paper, you ought to be able to hear yourself saying them. If you cannot, the chances are that what you have written is stilted, stiff and too formal. You can't write exactly as you speak, though, because it would be repetitive and rambling.

The advantage the written word has over the spoken word is that you can think a moment about what you want to say and how you want to say it instead of blurting it out. When we speak like that, we usually recognize that we haven't said what we meant accurately so we rephrase it and say it again. On paper, you have the opportunity to say it right the first time.

There is one punctuation mark I don't understand so I never use it. That is the semicolon. The colon is a practical divider of ideas and I often use one, but I never use a semicolon because I don't know what it does. I don't even know why it's spelled all one word instead of being hyphenated as "semi-colon." The semicolon is a period over a comma. If you use a period, a comma, a colon, question mark, quotation mark, hyphen, dash or bracket, you know what you're doing, but what does a semicolon do? Is it sort of a colon? Is it used to separate ideas in a sentence that are more different than when you use a comma, but not so different as when you use a period? This bears no likeness to the use of a colon and I hereby call for a worldwide English language boycott of the semicolon!

THE SOPRANOS, A BASE VOICE

I'm not sure "amuses" is the right word—but it amuses me that a good newspaper, appealing to the same audience, would never use the words that are commonly spoken in some movies and television shows.

The whole idea behind the word tolerance is good and we're all occasionally disappointed with ourselves for not being tolerant, but a little intolerance is a good thing too.

I am intolerant of the television hit *The Sopranos*. I fail to understand why so many people accept and enjoy a show that incessantly uses language so foul that I can't use it here because no newspaper would print it. Do dirty words turn people on? I am revolted by them.

I read a review in the *New York Times* describing *The Sopranos* as sophisticated and intellectual. The reviewer never mentioned the word used most often in the show because the *Times* would not have printed it if she had. She did not ever refer to the language used, which so dominates the dialogue that it's hard to follow the plot.

I spent four years in the Army and I'm familiar with all the words, but I don't use obscenities and the words had never been heard in our living room until I tuned in to "The Sopranos." This is a well-acted and otherwise well-written show, but I must have been asleep during the intellectual part. I tune out of any television show that has a psychiatrist, and *The Sopranos* has a few.

The use of foul language on the show is not limited to the lead character, mob boss Tony Soprano. (The creators of the show might argue that this language establishes his character.) In a recent installment, his teenage daughter used obscene language in an argument with her father and mother. Tony's wife, Carmela, wears a jeweled cross around her neck but uses profanity.

If I knew anyone in the Mafia, I'd ask if they really talk that way in their homes. I bet they do not.

There have been good movies in which obscenity and profanity were used effectively. I don't object to that. What I object to is the mindless profusion of both in some movies and television shows when such language does nothing for the plot or the characters.

I asked several regular viewers of *The Sopranos* whether the show's characters used profanity, obscenity and vulgarity, but most of them couldn't give me an answer because they didn't know the difference. Profanity is speech that is disrespectful of God or religion. Obscenity involves some sex act. Vulgarity is often associated with a body function.

Most newspapers don't print an obscenity even when it's part of a statement from a public figure. For example, when President Bush and Vice President Cheney were on a dais together and thought their microphones were off, the President described a reporter with a vulgar epithet involving a body aperture. Newspapers reporting the story did not use the word.

There have been a few times when newspapers found it necessary to violate their own policy. In 1974, when the texts of some of President Nixon's White House conversations were made public, many papers did print the worst of the language because they felt it was vital to a full understanding of the story.

Again in 1991, when the Supreme Court appointment of Clarence Thomas was at stake, newspapers printed some of the explicitly sexual language used in the harassment charge against him. Many newspapers also printed some of the explicit language in the text submitted to Congress recommending the impeachment of President Clinton. To avoid those words would have changed the meaning.

Newspapers that printed the actual text of the Clinton report omitted the same language in their news stories about it.

All this seems decent and responsible. I find *The Sopranos* indecent and irresponsible. Now, I suppose you can't wait to see it.

LAW AMONG THE SORRY LOTT

It's about time we stopped saying we're sorry when we aren't sorry at all. We have destroyed the meaning of a good word by using it a hundred times a day in all kinds of petty circumstances that don't call for being sorry. Well-meaning parents teach their children to say, "I'm sorry," before the kids know what being sorry means.

The word "sorry" does not seem to be related to "sorrow." Sorrow is a much more serious and sadder emotion than simply being sorry. The word "sorry" suggests regret but not remorse or grief as sorrow does.

We have established degrees of regret when we speak of it. We begin with the simply uttered "Sorry" and then progress to "I'm sorry," "I'm so sorry," "I'm awfully sorry," "I'm terribly sorry" and the ultimate, "I can't tell you how sorry I am." None of these statements is uttered with any real sense of regret.

Sen. Trent Lott of Mississippi and Cardinal Bernard Law of Boston don't have a lot in common but they did have one thing in common recently: They both spent a lot of time saying how sorry they were. Neither of them sounded like anything except they were sorry that the things they said and did became public. Their regret was not over what they said or did but over the attention they got.

Trent Lott was not sorry he held racist opinions for most of his career. He was sorry he made a dumb statement that made it apparent he had racist opinions. He went all out apologizing and it didn't work. Even though it would have been possible to vote against making Martin Luther King Jr.'s birthday a federal holiday without being a racist, Lott apologized for having voted against it, admitting, in effect, that he had been racist when he did.

One of Lott's Republican colleagues in the Senate was quoted as saying, "I'm sorry to say I think he has outlived his usefulness as a Republican leader." That's sorry on top of sorry and hardly sincere, either. Do you think that senator was really sorry to say that? He sounded pleased to say it.

Cardinal Law didn't seem anymore apologetic when he was shown kissing the Pope's hand before uttering words of abject apology for having helped perpetuate the sexual abuse of young boys by old priests. I'm sure he was sorry he lost his job and he was sorry everyone found out how wrong he was but it seems likely that, in his own mind, he did nothing that calls for him to be sorry. He no doubt has prayed for forgiveness and thinks he's been forgiven.

Both these experienced and worldly men should know that apologizing for something wrong that you have done or said doesn't work. An apology in the world these days means nothing. Everyone does it all the time. It almost never means that the person apologizing feels in any way apologetic or regretful. There's no evidence that prayer is any more effective in ridding a person of guilt than contrition, either.

We have ruined the whole idea of apology with meaningless repetition of the word "sorry," just as we have diluted "Thanks" by overuse. At least ten times a day we hear ourselves saying "Thanks" or "I'm sorry" when thankfulness or regret doesn't enter into our feelings. If someone bumps into us on the street, we instinctively blurt out, "I'm sorry," as if it was our fault. It is not an occasion that calls for an apology on the part of the person bumped into and it is just one more little thing that diminishes the significance of genuine contrition.

I'm sorry about this essay. Really, really, terribly sorry.

ENGLISH ISN'T EASY

Like the basement, the attic or garage, our language needs to be cleaned out once in a while. There are some words and phrases in our language that we ought to retire. I've made a small collection of some we could do without:

"Have a good one." This is a trite substitute for people who realize that "Have a nice day" is tired but don't know what else to say.

"Parental discretion advised." Does any parent advise their child not to watch when they see these three words on their television screen? What it's really saying is, "Hey, Kids! You might want to catch this dirty show."

Use of the word "experience" as a verb in advertising is annoying. The ads read, "Experience the ride of your life," or "Experience the taste of a great beer."

I have an unreasonably strong aversion to making verbs out of nouns like "parent." Here's a sentence from a magazine on my desk: "Parenting doesn't come naturally to some men." How about, "Being a father doesn't come naturally to some men."

"We're not getting the job done." The favorite post-game cliché of the coach of the losing team.

Use of the word "feel" for "think," as in, "I feel you're wrong about that." I use "feel" that way very often myself and feel I shouldn't. I use "very" very often, too.

We could do without subjunctives. No one knows what they are anyway and they sound pretentious. The indicative is always better, simpler. "I wish I was younger" is preferable to "I wish I were younger." I can take the subjunctive in a few places where the style fits the occasion, as in a meeting where the chairman uses the formal subjunctive: "I move the meeting be adjourned."

"In and of itself" should go. What does it mean?

"Your call is very important to us." Then why the hell don't you answer your phone?

Using "world class" for "good." This was a British expression used thirty years ago and we've taken it over. Americans use it to describe things that aren't much better than average.

A "bout" with cancer. People try to lesson the seriousness of the disease by using the word "bout" as though it was (not "were") a temporary affliction.

"Associate" for sales clerk. The loud speaker in the busy store says, "Attention! Will a sales associate report to the cashier!"

Using "unbelievable" for unusual. I heard the phrase fifty times listening to sports events last weekend. Football players made "unbelievable" catches. Golfers made shots that were "unbelievable." Sports announcers were all looking for some superlative to describe a good or unusual performance and they all lit on "unbelievable."

"Straight ahead" used by news announcers or anchormen meaning, "Coming next."

A mistake I hear too often is use of the adjective "Reverend" as a title. It is improper to address a clergyman named Paul Reynolds as "Rev. Reynolds." He is either "the Rev. Paul Reynolds" or "the Rev. Mr. Reynolds."

It's easy to get proud of yourself for knowing a little grammar. I'm not much of a grammarian, but I am always annoyed when I hear people misuse the word "comprise." The whole comprises the parts. The whole is not "comprised of" the parts.

The favorite term used by immigrants who know very little English is, "No problem." It seems to give them a sense of security with our language because it suggests they have mastered a bit of our jargon.

The word "shall" is too complicated for me. Look it up if you don't think so. I use "will" in every case.

Use of the word "negative" for "bad," as in, "The weather had a negative effect on attendance."

Class dismissed.

HUMOR ISN'T FUNNY

Whenever I see the word "humor" written, I wish we spelled it the way the British do: H-U-M-O-U-R. It's a better word with the "U" in it.

A sense of humor is one of the most universally admired qualities a person can have. You can accuse a friend of being dumb, cheap or fat but if you want to keep him as a friend, don't tell him he has no sense of humor, even if he doesn't.

Humor is held in high regard by all of us. We like to think we "get the joke." As the ultimate put-down, men have always said women have no sense of humor. It never seemed to me to be a gender-specific characteristic. Oscar Wilde wrote that "nothing spoils a romance so much like a sense of humour in the woman."

Disagreement about what's funny comes from the fact that there is no measuring device for humor. What's funny to me might not be funny to you.

I got thinking of humor when I read that Art Carney had died. He was my idea of a really funny performer. Art was second banana to Jackie Gleason on the television classic *The Honeymooners*, and even if you're too young to have seen it when it was originally broadcast, you've probably seen reruns. Art was a comic genius. He could make you laugh with a gesture, a small facial change or a couple of words. I knew Art because his brother, Jack Carney, was producer of *The Arthur Godfrey Show* when I worked for Godfrey, and I met Art often.

Art was not a particularly funny guy. In all the times I was with him, I never recall anything funny he said. What he was, was an actor who knew how to act funny and be funny on camera or on stage.

Humor is one of the most pleasant aspects of our lives and one of the most evanescent. When we laugh, we're happy even if it's for a fleeting moment. A laugh relieves tension. I use humor in my writing, but it's a mistake for a writer to set out deliberately to be funny. If it sounds like a joke, it probably isn't funny. Spontaneity is prerequisite to humor and jokes are the kind of intentional humor most apt to fall flat.

David Letterman and Jay Leno are popular, but I've never liked their opening monologues because they seem contrived. You can hear the writers in the background. Humor is best when it's spontaneous, and there's nothing spontaneous about those carefully written opening series of jokes even when the material itself is clever.

Nothing is funny that tries to be funny. Laugh tracks designed to indicate to people at home what's funny on television ought to be outlawed. When I'm home, clicking through the channels, there are a dozen shows that don't take me half a second to reject. I don't watch "survivor" shows; I don't listen to television evangelists; I don't watch hockey games; I can't stand anyone in a toque blanche telling me how to cook; I don't watch stand-up comedians or quiz shows; and if a program comes up and I hear a laugh track, I move on in an instant. I don't need recorded laughter laid in by a producer to let me know what he thinks is funny.

So-called "stand-up" comedians ought to sit down and relax.

They're trying too hard. My idea of funny on television is what Bob Newhart or the Smothers Brothers did. Their humor wasn't in the form of jokes. It played off real-life situations that we all recognize. Right now, I find Al Franken genuinely funny quite aside from his political opinions. We don't have anyone in the same league with the Marx Brothers anymore. We don't have Mark Twain or Will Rogers.

Humor doesn't take kindly to being explained, analyzed or written about (like this). E. B. White said that explaining humor is like analyzing the theory of flight by dissecting a sparrow.

THE COMPLEXITIES OF LANGUAGE

One of many reasons I'm pleased to be an American is that I'd hate to be a foreigner and have to learn the English language.

It's so complex. I've been making notes:

Last night, the news anchorman paused for a commercial and said, "We'll be right back."

What a strange use of the word "right," I thought, missing the whole commercial as I considered some of the many meanings the word right has. There must be twenty. "You're right," meaning correct. "Take a right." "He hit him with a right." "It's a right angle." "You have a right." "He's right wing." "That's not right to do." "It doesn't fit you right." "The canoe tipped over and he righted it."

How would you teach anyone all those meanings?

"A slip of the tongue." Slip? What's a tongue got to do with slipping? Isn't a slip underwear? "Slip and fall?" "She's a slip of a girl." "Put the boat in the slip." And consider:

Censor, censure.

Council, counsel.

Complement, compliment.

Affect, effect.

Proscribe, prescribe.

Why does someone "go to the hospital" but "go to prison"? "I'm afraid we can't go tonight." What do you mean you're "afraid"? What are you afraid of?

And why do we spell "embarrass" with two r's and two s's when we spell "harass" with just one r but two s's?

If you live in Chicago, you say, "IlliNOY." Many others call it "Illi-noise." Same with Colorado. Natives call it "ColaRADo." I say, "Cola-RODo." Sounds better.

"Till" is not a contraction of until. It's a word all by itself. People who spell it "'til" don't know that.

Is gray a darker color than grey? Why do we spell it two ways?

We say, "I could of hurt myself," but if we wrote it, we'd know it should be, "I could have hurt myself."

High school English teachers are still insisting on "dived" instead of "dove" and "hanged" instead of "hung." They're fighting a losing battle.

We still accept "mankind," but it's politically incorrect to call a woman "chairman." I don't like just "chair" and "chairperson" doesn't have much authority. I don't see anything wrong with a woman being chairman.

"OK" has been one of the most useful American additions to the English language. It's old and no one knows its derivation. There are at least twenty theories.

I don't understand the punctuation of "Rock 'n' Roll." (Of course, I don't understand Rock 'n' Roll, either.)

You don't hear people say "PDQ" much anymore.

"Jock" and "closure" have become popular recently.

The English language has three times as many words as French because we take in new words that are useful and have a different nuance of meaning than anything we already have. The stuffy French Academy doesn't allow that. They wouldn't have taken in "pizzazz," for example. French is nice, though.

A FEW WORDS ON WORDS

During the hearings held by the commission investigating the 9/11 attacks, one member, Richard Ben-Veniste, questioning Condoleezza

Rice, kept referring to the "PDB." It was irritating. I felt dumb because I didn't know what PDB stood for and he used it as if everyone should know. I've since found out it stands for "President's Daily Brief." Now I know Ben-Veniste was dumber for using it than I was for not knowing the meaning.

There are always people who try to make themselves sound special by using words familiar only to the people in their profession. Doctors do it, lawyers do it, scientists do it.

There are hundreds of initials we use as shorthand without thinking of the words they represent. A newspaper using them doesn't have to spell them out every time because we're all familiar with their meaning: USA, AFL-CIO, NATO, YMCA, AMA, FBI, CIA, OSS, AIDS, ROTC, PCB, USAAF, AP, ABC, NBC, CBS, CNN.

In many cases, it's just more practical to use initials or acronyms. What road crew would plant a stick of trinitrotoluene under a rock? They'd use TNT. Acronyms and initials have been very handy and good if not abused. No one has to post a sign outside a Hollywood block-buster saying, "Standing Room Only." All we need is "SRO."

Some familiar initials turn into words called acronyms because you can pronounce them. We say "OK" as the acronym "okay." Other sets of initials don't lend themselves to becoming words.

"RADAR" is an acronym so familiar that we don't think of it as anything but a word. Originally it came from the combined first letters of some of the words in the phrase "Radio Detecting and Ranging." "SONAR" came from "Sound Navigation Ranging." "SCUBA" is short for "Self Contained Underwater Breathing Apparatus."

"BASIC" is an acronym in computer-talk that stands for "Beginners' All-purpose Symbolic Instruction Code." The acronym "MOUSE" refers not to a computer "mouse" but to a proposed "Minimum Orbital Unmanned Satellite of the Earth."

The most familiar acronym to come out of World War II, which is still part of the language, was "SNAFU," which I won't translate here. The sanitized version is, "Situation Normal All Fouled Up."

"AWOL," meaning "Absent Without Leave," originated in World War I. The most unfortunate military acronym in World War II was "CINCUS," meaning "Commander in Chief of the United States Navy." It was pronounced, "Sink us."

The federal government loves initials and acronyms. Franklin Roosevelt's administration brought in hundreds like WPA, NRA, OPA. Even the name "Franklin Delano Roosevelt" is often replaced by the initials "FDR." John F. Kennedy was often called simply "JFK." Lyndon Johnson was "LBJ."

It's hard to know why that happens to some Presidents and not to others. It didn't happen to Presidents before FDR and it didn't happen to some of our most recent presidents. No one called Richard Milhous Nixon, "RMN." They didn't call Jimmy Carter "JC" or Bill Clinton "BC." It may take three letters to give it the right ring.

Big Business didn't leave itself out of the initial and acronym business. We have words like "NABISCO" for "National Biscuit Company," "SUNOCO" for "Sun Oil Company," and "ALCOA," for the "Aluminum Corporation of America." "IBM" is familiar as a name but it's not an acronym because you can't pronounce it as a word.

I have to get out of here PDQ. I hope the essay is OK, pronounced as the acronym, "okay."

THE HANDWRITTEN WORD

If it were not for the fact that mine is worse than any of theirs, I would complain bitterly about the people who write me letters with handwriting I cannot read. I often give up on a letter and throw it in the wastebasket because it's too difficult to decipher. I always think there's a good chance the writer wasn't trying to tell me anything I wanted to know anyway.

People become enamored of the scrawl they use for their signature even when it's illegible. I have no objection as long as the name is printed clearly under it. I do object to letters I can't read. The ones with the worst handwriting are always the longest.

The letters of our alphabet are not all beautiful. Cursive writing—the name for handwriting in which the letters are connected to each other, is supposed to be quicker because you don't lift the pen or pencil off the paper between each letter. This type of handwriting may be quicker but it is not pretty. The letters a, b, c, d, e are nice enough but some others are not.

Generally speaking, our capital letters are better-looking than the small ones. The big, looping B and the moving S are fun to scrawl. G's are not.

When I was growing up, I was taught something called "The Palmer Method." The writing instrument was held between the thumb and the forefinger and went almost straight up before the second joint and the knuckle. You were not supposed to use your fingers to move the pen or pencil. The motion all came from the shoulder moving the whole arm with the writing tool held between the thumb and forefinger. The teacher insisted that she be able to see light under your wrist.

In the 1930s, 80 percent of all American schoolchildren were taught "The Palmer Method." It was stupid and awkward and may account for why my handwriting is so bad.

The typewriter should be ranked in importance to civilization with the light bulb and the telephone, I don't write anything except a grocery shopping list by hand anymore.

For fifty years, I wrote on a great typewriter known as an Underwood No. 5. It was satisfying to hit the keys with my fingers because the lever with the letter on the end of it rose quickly and struck the inked ribbon in front of the paper to make its mark. It made a good sound, too. The computer is not so satisfying physically but it's a major improvement as a writer's tool.

About fifteen years ago, I fought a losing battle to resist giving up my faithful old typewriter for a computer. I was embarrassed to tell people I was writing on one, but now you couldn't get me to go back to the type-writer any more than you could make me use "The Palmer Method." A computer makes it so much easier to make changes that it improves the work of any writer who uses one. Writers make changes now they wouldn't have bothered with twenty years ago because it's so much easier. They don't have to throw away the page or make marks on the paper they're writing on.

Reading this, you may not be convinced I write better on a computer.

PART TEN

The Sports Fan

In the winter Olympics, they keep adding things to slide downhill on and then call the competition an "event." It used to be just skis and bobsleds. Now they've added luge and snowboarding. I'm waiting for them to have an event exclusively for Flexible Flyers. I'd get out my old sled.

THE GOOD-BAD WORLD OF SPORTS

Here are some thoughts on sports:

Baseball players are talking about a strike again. A strike by ballplayers is ridiculous. It wouldn't be a work stoppage. It would be a play stoppage. It seems unlikely, though, that any ballplayer making two million dollars a year at age twenty-six would be in favor of walking out. Most of the owners are already rich, but they aren't making as much from the game as the players—which is the way it should be.

I don't know what's happened to baseball. Even Little League baseball is close to being Big League. Don't kids ever get together anymore, divide themselves into teams without any adults around and play a game on Saturday morning?

. . .

Size is too important in several sports. Most offensive linemen in the NFL weigh more than 300 pounds. A few weigh 400. There are more players seven feet tall in the NBA than there are players under six feet.

. . .

The worst idea the producers of televised football games have had is putting good-looking young women on the sidelines to ask inane questions of coaches and players.

. . .

The crashes that race car drivers survive, usually without serious injury, are amazing. They are poured into that cockpit and fit so tight that they can't rattle around if they flip. They can't move much of anything. What happens if they get an itch?

. . .

Lance Armstrong, the Grand Prix bicyclist, is one of the greatest athletes alive. Armstrong rides with something called the U.S. Postal Service Team. I've never seen one of our mailmen on a bicycle.

.   .   .

August is too hot to play football. It's too hot to watch football. That doesn't stop the NFL from trying to make money on football in August.

.   .   .

Pete Sampras wasn't famous for very long. For a few years they were saying he was the greatest tennis player who ever lived, but he never was. They have said that about every great player during his time at the top. They said it about Bill Tilden, Ellsworth Vines, Fred Perry, Don Budge, Don McNeill, Jack Kramer, Frank Sedgman, Ken Rosewall and Rod Laver. There were all great—and so was Sampras.

.   .   .

It's wrong to try to pick the all-time best in any sport. There's no way to compare Red Grange with Jimmy Brown, Babe Ruth with Barry Bonds, Ty Cobb with Derek Jeter or Walter Johnson with Roger Clemens. No way to compare Jack Dempsey with Joe Louis or Lennox Lewis.

.   .   .

Swimming is a sport only followed by people who used to swim on their school team. I look with amazement at the winning times. Women are now swimming 100 meters, about 109 yards, ten seconds faster than I ever swam 100 yards. In a 100-yard dash, the men would lap me.

.   .   .

Golf is an interesting game but it isn't much exercise for the players since they started using those little carts to take themselves from hole to hole.

. . .

For two years I thought that the Williams sisters, Venus and Serena, had ruined women's tennis because they were too good, but they didn't last long. No one does in sports.

. . .

There are golf and tennis players in every country. Soccer is an international sport but has never been big in the United States. Basketball is the only American sport that is becoming international. Several South American countries play baseball, but the Japanese are a surprise. They seem to really like the game.

. . .

It is a mystery to me why anyone who has ever watched one of our football games could still think that what we call "soccer" is a good game. It doesn't compare with football in any way. The only thing I concede is it has more right to be called "football" than our game does. I don't know what our game should be called.

. . .

The NFL has tried to push football in Europe, but no other country except Canada plays much football. They don't know what they're missing.

. . .

For entertainment at halftime during the next Super Bowl game, I'd like to see a track meet among players from other teams. It would be fun to see which football player could run the fastest 60 yards, 100 yards or mile. They could have a mile relay.

THE TROUBLE WITH BASEBALL

Other than being pretty sure that the New York Yankees will win the World Series again this year, I don't know a lot about baseball. It's not my favorite game because there's too much emphasis on numbers. Being a fan involves knowing such arcane facts as which player struck out most often in his career when he came to bat with the score tied and the bases loaded in the bottom of the ninth.

I'm not alone. Baseball is no longer the Great American Pastime. It's getting to be the Great Central and South American Pastime. More and more good players come from those parts of the world. Attendance at games is down and there are many fewer kids playing baseball after school in vacant lots in the United States these days because the lots are no longer vacant. City kids play basketball. It takes less space. The song should be rewritten. It would go, "Take me in to the basketball game."

As a result of this trend, there are fewer and fewer Americans playing major league baseball. The names are more apt to be Rodriquez and Lopez than Ruth, Gehrig, or Mays. More than 25 percent of the players on the Yankees this year were not born in this country. It seems likely that this is a league average and there's no statistic comparable to it in football or basketball.

Having watched several football games, parts of five baseball games and a little basketball in the past week, I've concluded that the main thing wrong with sports coverage on television is that the men in the anchor booth won't shut up and let us watch the game.

A lot of the announcers are good, but even the good ones talk too much. We don't need to be told what we've just seen. John Madden knows the game and thinks of interesting things to say. But he often gets bored and talks over a play we want to watch without being distracted by his comments about something else. He repeats himself incessantly.

When there are two men in the booth on television as is usual, they always seem uncertain about whether they should be talking to the audience or each other. It's awkward. If they look at each other while they're explaining a point, one announcer may end up telling his partner something about the game that he already knows. The only response the guy can make is, "You are absolutely right."

Baseball needs some rule changes. There are too many substitutions. The pitcher who starts the game ought to be required to finish it no matter how many runs the opposing team scores.

The baseball gloves are too big. I was in a sports store where I measured a glove. A $200 first baseman's glove was twelve-and-one-half inches across. When I played as a small boy and someone dropped a ball, we'd all say, "Get him a bushel basket!" Well, the gloves the pros use now are bushel baskets. Smaller gloves would make the game more interesting by producing more errors. A fielder almost never drops a fly ball anymore. If there were more doubt about whether he'd catch it when the ball was in the air, it would make the game more interesting. It's wrong that a ball landing a foot short of being a home run is a certain out because the ball is invariably caught in the outfielder's bushel basket.

The other change I have suggested is to score one point for each base a runner reaches. If he hits a home run, he would get four points. For a double, he would get two points.

EAT YOUR HEART OUT

As I left the office with my suitcase, friends asked where I was going. I hoped they would and I said, in a voice louder than was necessary, "I'm going to the Super Bowl."

Everyone was impressed or envious except for one guy I never liked anyway who said, "Who's playing?"

A lot of hanging around hotel lobbies takes place at this event every year. "How many have you been to?" is a usual question in small-talk conversations. I have been to nineteen now. I can count them because every year, on every seat in the stadium, there's always a foam cushion, provided by an advertiser, with the name and date of the game emblazoned on it. I always take my cushion home. All I have to do to determine how many Super Bowl games I've been to is count the cushions.

If the game is going to be fun for a fan, the fan has to hope one team wins. He has to hate the other team to make it interesting. It doesn't take much. Maybe you once stayed in a bad hotel in the city the team represents. Maybe you have some prejudice against the coach, the spelling of the quarterback's name or the way the owner got together the millions of dollars it took to buy the team. It can be anything.

There are many reasons to like or dislike a team. For instance, if you like the city a team plays for, this is reason enough to root for it. It accounts for why so many people love to see Green Bay win. Everyone loves an All-American small town in Wisconsin. San Francisco, Pittsburgh, San Diego, Buffalo and Seattle are likable.

On the other hand, it's easy for nonresidents to dislike cities like Miami, Dallas or Atlanta and root against their teams. I have a friend who always roots against any college team from Florida unless they're playing Notre Dame.

There are dozens of petty reasons to prefer one team over another as you watch on television. It can be as simple as the color of their uniforms. The tacky, no-class, mini-skirted Dallas cheerleaders offend me. One show-boating wide receiver who does a victory dance in the end zone after scoring turns me off a team.

The NFL has done a lot of things wrong, but affixing a Roman numeral to each successive Super Bowl was a stroke of genius. There's something classy about a Roman numeral that Arabic numbers don't have. The use of Roman numerals had all but died out until they started identifying Super Bowls with them.

WHY I LOVE THE GIANTS

The opening of the baseball season is something I look forward to because every game they play brings me closer to the football season.

I've missed very few New York Giants home games in forty-five years in spite of the Giants' management's incessant efforts to discourage me from coming.

In April this year, the Giants started their campaign to drive me out of the stadium again for next season. It was a letter I got as a season-ticket holder.

"Please note," they say at the top of their message, "that we have increased our ticket prices by $5.00." Well, of course you have. You always do. Why should this year be any different? My bill for ten games, including two preseason games that I have no interest in attending but must buy tickets for, is $750. That $750 is $250 more than Tim Mara paid to buy the Giants in 1925.

This was just a start in their effort to keep me from coming to games this year. The letter goes on to say, "Games scheduled during Weeks 10–15 and Week 17 will be scheduled for 1 P.M. starts but will be subject to being moved to either 4 P.M. or 8:30 P.M." That's nice for fans trying to plan their weekend, isn't it?

The so-called New York Giants play their home games in New Jersey. It can take me an hour and a half to drive the traffic-clogged nine miles from Manhattan through the Lincoln Tunnel to the stadium to find a parking place walking distance to my seat. It's always a long walk. With new security rules and not enough people to frisk each of us entering the stadium, I have to allow another half hour to make the kickoff.

We are no longer allowed to bring anything to eat or drink into the stadium. A sandwich in a bag or a bottle of beer or water must be discarded at the gate because of "security," they say. Because they make money selling food and drinks to us for outrageous prices at the concession stands, I say.

I try not to arrive at the stadium hungry or thirsty. A small bottle of plain carbonated water, which you stand in line for fifteen minutes to buy, costs $3.50. A twelve-ounce bottle of mid-quality beer is $6.50. A bag of popcorn is $6.50.

If the game is moved to 8:30, it means I do not get home from the Meadowlands until sometime between 12:30 and 1 A.M. I enjoy reading about a game I have attended but Monday morning newspapers often do not carry the result because they went to press before the game was over.

Several years ago, it snowed the night before a game and when we arrived at the stadium the seats were covered with snow. Fans did what came naturally: they balled up the snow on their seats and threw it at officials down on the field. Giants management was furious with what they called "unruly fans." It had apparently not occurred to them that they could have avoided having us throw snow if they had cleared it off our seats before we got there.

You might think that by being at the game you'd avoid the tediously frequent television commercials during a game but such is not the case. The public address system in the stadium is never quiet and is usually trying to sell something.

At home, a fan can avoid the sales pitches by going to the refrigerator for a snack. In the stadium, we're captives forced to listen to the sales pitches that constantly appear on the huge screens at either end of the stadium. Commercials are not solely a halftime intrusion. They come up between plays, during time outs and during the thirteen-minute intermission.

The time between halves was extended by a minute in 1990 not to provide the players with more rest but to allow more time for commercial announcements.

After the game, anyone who comes by bus, as I sometimes do, walks three-quarters of a mile to where the buses are parked for the ride home. Passengers are a somber crowd if the Giants lose the game ... joyous if we've won. Passengers have been somber on 41 occasions during the last 100 New York Giants home games—in New Jersey.

PITCH AWAY FROM BALLGAME

I don't dislike baseball; I'm indifferent to it. Last Monday night, when they played the fifth game in what fans were calling one of the great series in baseball history, I watched an undistinguished Monday night football game between St. Louis and Tampa Bay. The football game started a few minutes after 9 and ended about 11:45 P.M. The baseball game started four hours before the football game and ended only forty-five minutes earlier.

I watched twenty minutes of the interminably long Saturday night baseball game that started a little after 8 and ended about 12:40 A.M. The Sunday night game was even longer. It ended about 1:10 A.M. It should not take that long to determine which group of nine men throw, catch and hit a small ball better.

My granddaughter, a college senior who grew up in Boston, called the next day to ask, somewhat critically, if I had watched until the end.

"No," I told her. "Some of us have to go to bed at night so we can get up in the morning and go to work to make enough money to send children to college."

There are fans who like both baseball and football but almost all of them have a preference. Some older baseball fans try to justify their enthusiasm for the game by endowing it with some mystic intellectualism that escapes me. Columnist George Will is their guru.

The Yankees are the best team in baseball year after year because their owner, George Steinbrenner, spends the most money to buy players. Something wrong there. If another team beats the Yankees, which happens, it's because the best team doesn't always win in baseball. Doesn't even usually win, it seems to me.

I get fidgety watching baseball because the players are fidgety. The pitcher stands on his little hill looking down from his elevated position toward the man with the stick at home plate. He tugs at his cap. He shifts his shirtsleeves. He looks toward first base. He looks at the catcher and nods or shakes his head. On television, the camera shows someone in the dugout spitting tobacco-infused saliva. The pitcher seems to be afraid to throw the ball. The catcher is telling him where it should go even though no pitcher can accurately predict, within a foot or so, where any ball he throws is going to end up.

It's not clear to me why a catcher is supposed to know where the ball should be thrown better than the pitcher does. The pitcher's only input is negative. He shakes his head if he doesn't like the catcher's suggestion. Eventually he's ready and at that instant, the man waggling the bat steps away from the plate and the inaction continues. It's no wonder games last five hours.

If the pitcher fails to throw the ball within the designated boundaries over the plate four times, the batter gets what is called "a walk." When a batter is "walked," he doesn't walk, he trots to first base. After playing from early spring until the day before November, they still have not decided which team is best, so they play what baseball arrogantly calls "The World Series." No other country in the world but Canada is allowed to play. If Japan could play and won the World Series, not an improbable outcome, it could destroy the image the game has of itself as all-American.

NOT WATCHING TELEVISION

Every evening after dinner, millions of Americans decide what they don't want to watch on television that night. It's easier than deciding what they do want to watch.

There's so much fake drama on television that poses as "reality" that it's a relief to turn the dial to sports and watch something that's really real. A lot of us do that. When a game starts, no one knows how it's going to end, so the drama may have no importance but it's genuine. It accounts for why five of the ten most-watched shows in the history of television have been sports events. (Four Super Bowl games and the 1994 Winter Olympics. The World Series never made it. If there had been television in the 1920s, a fight between Jack Dempsey and Gene Tunney would have been watched by everyone, but boxing has lost its appeal.)

Football is easily the best sport to watch on television. Four downs for a team to move ahead ten yards sets up a dramatic situation every time a team gets the ball. The brief pause between plays gives viewers an opportunity to assess their team's options, and to that extent they're playing the game themselves.

The two worst games to watch on television are hockey and soccer. The trouble with them, from a viewer's standpoint, is the lack of predictable continuity. One player kicks the ball or hits a puck with a stick but, as many times as not, the ball or puck doesn't end up under the control of the person to whom it was directed. This is not satisfying. Even if you're sitting in a cushy armchair, it's frustrating.

Baseball has good dramatic form with nine innings, each divided in half, and the three-strike and four-ball rules work well. After three outs, the sides change positions on the field and that gives fans time to savor their team's situation. That's the most I can give baseball.

Golf is a slow game to watch on television, but if you don't have anything to do at home on a Saturday or Sunday afternoon, the courses are the way you'd like to have your back yard look, and every once in a while there's some drama. The trouble with golf as a television sport is that the action of a golfer hitting the ball with a stick takes so little of the to-tal time involved in watching a four-hour, eighteen-hole match that the game is more apt to induce slumber than excitement.

Tennis is good on television because, shooting from one end of the court, a camera can get the whole picture of the action and can also pro-vide close-ups of the most interesting shots. Unlike golf, the action in a tennis game is interrupted only briefly while the players serve the ball or change sides. You also get a better idea of the appearance and personal-ity of tennis players from watching them on television than you get of other athletes. You know a lot about Andre Agassi or Andy Roddick just from watching them play.

Basketball is moderately interesting, but there are no pauses during which a fan can relish the situation on court. It's incessant scoring. When a team gets the ball, it moves down the court, and more often than not, puts the ball in the basket.

It's a mystery to me why anyone watches some sports on television. NASCAR (National Association of Stock Car Auto Racing) has a huge following and I've tuned in once in a while but unless there's a crash, it's about as interesting as a traffic jam during rush hour.

When I'm dull on television, at least it doesn't last long.

BEFORE JOINING THE HUDDLE . . .

All normal readers should be aware that there's a small minority of dis-sident, dysfunctional Americans who don't like football. These Ameri-cans, if you can call them "Americans," think watching a game is a waste of time, and further, they completely fail to understand the loyalty foot-ball fans have for one of the thirty-two NFL teams.

It is to these misguided, uninformed individuals that I address my re-marks here.

Football is watched by a great many more people than play it for a va-riety of good reasons. First off, it is not a game that's practical for a lot of Americans to participate in the way they play golf or tennis because, second off, a uniform costs about $950. The hat alone, known as a helmet, goes for $250.

There are eleven players on each team on the field, although thirty-four other players stand around on each sideline, hoping an emergency occurs, such as an injury to one of the players that will make it necessary for one of the coaches to send in a substitute. (In baseball, the person telling players what to do is called "the manager." Although his function is more or less the same, in football that person is referred to as "the coach.")

To begin the game, a dozen or so players from each team called "captain" or "co-captain" gather with officials in the middle of the field and flip a coin to decide which team will kick the ball and which team will catch it, then try to run with it toward the kicking team's goal line.

It's important to note that while we play different games with twenty-seven different size and shape balls (My estimate. Don't forget squash and croquet.), the football is the only one that is not round. The ball not being round substantially differentiates the game of football from other ball games.

The mission of the team with the ball is to advance it by at least ten yards in four tries. The ball can be moved either by throwing it or running with it. If you care who wins, the fact that the ball must be moved at least ten yards in four tries or returned to the other team adds constant drama to the game.

Part of football's popularity derives from the fact that the players are easy to see. Many of them are over 300 pounds so they can wear big numbers on their broad backs.

The defensive lineman tries to tackle the quarterback before he gives the ball to another player or throws it. This is enjoyable to watch because the quarterback makes a lot more money than the other players, and everyone likes to see him get knocked to the ground—or even out.

If you don't care who wins, it isn't any fun to watch a football game, so what you have to do in order to enjoy the game is to transfer your allegiance to another team. When Pittsburgh plays Seattle I root for

Seattle because I like the sound of their city's name and I don't care for the color of the Pittsburgh uniforms.

I hope this explanation will help non-fans enjoy the Super Bowl. This is one of the most important events of the year—the results of which don't matter one bit to our lives.

TOO MANY GAMES

One trouble with sports now is that their seasons overlap. It used to be that football was played in the fall. Baseball was spring and summer. Basketball was a winter sport.

Hockey was played in the winter because that's when the lakes and ponds it was played on froze. Now hockey starts in September and ends in February.

Baseball starts in April and keeps going until they play the World Series during the football season in September. The basketball season overlaps both football and baseball. Professional basketball starts in November and doesn't end until June.

Basketball is a flawed game now because it depends too much on the height of the players. Maybe it's because I'm only five-foot-nine myself, but I object to a sport in which it's so important to be seven feet tall.

Basketball doesn't depend much on the marks the players get in the classroom—if they go at all. When I see two college teams playing basketball, I always wish all the players had to take an exam to make sure they can count. Any player who couldn't count to ten or spell C-A-T wouldn't be allowed to play.

I also think there's too much scoring in basketball. One pro team will often beat another by 116 to 112, and the report in the newspaper will refer to the winner's "dominance."

The fact is, in a basketball game these days, the team with the ball almost always scores. A player drives to a point under the basket and simply reaches up and drops the ball through the net.

Maybe they ought to figure out a handicap system. Officials would measure all the players, and if twelve players from one team had a cumulative height of 72 feet (six feet each), and the other team's total height was 70 feet, the shorter team would start with something like a two-point advantage on the scoreboard.

Sometimes, when there's nothing else on I want to watch, I've looked at some of the NCAA tournament games. I haven't enjoyed watching these games because half the time I've never heard of the colleges playing. I was looking though the names of the sixty-five colleges entered in the NCAA tournament this year and I never heard of seven of them. I suppose it will make someone mad, but the mystery colleges to me are: Belmont, Murray State, Northern Iowa, Pacific, Southern Alabama, Southern and Winthrop. I have just barely ever heard of the early favorite to win the tournament: Memphis. I hardly know George Mason College or University, and that was an early favorite.

I suspect some of the colleges are nothing more than basketball teams attached to something that calls itself an educational institution to get into the tournament.

I've often dreamed of going back to college. I'd appreciate learning more now than I did then. It would be fun to register in one of these basketball colleges just to see whether I could pass any of their courses. I certainly couldn't make their basketball team.

A high school basketball game between two local rivals is healthy fun for a community, but too often, one of the teams with an overly ambitious coach starts cheating. Maybe he encourages a six-foot-eight-inch kid from a town fifty miles away to move to town in exchange for a place to live, or perhaps a car. Maybe he talks a couple of players into repeating their senior year.

There's often a conflict in a school between the serious teachers who believe that education is of primary importance and the boosters who want to see their team beat the team from the adjoining town. Too often, the teachers lose. If Belmont, Winthrop or Northern Iowa wins the NCAA tournament, I'll apologize.

IT SHOULD HAVE BEEN SUPER

One regular ticket for the Super Bowl costs about $600. If someone offers you a ticket for $10, don't buy it if you want to see the game. In the stadium, the game is an afterthought. It's treated as though it was an intrusion on the mindless noise flowing endlessly from the stadium speakers.

I have been to all but two Super Bowl games since 1967, and this year may be my last. Going to the game should be a good experience for a football fan but it's not. Everything about going to the game is unpleasant. The game of football is the last thing the people at the National Football League think of. I realize that I'm probably not the audience they're aiming at, but I talked to a dozen people at the game and in the bus going back to the hotel who were as offended by the production as I was.

Last year I stayed at the NFL headquarters hotel, the Marriott at the Renaissance Center, and it is in a complex of buildings so confusing to get around that only a master architect like John Portman could have designed it. General Motors uses part of it for executive offices. I was in an elevator with several reporters Saturday, and one of them said maybe the reason GM's business was in such trouble was that none of the executives could find their way to their offices.

Detroit desperately wanted to have people like their city. It was sad. I was asked a hundred times how I liked Detroit. It amused me because when there's a big event in New York like a political convention, New Yorkers don't give a damn whether out-of-towners who come like the city or not.

There were people in red vests who'd been assigned to help strangers find their way around the maze, but they appeared to have been shipped in from Toledo. They had no answers to such basic questions as, "Where is the newsstand?" "Which floor is the newsroom on?" or "Where are the buses to the stadium?"

I arrived at Ford Field more than two hours before kickoff and by the time the game started, I was numb from the noise they were passing off as music. I would have been willing to pay for silence. I kept hoping some disgruntled fan would cut the power line.

The half-time extravaganza took forty-three minutes. I wasn't interested in watching the half-time show, so I went out back to get some $5 popcorn and a $2.50 bottle of water. I just wandered around, noting, for instance, that Tropicana was "the official grape juice of Super Bowl XL."

I didn't want to miss the second half kickoff so, after twenty minutes I went back to my seat. The half-time show wasn't over. I was shocked to find it hadn't even started yet. Stagehands were still dragging large pieces of the stage into place on the field. Mick Jagger and his entourage finally came out and performed for about twelve minutes with an inadequate sound system, then workers started the long process of breaking down the stage and dragging the pieces back where they came from.

The blaring from the loud speakers was unremitting throughout the game. During any break in the action—even between plays—the huge screens at either end of the field showed one highlight after another from previous games. No one in the stadium had time to savor the action, anticipate the next play, or exchange a comment with someone sitting near him. Noise was the dominant element in the stadium.

The NFL ought to start putting more emphasis on the football game and less on making money, or it's going to kill this golden egg-laying goose.